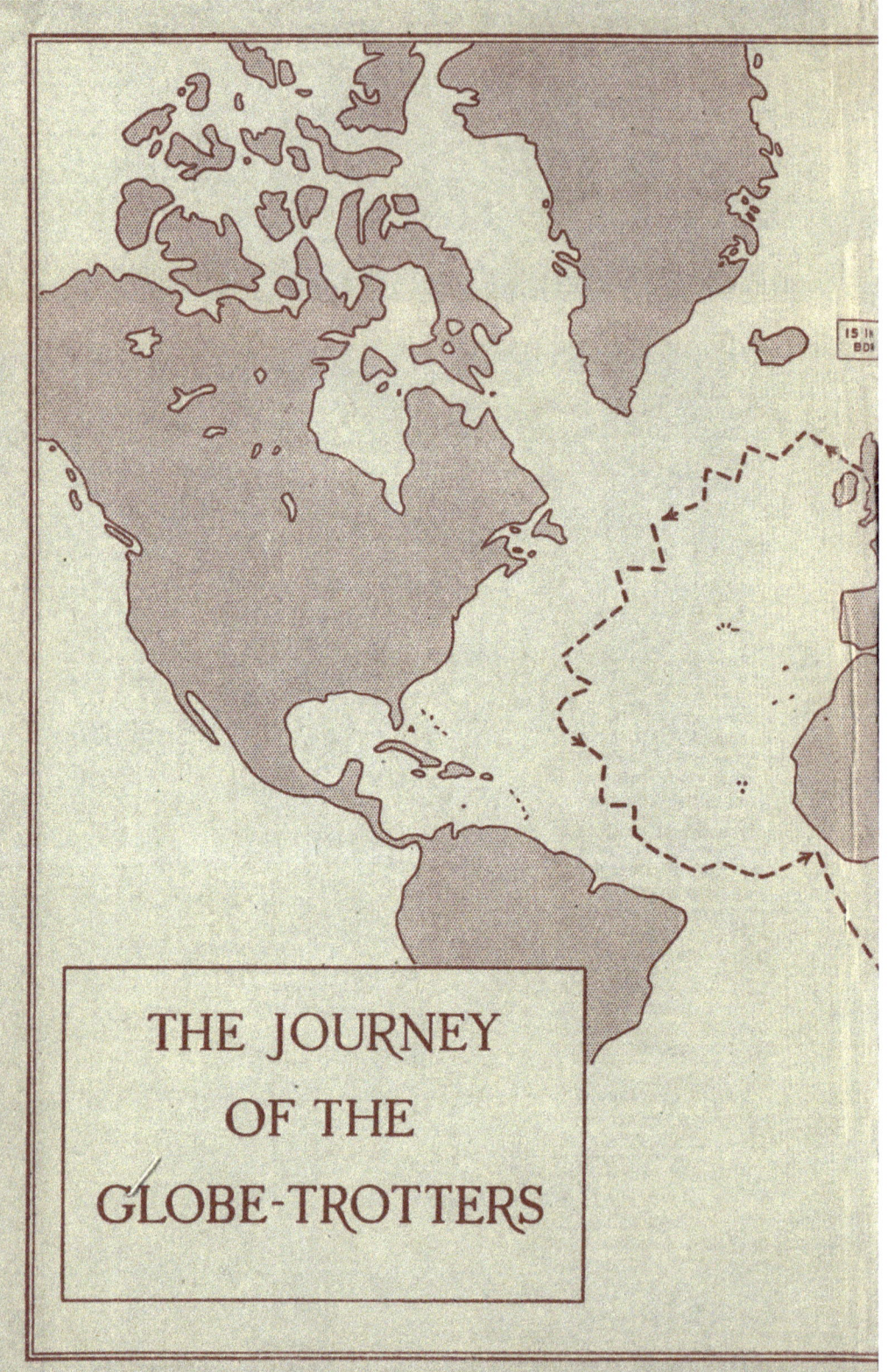

THE JOURNEY OF THE GLOBE-TROTTERS

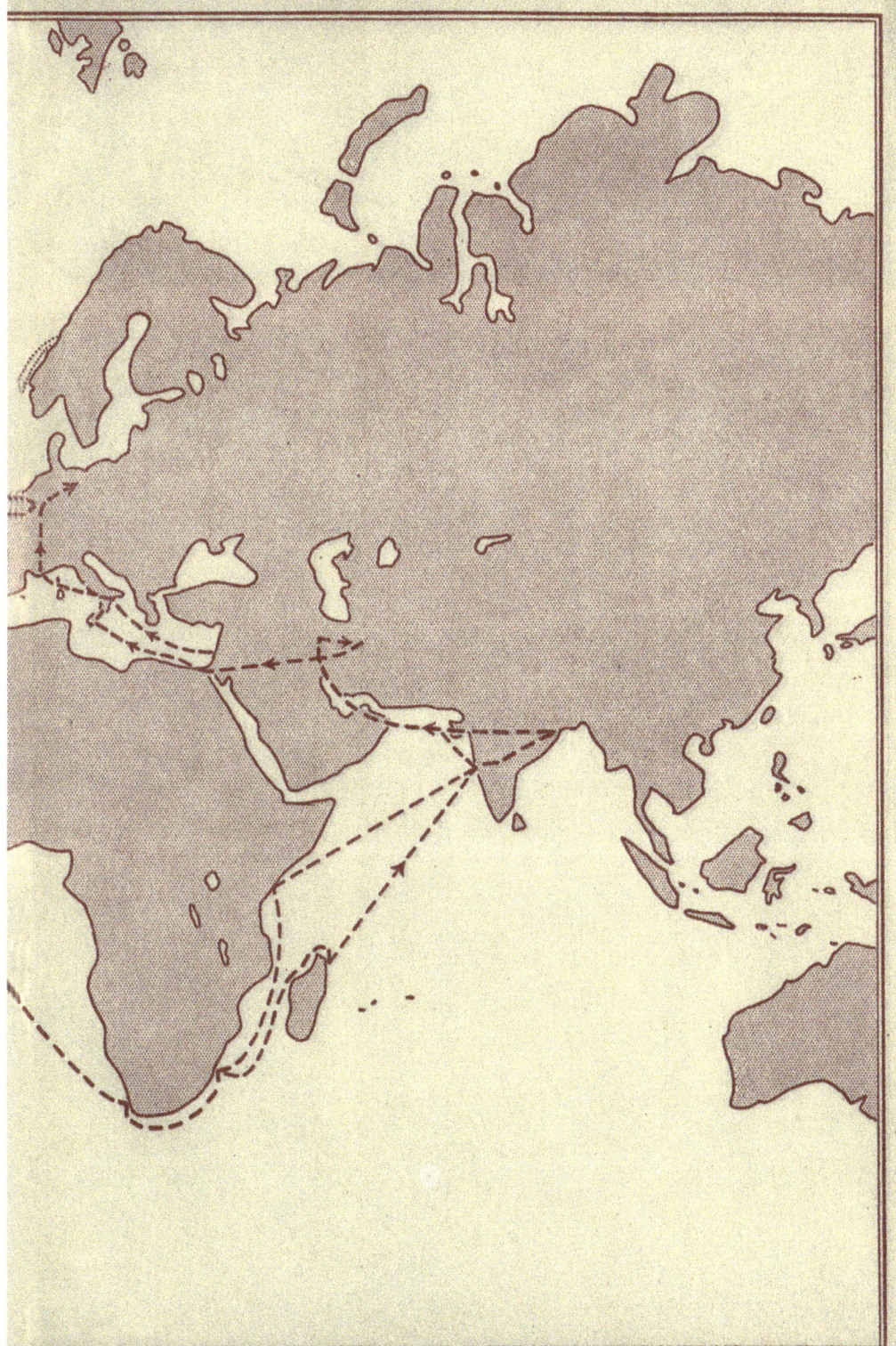

The Fifth British Division

1939 to 1945

Being an account of the Journey and Battles of a Reserve Division in Europe, Africa, and Asia

BY GEORGE ARIS

Edited by
LIEUT.-COLONEL C. S. DURTNELL, O.B.E.

The Naval & Military Press Ltd

Published by

The Naval & Military Press Ltd
Unit 5 Riverside, Brambleside
Bellbrook Industrial Estate
Uckfield, East Sussex
TN22 1QQ England

Tel: +44 (0)1825 749494

www.naval-military-press.com
www.nmarchive.com

In reprinting in facsimile from the original, any imperfections are inevitably reproduced and the quality may fall short of modern type and cartographic standards.

CONTENTS

FOREWORD By Major-General H. P. M. Berney-Ficklin, C.B., M.C.   ix

INTRODUCTION By the Editor   xi

I   CONCENTRATION AND SERVICE WITH THE BRITISH EXPEDITIONARY FORCE UNTIL APRIL 1940   1
The Traditions of the Reserve Division—The Concentration in France—The Gort Defensive Line, Winter 1939–40—Interlude on the Saar Front—Final Collective Training

II   THE 15TH INFANTRY BRIGADE IN NORWAY   10
The Setting—The KOYLI at Kvam—The Y and L Regt at Kjörem—The Green Howards at Otta—The Evacuation

III   CAMPAIGN WITH THE BRITISH EXPEDITIONARY FORCE, MAY 1940   25
The Background to Plan "D"—The Advance to the River Senne around Hal—The Withdrawal from the Senne—The Task of Frankforce—The Defensive Battles of Arras, 22nd–23rd May—The Ypres-Comines Canal Line

IV   TRAINING IN THE UNITED KINGDOM   47
Concentration Again in Scotland—North-West England—Northern Ireland

V   LONG SEA VOYAGE—THE 13TH AND 17TH INFANTRY BRIGADES IN MADAGASCAR   57
A Voyage to the Indian Ocean—The Setting for Operation "Ironclad"—The Assault on Madagascar—The Battle for Antsirane—On the Defensive

VI   ACROSS INDIA   70
The Gateway to India—Across India by Road—Training at Ranchi—The Threat to the Middle East—The Move to Persia

VII   AUTUMN AND WINTER IN PERSIA, 1942–3   84
Winter at Qum

CONTENTS

VIII PREPARATIONS FOR THE MEDITERRANEAN OFFENSIVE, SPRING AND EARLY SUMMER 1943   93
From the Defensive to Planning the Offensive—The Journey from Persia

IX CAMPAIGN IN SICILY   106
The Setting—The Plan—The Beaches—The Approach—The Landings and Capture of Syracuse—The Advance Continued to Augusta—The Battles on the Catania Plain—Fighting in the Foothills—Preparations for Crossing the Straits of Messina

X THROUGH SOUTHERN ITALY TO THE ADRIATIC   140
The Setting and the Plan—The Landing and Securing of the Beachhead—The Advance from the Bridgehead to Potenza—Across the Foggia Plain into the Central Apennines—The Rionero Sector—The Adriatic Sector

XI CROSSING THE GARIGLIANO RIVER   175
The Setting and the Plan—The Night of 17th–18th January—The 18th–19th January—The 20th–21st January—22nd January—23rd January—The Battles for the Natale Feature—27th January—30th January onwards

XII THE ANZIO BEACHHEAD   205
The Setting—The Corps Perimeter—The Divisional Sector—The Take-over—The Routine Defensive Battle—The Break-out and Advances on Rome—Operation "Wolf"—The Battle for Ardea—Advance to the Tiber

XIII THE MIDDLE EAST REVISITED   241
The Move Back Again—Training in Palestine and Syria—Advance Parties to Italy and Back

XIV RETURN TO NORTH-WEST EUROPE. THE END OF THE JOURNEY   249
The Move into Italy and France—The Advance to the Elbe—The Crossing of the Elbe and on to Lübeck

CONTENTS

APPENDIX "A"   264
    Senior Commanders, 1939–45

APPENDIX "B"   265
    Corps and Regiments which served with 5 Div,
    1939–45

LIST OF LINE ILLUSTRATIONS
Drawn by COOPER BELL, A.R.I.B.A. (A.A. Hon.Dip.)

THE SAAR VALLEY	9
NORWAY	24
MALINES: THE GRAND PLACE AND CATHEDRAL	27
TOURNAI CATHEDRAL	31
ESTAMINET IN A FRENCH VILLAGE	35
GHENT: THE CHÂTEAU DES COMTES	38
TABLE MOUNTAIN	69
TAJ MAHAL	83
QUM: THE GOLDEN DOMED MOSQUE	92
THE SUEZ CANAL	105
MOUNT ETNA FROM POMPEII	139
THE BAY OF NAPLES	204
BETHLEHEM	248
ROME: THE COLOSSEUM	263

LIST OF MAPS

Specially drawn for this history by F. RODNEY FRASER

THE GORT-LINE	4
THE SAAR	7
NORWAY	13
FRANCE–BELGIUM	facing 40
ARRAS TO DUNKERQUE	facing 46
IRAQ-PERSIA	85
MIDDLE EAST	96
RIVER SIMETO	facing 134
SICILY	facing 138
SOUTHERN ITALY	facing 164
ADRIATIC SECTOR	166
CENTRAL ITALY	facing 174
RIVER GARIGLIANO	facing 204
THE FORTRESS	216
BATTLE OF L'AMERICANO	228
ADVANCE TO THE RIVER TIBER	236
THE ANZIO BEACHHEAD	facing 238
MIDDLE EAST REVISITED	242
ELBE-BALTIC	252
THE RETURN JOURNEY	facing 260

NOTE. All pull-out maps are at the end of the chapter or section to which they refer.

ERRATA

RIVER SIMETO		facing 134
For "Primosole"	read	"Prima Sole"
For "Semeto"	read	"Simeto"
SICILY		facing 138
For "Cassible"	read	"Cassibile"
RIVER GARIGLIANO		facing 204
For "Pontifiume"	read	"Ponte Fiume"

FOREWORD

By MAJOR-GENERAL H. P. M. BERNEY-FICKLIN, C.B., M.C.

THIS is necessarily a very concentrated account of the journeyings and battles of 5 Division during the war 1939–45. As will be seen, the Division covered a tremendous amount of ground and its movements carried it to many places inside an area bounded by Kvam (Norway); Qum (Persia); Madagascar; Ranchi (India); Loch Erne (Ulster).

I am certain—as I am sure are many other Commanders—that the two most important things in the training of the soldier, of whatever arm, are discipline and *esprit de corps*. These two are really complementary and given that they are properly inculcated I am quite convinced that there is nothing that you cannot teach troops or, having trained them, ask them to do. Units, other than perhaps Artillery previously regimented, and Infantry previously brigaded, which suddenly find themselves an integral part of a larger formation—as happened in 1939—take a little time to settle down. We in 5 Division had initially many problems to face. We were really a hotch-potch collection, including units from Northern and Southern England, the Highlands and Lowlands of Scotland, and Ireland. However, we soon managed to weld ourselves into one solid whole. Although some units were Regular and others T.A., there was no differentiation between them. I have often thought that the mutual trust and confidence which became engendered between all arms and services in the Division was directly due to the fact that 5 Division regarded itself as a composite whole and not as a collection of Infantry Brigades, Gunners and a lot of other units. It has also always seemed to me that many of the successes, the good behaviour and cheerful acceptance of things by the Division were due to an extremely high *esprit de Division*.

I always felt that though the Division might have to fight, as it so frequently did, in Brigade groups, it was essential that there should be a strong Divisional spirit; for this ensured, in cases of necessity, real flexibility in switching units, supporting arms and services. Such flexibility was therefore not only a matter of

FOREWORD

technical regroupment, but also the foundation of continued mutual confidence.

I see no reason why I should have been asked to write this Foreword as there were four other war-time commanders—more distinguished than myself—who commanded 5 Division at various times. I have agreed to write it only because I happened to command it for the longest period and was, perhaps, in 5 Division service the oldest soldier in the Division; I first joined it (although of course, my service in it was not continuous) before the 1914–18 War, some time before a great many of its members serving under me in the period 1940–43 were born!

This short history shows, I feel, that the 5 Division of the 1939–45 War succeeded under its various commanders in maintaining all the traditions and prowess in battle of the several 5 Divisions of the past.

Finally, in 1958, we are most happy to know that 5 Division is in being again and that our "Y" once more is being worn by our successors as proudly as we wore it during the Second World War. To the present 5 Division we wish the best of luck, and venture to hope that the adventures recorded in this book may perhaps be of more than passing interest to them.

INTRODUCTION

We are all pleased that the history is now published. Just as 5 Division in war acted as a team, so the recording of these adventures has been the result of team work. The delay in publication is regretted; there have been many difficulties to overcome.

The thanks of all members of 5 Division are due to many people; to Major-General H. P. M. Berney-Ficklin, C.B., M.C., to the late Major-General P. G. S. Gregson-Ellis, C.B., O.B.E., and to Lieut.-General Sir Richard Hull, K.C.B., D.S.O., for their enthusiasm, encouragement and advice and, above all, for their great patience. Brigadier W. Buffey, D.S.O., T.D., D.L., has been a tower of strength; without his unfailing help and determination, this book would not now be published. Lieut.-Colonel C. D. van Namen, M.B.E., has done much of the donkey work behind the scenes as Secretary of the 5 Division Benevolent Fund. We were also most fortunate in having had serving in the Division Captain J. P. Mackay Miller, whose firm has undertaken the printing of this history. He was able to arrange for much of the book to remain set up in type for over four years and so gave us the opportunity of eventually finishing the work.

In my task as Editor, it has been a delight to work with such a team. One feels that one is working with and for 5 Division and there is a great deal of satisfaction in that.

C.S.D.

Major-General H. E. Franklyn, C.B., D.S.O., M.C.

CHAPTER ONE

CONCENTRATION AND SERVICE WITH THE BRITISH EXPEDITIONARY FORCE UNTIL APRIL 1940

In which the brigades and units of the 5th Division concentrate in France as part of the British Expeditionary Force, and prepare themselves for the beginning of a long and great journey.

The Traditions of the Reserve Division
To be in reserve had for long been the traditional rôle of the 5th Division of the British Army. Over 120 years before the second World War, it had served as Wellington's reserve at Waterloo under the picturesque and forceful leadership of its top-hatted Commander, Sir Thomas Picton. Consisting then of the 8th and 9th British Brigades and the 5th Hanoverian Brigade, "General Picton's Division did wonders, and the gallant General himself fought at the head of it in a manner to astonish the greatest veterans", according to *The Times* of 22nd June, 1815. Although a few days previously they had suffered grievous casualties at the battle of Quatre Bras, the men of "Picton's Fighting Division", and particularly those of the 92nd of Foot, famous as the "Gay Gordons", of the Cameron Highlanders, the Black Watch, and the 1st Royal Scots, distinguished themselves again at the fierce little battle that raged around the farm of "La Haye Sainte". In all, in those few days, they lost more than a third of their numbers, but fought with such inspiration that could not fail to be reflected in their record and that of their successors, ever since. Although the regiments and battalions themselves changed, the spirit of the Fighting 5th Division grew and lived on.

The character of the Division as it became known in the second World War, first revealed itself in the South African War. Both the 1st Battalion the York and Lancaster Regiment and the 2nd Battalion the Royal Scots Fusiliers served with the 5th Division throughout both occasions. During the South

African War the 5th Division, under Lieut.-General Sir Charles Warren, particularly distinguished itself with the Natal Army, when crossing the Tugela River and in the final battles for the relief of Ladysmith during which the 11th Brigade Column included the 1st Battalion the York and Lancaster Regiment.

During the Great War of 1914–18, the 5th Division fought with II Corps of the B.E.F. (General Smith-Dorrien), as it did later in 1940, and gave good account of itself during the retreat from Mons, on the Marne, the Aisne and at Ypres, where again history was to repeat itself in 1940. In the order of battle of the B.E.F., two of the 1939–45 Infantry Brigades, the 13th and the 15th, were part of the 1914 Division, although the battalions that composed them were quite different.

In between the wars, the nucleus of the Division was based on Catterick. It was basically a Yorkshire Division, having a Yorkshire Brigade, the 15th. To all who were to wear the "Y", it became a proud and precious symbol of the difficult and ubiquitous rôle of a reserve division moving restlessly from theatre to theatre and fighting long intervals of boredom in between. It became a formidable reserve that certainly let no opportunity for distinction slip by, a reserve that was to earn the admiration of every commander privileged to wield it.

The Concentration in France

The complete division was not to take its place in Lord Gort's British Expeditionary Force until the last days of 1939, but most of its formations and units had been among the first to arrive in France. As already mentioned, 15 Inf Bde H.Q. with 1 Green Howards, was based on Catterick; 1 KOYLI at Strensall and 1 Y and L at Scampston. Part of the 13 Inf Bde, 2 Cameronians and 2 WILTS were also at Catterick and were joined later by 2 R INNISKS who came from Omagh, their depot in Northern Ireland. From Northern Ireland also came 2 Northamptons, to concentrate with 17 Inf Bde at Aldershot. The other two battalions of that brigade, 2 RSF and 2 Seaforth, came to Aldershot from Scotland.

Almost all these infantry battalions and other Divisional units had been manning some part of the main defensive position in France, or digging reserve positions behind it, until they met up in the final divisional area. All were Regular battalions, although two of them were later replaced by Territorials, but the remainder of the division was predominantly Territorial. Of the divisional artillery, 9 Fd Regt was a regular unit stationed at Bulford, later to be replaced by a Territorial unit, but 91 and 92 Fd Regts and 52 A Tk Regt were Territorial units from London, south of the Thames. The RE, RASC, R Sigs, RAOC, RAMC were partly Regular and partly Territorial from Liverpool, Wales, the Midlands and almost all parts of the United Kingdom. 7 Cheshire, which later became the Divisional Machine-Gun Battalion, was the first Territorial battalion to land in France in 1939, from its mobilization in Aldershot. Other units joined as the division went on its way and all of them quickly and completely assumed the remarkable divisional spirit.

The Gort Defensive Line, Winter 1939-40

By the end of 1939, commanded by Major-General H. E. Franklyn (later General Sir H. E. Franklyn, K.C.B., D.S.O., M.C.), 5 Div came under Lieut.-Gen. Sir Alan Brooke's II Corps. The latter was directly under the command of Lord Gort who was responsible to the French General Georges, commander of the French Army of the North-East, under the Supreme Allied Commander, General Gamelin. The main task of the division was to take over the Halluin Sector from the 51 French Division, improve it, and train themselves to man it in the event of a German attack. This sector around Halluin was a salient north-east of Lille, stretching from the northern outskirts of Tourcoing around Halluin and westwards along the line of the River Lys, parallel to the Franco-Belgian frontier, as far as Armentières. This was at that time the left flank of the British Expeditionary Force (B.E.F.), joining there with the right flank of the French Seventh Army which stretched northwards from there to the sea.

The French had constructed a large and continuous anti-tank ditch laced with various sizes of pill-box running along this line as an extension, albeit a feeble one, of the Maginot Line farther to the south. It had been hoped that from Halluin it could have been extended to the sea by the Belgians to make the Halluin sector unnecessary, but the Belgians remained strictly neutral until it was too late.

During the appalling weather conditions of the 1939-40 winter, first wet and muddy, then cold and hard, the divi-

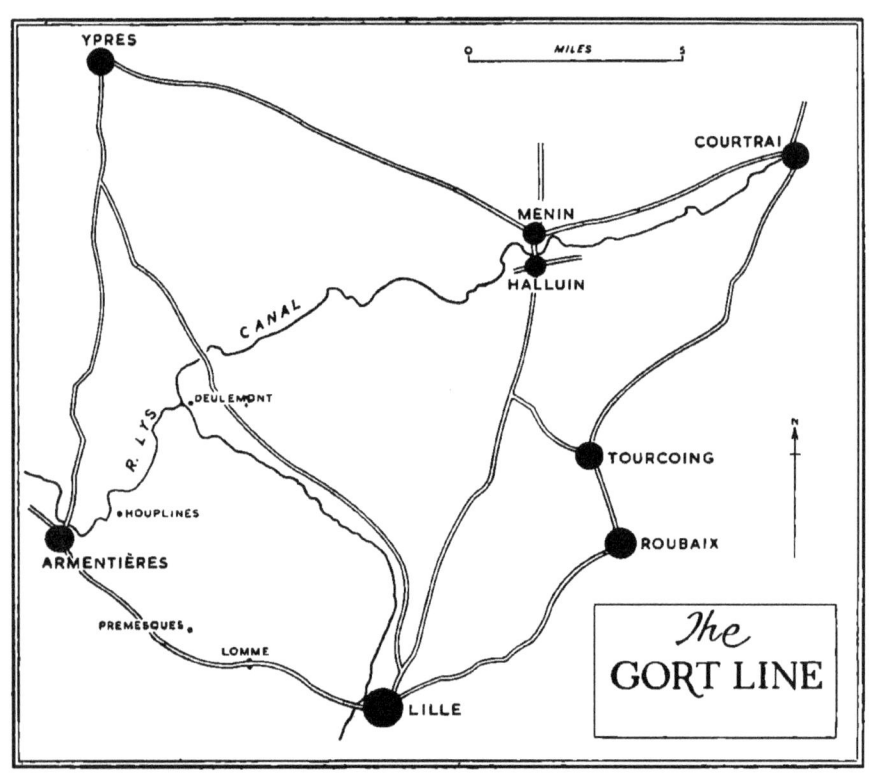

5th Division Sector

sion worked strenuously to improve their positions; digging deeper, revetting and wiring. Field and anti-tank guns, machine-guns and other support weapons were cunningly concealed in the then fashionable disguise of houses, haystacks and chicken sheds. Much cable was laid, much water baled out, many tempers momentarily lost, but the work was carried out efficiently and cheerfully. It was difficult, however, to believe that there was a war around the corner.

This defensive line was multiplied to give depth and the various courses open to the enemy were rehearsed in every possible way. It was not possible to reconnoitre forward into the neutral Belgium that lay between the divisional front and the Germans, although mistakes did occur at times: for instance, the Beagle pack run by the Cameronians frequently had to be bailed out until someone suspected that the Belgian half of Comines might be in league with the French half !

Amid all this work and training there was a lighter side as well. Lille abounded with entertainment to suit every taste and pocket for those who liked the gay city life. For those who were a little more cautious with their money, the local estaminet provided some sort of substitute for the pub at home. The new organization of ENSA, with its all-star bills, or the more modest concert parties run by the soldiers themselves, helped to make more cheerful what spare time there was.

Mail from home became regular and more and more prolific until the necessary censorship of outgoing mail became one of the major tasks of most officers. During all this time, each man got to know the men he was going to fight next to rather more than well: this was to serve the division in good stead when these men later found themselves facing difficulties and danger side by side. There was always leave to look forward to; and there was always the inner satisfaction of knowing that the call had been answered promptly even if it was no more than a whisper just then.

This gift of time to prepare for battle, particularly necessary to the semi-trained Territorials, had been denied to 5 Div of the first Great War. Good use of it was now made to build up an elaborate administrative organization, a long soft tail that was soon to be closer to the enemy than was then thought possible, although this was much as it was in the first war, unprepared for all-round defence.

Interlude on the Saar Front

There was hardly a unit, Regular or Reserve, in the B.E.F., that was unaware of its own training shortcomings. The Regular and Territorial armies of pre-war days had been woefully short of manpower and equipment, and the officers of the former had become sadly depleted in numbers. There had been few high level combined exercises in England prior to 1939 and the staff necessary in modern warfare had had little chance to gain enough experience. Whenever possible, intensive training, to make good the obvious deficiencies, was now obligatory. This for some culminated in a short spell in the Ligne de Contacte in front of the Maginot Line as part of a French Division on the Saar front. As far as the division was concerned, most of this was done by 15 Inf Bde in the snow period of January and February 1940 when Brigadier Berney-Ficklin's Brigade H.Q. at Kedange controlled a small sector around Halstroff and Waldweisstroff some thirty miles north-east of Metz. Although there was little fighting in this sector, there were many ideal opportunities for patrolling with the chance of the odd light skirmish with an opposing German patrol. These opportunities instilled experience and with it self-confidence in those most important members of the division, the Junior Leaders. 1 KOYLI moved there in January, followed by 1 Y and L, 1 Green Howards and a composite company of 7 Cheshire commanded by Major C. S. Durtnell, later Commanding Officer of that battalion. Some of the divisional Artillery officers went down attached as liaison officers to the French divisional and corps artilleries. The French gunners occasionally supported the brigade when they felt the latter's enthusiastic demands were not such as were likely to cause them too much discomfort when the inevitable German round-for-round reply arrived back on them. Many are the memories of this little interlude in the Saar; of the international arguments at the junction point in the Grossenwald; of the skeleton of Remling, a deserted shelled village in no-man's land; of George the sentry in a German railway truck who continually ate and read newspapers "on sentry" unmolested, as if charmed, by French or British intervention; of the German loudspeakers which frequently informed the French soldiers that while they fought in the Maginot, the English were misbehaving with their wives and daughters in

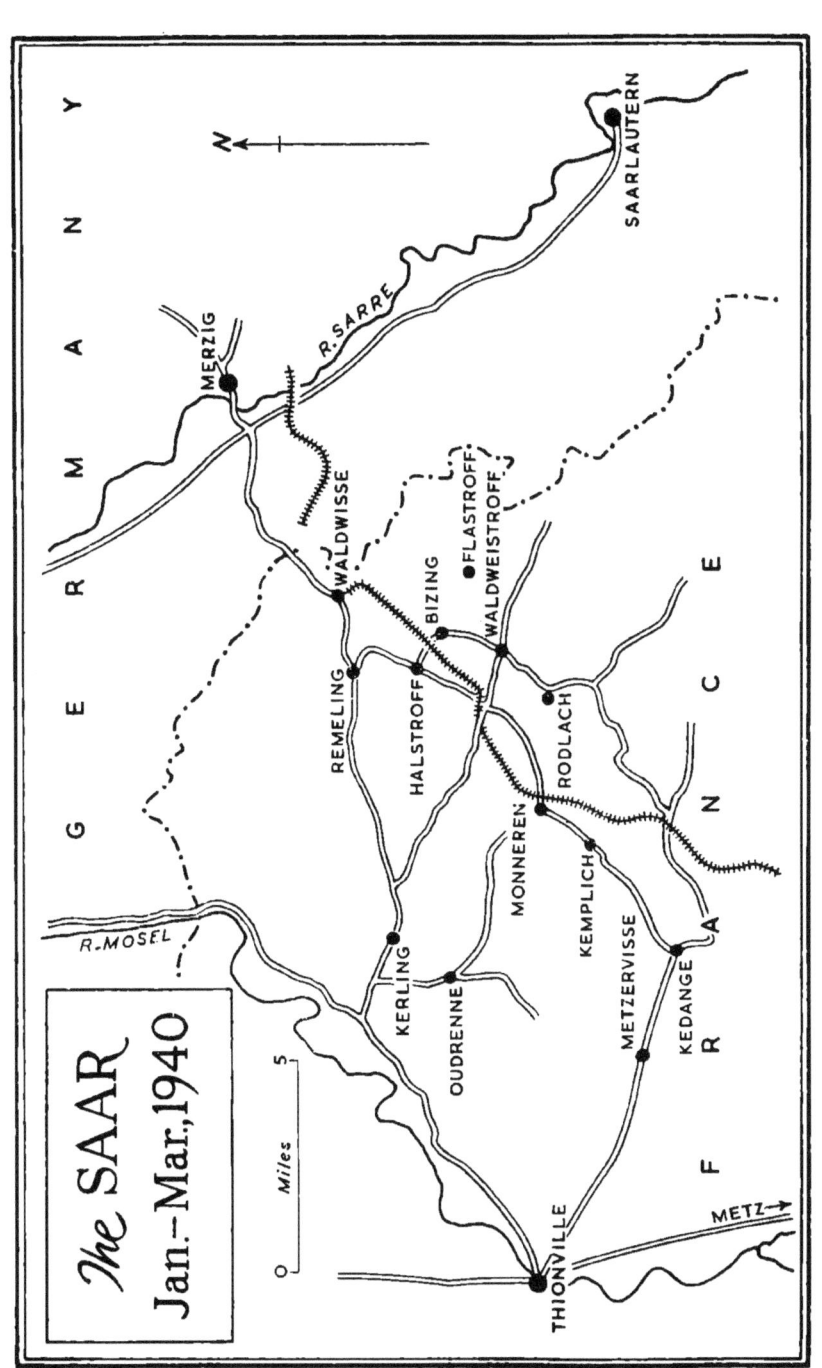

the north, apparently unaware that the French opposite them were Provençals from the south; above all of the quietness, and of the snow and hoar-frost which in the case of 15 Inf Bde were soon to become more significant in Norway.

Final Collective Training

Other training and courses took place, the gunners fired their guns at Oppy near Arras and Sissonne near Laon. Regiments, battalions and brigades went down to the Somme for short periods and often returned almost as quickly to face a rumoured German invasion. At one time the division was earmarked to rush to the aid of Finland against the Russians, and at another to the aid of the Norwegians against the Germans. The latter help was eventually supplied by 15 Inf Bde. These alarms and rumours of war were to be more the feature of a reserve division than of any other, and served early to instil the vital sense of security so essential in every man of such a formation.

The last of these collective training periods was in the latter part of April when the Division, less 15 Inf Bde, concentrated for manœuvres in the Somme country. This came as a welcome relief, particularly as the cold, hard and dreary winter had given way to a gloriously lovely spring which made the open simple landscape of the Somme look so remote from the sordid, flat and uninteresting north. But these halcyon days were not to last long. First there was the threat of a move to Norway, and some units got as far as the French ports of embarkation; the next alarm was more than a threat, and much nearer the B.E.F., but before considering this, the adventures and exploits of 15 Inf Bde, who had left France and the division in mid-April, must be followed to Norway.

Before the brigade moved, Brigadier H. P. M. Berney-Ficklin, M.C. (later Major-General H. P. M. Berney-Ficklin, C.B., M.C.), had been sent back to take over command of the force that was to operate against Trondheim, to replace Major-General Hotblack the first chosen commander, who had had a stroke in London. Brigadier Berney-Ficklin was on his way to the Orkneys when his plane crashed near Kirkwall and he was so injured that he was out of the running until he came back to command 5 Div a few months later. Major-General B. C. T. Paget (later General Sir B. C. T. Paget, G.C.B.,

JOINING THE B.E.F.
2nd Battalion the Royal Inniskilling Fusiliers board the *Royal Sovereign* on their way to Cherbourg on 15th September, 1939.

1st Battalion the Green Howards arrive in France.

CHANGING THE GUARD.—1st Battalion the York and Lancaster Regiment at Quesnoy, their billeting area.

MANNING THE GORT LINE.—The Command Post of 365 Bty. of 92nd Field Regiment of Mouchin on an exercise. From left to right: Lieutenant R. P. H. Stables, Major D. Cragg-Hamilton, 2nd Lieutenant P. W. Foster and Gunner Hill.

BREN GUN TRAINING.—1st Battalion the King's Own Yorkshire Light Infantry in their billeting area.

13TH INFANTRY BRIGADE STAFF.—Brigadier Dempsey and his staff, not forgetting their mascot "Tiny", at Wervicq on the 15th March, 1940.

Lieut.-Colonel R. L. Owen giving orders to some officers of 7 Cheshire.

2nd Lieutenants J. B. Bassett and D. H. Mays-Smith take a breather during the construction of gun pits at farm de la Rive near Bondues.

D.S.O., M.C.) took over from him and controlled the destinies of the brigade in Norway, now commanded by Brigadier H. E. F. Smyth, M.C., lately Commanding Officer of 1 KOYLI.

Bde H.Q. and the battalions left France on and about 17th April, arriving at Dunfermline in Scotland thirty-six hours later. Little time was wasted there before sailing from Rosyth to Norway where the Germans were having things much their own way.

This is the beginning of a long and great journey. During the second World War, from 1939 to 1945, 5 Div, as already mentioned, was predominantly a reserve division prepared to serve in any theatre of war. It did, in fact, at some time or other, appear in every theatre except the Pacific; consequently, it travelled some 30,000 miles, in and out of battle, sustaining long periods of waiting in between. It was to become by far the most travelled British division of the war.

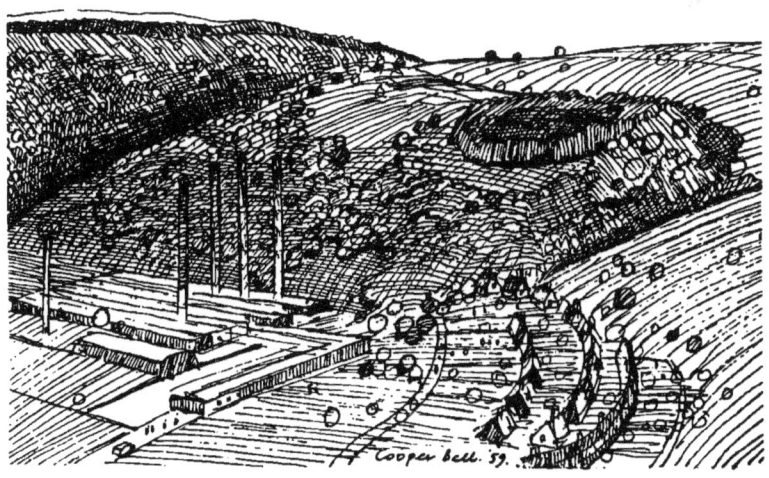

CHAPTER TWO

THE 15TH INFANTRY BRIGADE IN NORWAY

In which the 15th Infantry Brigade disembarks at Andaalsnes and tries to stem the German advance northwards from Oslo and in which the stands at Kvam, Kjörem and Otta provide the first distinctions of many to be gained by the Division on its journey.

The Setting

The opportunity Hitler had been waiting for to strike at Norway first came when Admiral Vian's "Cossack" daringly liberated the merchant seamen held prisoner in the *Altmark* during February. He believed, or found it convenient to believe, this incident to be a prelude to an Allied invasion of Norway; an event that would cut his supply of iron ore and timber which he was blatantly shipping from Sweden by violating Norwegian territorial waters. He was further inconvenienced when the Allies started to lay intensive minefields in these waters during March. The Allies, partly prepared for a sharp reaction to this manoeuvre, had earmarked a scratch British division and a French Alpine division which were to land, by arrangement with the Norwegians, should the Germans invade that country in reprisal. But they were not prepared for that reaction to be so immediate and so decisive. The Germans had planned to seize the main Norwegian ports with *coups de main* knowing full well that their defenders alone could not stand up to the mighty Wehrmacht. But just to make quite sure, they had taken the precaution of planting many agents, of whom the foremost was Quisling, who between them saw to it that that resistance was even less effective than it might have been.

On Tuesday, 9th April, after much preliminary Naval manœuvring, Oslo, Bergen, Stavanger, Trondheim and Narvik were entered, the former by airborne troops, preceded by their own brass band imported to soothe and distract the Norwegians from more nefarious deeds elsewhere. Although, by unfair means, most of the keypoints had fallen, the Nor-

THE 15TH INFANTRY BRIGADE IN NORWAY 11

wegians were fighting back and the Anglo-French force already mentioned set out to re-take Narvik. Two other forces were ordered to recapture Trondheim; the one known as "Mauriceforce" was to land at Namsos and attack from the north, whilst the other, "Sickleforce", approached from Andaalsnes to the south. These two forces were to converge on the port. It was to the deep valleys to the south and south-east of Trondheim where "Sickleforce" was meeting severe opposition, that 15 Inf Bde were now rushed. The task of this force was to co-operate with the Norwegian 2nd Division in preventing the Germans advancing northwards from Oslo; at the same time it was to hold off the Germans already in Trondheim, and deal with any parachutists that might land between the two forces. 148 Inf Bde (Brigadier H. de R. Morgan) advanced 150 miles from Andaalsnes and, without much opposition, established themselves to the south of Lillehammer; their lines of communications, however, ran down the narrow valley, the Gudbrandsdal, using the railway as their main artery as they had only a few road vehicles provided by the Norwegians. The enemy completely mastered this valley from the air and had the only artillery and tanks of either side. It was soon appreciated by the Brigade Commander and the Norwegian Commander-in-Chief, General Ruge, both of them unaware of the Allied plans for a follow-up force, that the brigade was now in a very dangerous position. The Allied plan, as conceived in London, was for 15 Inf Bde to support 148 Inf Bde by advancing down the next and parallel valley, the Osterdal, on the latter's left flank, and to come up into line with them at Elverum, south-east of Lillehammer; they were then to continue south to Hamar and thus, as the two valleys converged, the brigades would meet up north of Oslo. But this plan did not account for a forestalling enemy advance from Oslo.

The first serious clash between 148 Inf Bde, now scattered and mixed with Norwegian troops, and the Germans occurred on 23rd April at Tretten, which was held for a short time against heavy odds. The Germans eventually broke through and dispersed the remnants of the brigade of which few got back to the Norwegian support position at Faavang.

It was while this retreat was taking place on the 24th and 25th April that 15 Inf Bde disembarked at Molde and 1 KOYLI, commanded now by Major E. E. E. Cass (later

Brigadier E. E. E. Cass, C.B.E., D.S.O., M.C.) and 1 Y and L, Lieut.-Colonel A. L. Kent-Lemon (later Brigadier A. L. Kent-Lemon, C.B.E.) arrived first, to be followed by Bde H.Q. and 1 Green Howards, Lieut.-Colonel A. E. Robinson (later Major-General A. E. Robinson, C.B., D.S.O.) It was soon obvious that Brigadier Smyth's force would have to abandon the parallel valley project and rush to stem the ugly gap that was fast growing in the Gudbrandsdal over and around the almost non-existent 148 Inf Bde whose Norwegian allies were not likely to last much longer either. It was fortunate for "Sickleforce" that the Germans were in the habit of calling off the engagement in the evening and thus not following up their successes gained in the daytime. Both KOYLI and Y and L were able to take up their positions in time, molested only from the air. Although not a large force, the German Battle Group commanded by General Pellenghar, consisted of seven infantry battalions, some of them from the Hermann Goering Division to be met again elsewhere by 5 Div. One was a ski-mounted unit trained for mountain fighting. There were also a motorized machine-gun battalion, a troop of tanks, some 5.9-in. guns; in all, about 9,000 men with air and ground support superiority against three battalions, an anti-tank company, some LAA guns borrowed from 148 Inf Bde and a handful of sappers with a very limited supply of explosives.

There now followed an almost classical continuous withdrawal by 15 Inf Bde from Kvam to Andaalsnes, a withdrawal carried out against overwhelming odds and with inadequate supporting weapons and transport, and in the most severe physical conditions, demanding the highest of mental and bodily toughness laced with an iron discipline.

It must be remembered that the deep snow hampered movement, although it prevented high altitude flanking moves; that many miles of ice-covered roads had to be negotiated in ordinary ammunition boots which gave no real grip for those marching. It must also be remembered that the northern nights were short and that first light came before three o'clock in the morning. When day came, it became so hot that the snow melted, only to crust up again in the cold night.

These were the conditions under which its battles were to be fought by 5 Div in Norway.

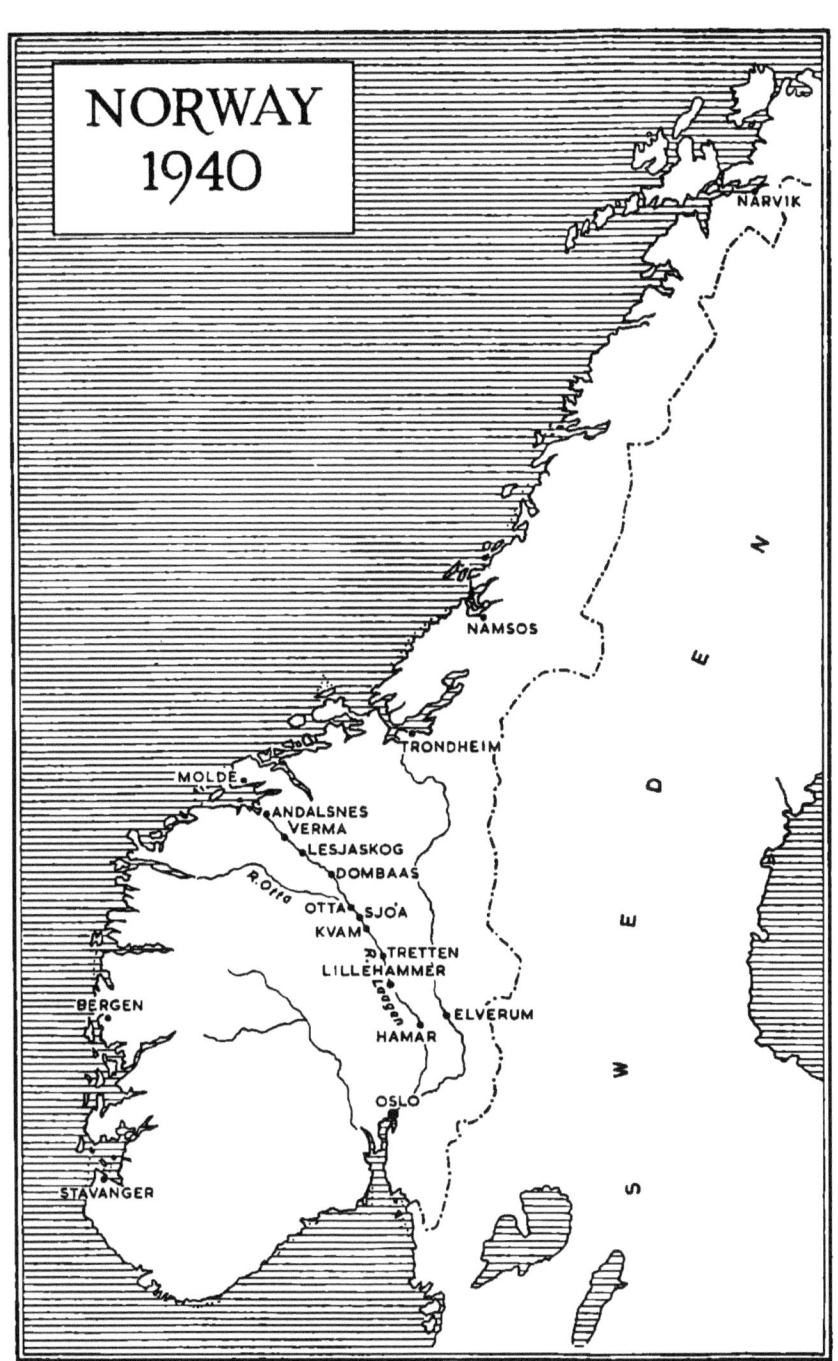

The King's Own Yorkshire Light Infantry at Kvam

On the morning of the 24th April, it was decided that 15 Inf Bde should make a stand at Kvam some thirty miles nearer the coast from Tretten and covering what was left of 148 Inf Bde. Again the Germans moved swiftly and it was 1 KOYLI alone that barred their path at Kvam, having had to march the last ten miles or so from railhead at Otta. The valley was too narrow and too easy a target for the Luftwaffe to make the use of motor transport possible. The battalion were attacked from the air often that day, but were able to dispose themselves in a fairly strong position by first light on the 25th. This was astride the wide but shallow river Laagen with "A" Company (Captain R. L. N. Gowans) and "C" Company (Captain S. F. Fox, who was killed that day) in depth on the island near the right-angle bend on the river, east of Kvam. This island was little more than half a mile long, almost without cover save for a few willows on the banks at the ice-covered water's edge. On either side of the main river the banks rose so steeply in tiers of pine and birch-covered slopes as to prove a difficult approach for German flank infiltration. There were, however, here and there, small clearings and lonely farmsteads, which could be useful in defence. On the south bank there was not even a road or track, so that "C" Company needed only to put out a detached platoon to give warning of an enemy approach that way. On the other side "B" Company (Major H. N. Burr) was sited forward at the village of Kvam, a collection of some fifty wooden houses, on the slopes about 250 feet above the river.

"D" Company, in depth, were covering the neighbouring village of Veikle, Battalion Headquarters and Headquarters Company being in Kvam itself. There was no artillery support and the eight 25-mm. French Hotchkiss anti-tank guns available, commanded by Captain P. H. D. Dessain of the Green Howards, were deployed in the best possible positions. Only two 3-in. mortars were in action, there were no high explosive bombs for the 2-in. mortars, and very few tools for digging into the hard ground.

The advancing Germans were first encountered by a small battle patrol commanded by Lieutenant J. H. Oldman, who was wounded and captured by a leading German tank after he had stayed behind to cover the withdrawal of the patrol. He was later awarded the Military Cross for courage and determination whilst a prisoner of war. The sun was now up and the heat became intense. The Commanding Officer was heard to remark that it was just the day for a battle. It was not, however, until some five hours later that two more tanks and an armoured car, closely followed by guns and marching and lorried infantry, presented a wonderful target to the well-concealed battalion who, with great wisdom and restraint, held their fire until the last possible moment. The first shots were actually fired by the anti-tank gun with "A" Company, which knocked out both tanks and forced the armoured car back into cover. Despite the extremely limited area for deployment, the German gunners, particularly the 5.9's, soon rained a very heavy bombardment into Kvam, setting fire to the buildings, causing the KOYLI heavy casualties, particularly on the island from which "A" Company were forced to retire. Brigadier Smyth was wounded and was relieved by Lieut.-Colonel Kent-Lemon, who handed over 1 Y and L to Major D. C. Tennent.

This fierce shelling quickly set light to the wooded slopes and drove those taking cover there out into the fields of fire of the enemy machine-gunners. Under cover of all this, the German infantry steadily moved forward in small parties. Although "A" Company were practically wiped out, KOYLI held on grimly until last light, being considerably helped by the timely arrival of "C" Company of Y and L (Major F. H. Jordan, M.C.), who took up a position farther up the northern slopes above Kvam, and were able effectively to enfilade the enemy infantry. The Germans had failed to take full advantage of their enormous superiority in supporting fire, and, as expected, disengaged by nightfall. The anti-tank guns had done heroic work and at least two of them had been knocked out, one of them after killing two tanks, a feat which was made possible by the fearlessness of Captain A. F. McRiggs, M.C., Commanding "E" Company. Seeing that the tanks were screened from the vision of the anti-tank guns by a road block, he personally and under very heavy fire, removed the road block, being wounded in the effort. He survived to command the battalion later in Sicily.

During the calm of the night, the survivors from the forward companies were withdrawn into the rear company area.

That same afternoon the remainder of Bde H.Q. and 1 Green Howards arrived at Molde and Andaalsnes. General Paget also arrived with them to take over command of "Sickleforce", only to find that everything was in favour of the enemy. Even the few Gladiator Fighters, gallantly operated by the R.A.F. from a frozen lake near by, had been caught on the ice by enemy bombers, only three of them surviving to support the ground forces. This and the inadequate amount of anti-aircraft defence, enabled the Luftwaffe to dominate completely the main valley with its road and railway right back to the vulnerable base of Andaalsnes.

The Norwegians were, by now, showing the ill effects of the last three weeks and the roads were littered with their abandoned transport. There was also the prospect of a thaw in the immediate future which would worsen the bad state of the already inadequate quota of roads.

Few commanders have been presented with a more hopeless task than that which now faced General Paget, very much remotely controlled by the authorities at home. It was obvious, even if they could survive another day at Kvam, that it would only be a matter of time before KOYLI would be annihilated as 148 Inf Bde had been at Tretten. There was only one other suitable place for a stand in protection of the vital junction at Dombaas of the railways to Andaalsnes and Trondheim; this was at Otta, some ten miles behind Kvam. It was decided that 1 Green Howards should immediately prepare this position for defence, while the other two battalions held off the enemy as long as possible, and while General Paget tried to get urgent reinforcements from home to cover what he had realized at once must otherwise undoubtedly develop into an evacuation.

After the usual early morning reconnaissance sortie followed by bombing, the Germans attacked next day accompanied by a vicious artillery bombardment. "A" Company of Y and L on the left managed to hold the first attack, but this action only directed the persistent Germans farther up the slopes until they managed to get round to the rear of the village of Veikle and cut it off from the main KOYLI position. All the time our troops were mercilessly pounded from the air and from the augmented German artillery. A very gallant platoon counter-attack led by 2nd Lieutenant French saved the Y and L company from being completely pinched out by the German infantry. The latter were driven back fiercely and with many casualties, after having fired a prodigious amount of ammunition.

But this check to the enemy was only temporary, and it was very obvious that it would now be only a matter of hours before the position at Kvam became quite untenable. General Paget decided that he must now make a stand between Kvam and Otta to gain every day possible for the arrival of the help he had already sought. He ordered 1 Y and L, less their company forward at Kvam, to make a stand at Kjörem, two miles behind Kvam; and farther back still, the remnant of 148 Inf Bde, strengthened by a company of 1 Green Howards, were hastily organizing the defence of Dombaas.

Fortunately, once more, the enemy disengaged at nightfall and KOYLI with the remaining six anti-tank guns, withdrew without much trouble, although "D" Company with the Y and L company did not receive their orders to withdraw, and only discovered that the remainder had gone back when a runner sent down to Bn H.Q. found the village full of Germans and got back alive with a certain amount of difficulty.

This defence of Kvam by 1 KOYLI and 1 Y and L was the first firm and determined defence of the war by British troops and it had been made against heavy odds. Casualties had not been light, but less than fifty prisoners could be claimed by the Germans. This was a fitting prelude to the many battles that lay ahead, and it is noteworthy that in the churchyard at Kvam today there lie more soldiers who fell defending Norway in 1940 than in any other single place in that country.

The York and Lancaster Regt at Kjörem

On 27th April, 1 KOYLI moved back through the other two battalions to join 148 Inf Bde's position at Dombaas. 1 Y and L, now reinforced by "B" Company 1 Green Howards (Captain P. G. J. M. D. Bulfin) and the Carrier Platoon also from the Green Howards (Captain G. R. Lidwill) had very much the same problem at Kjörem as 1 KOYLI had had at Kvam. The battle that followed was almost a repetition of the previous one. Although the valley at Kjörem was much narrower than at Kvam, both banks of the river were so accessible to the enemy, that it was found necessary to put "A" and "B" Companies (the latter less two platoons) and 1 Green Howards on the south bank, whilst the remainder held the two islands and the north bank.

"D" Company were forward at the village with "C" Company strengthened by the two "B" Company platoons, close together on a steepish slope behind the village. H.Q. Company prepared to defend the islands. Standing patrols were put out farther up the slopes.

After their customary air activity, the Germans attacked early in the morning and, as at Kvam, the infantry took to the wooded slopes as soon as they were fired upon and the few tanks that could be deployed moved along the road to give them covering fire. Once again artillery fire was intensive and soon set fire to the woods to such an extent that a protective smoke screen partially covered the advance on either side of the road. 1 Y and L had some mortar support but it was inaccurate enough to be more of a hindrance than an advantage. By the evening, the enemy had repeated his flanking performance and had actually succeeded in placing a road block, covered by fire, behind the battalion position. This was dealt with by an energetic battle patrol whose immediate determination cleared what would have quickly become a disastrous situation for Y and L.

In the afternoon, an attempt was made to detach the two companies south of the river with the intention of their forming an intermediate position at Sjoa, two miles behind Kjörem, but in the darkness they lost their way, eventually arriving at Dombaas two days later, having suffered heavy casualties. Meanwhile, H.Q. "C" and "D" Companies held the position almost until midnight, but had considerable difficulty in disengaging as the enemy had this time succeeded in getting small ambush parties right amongst Y and L, causing many losses. The Commanding Officer, Major Tennent (later Brigadier D. C. Tennent, C.B.E.) was among those missing and Major F. H. Jordan took over command. So heavy were the losses that his command was now reduced to thirteen officers and three hundred men. Nevertheless, 1 Y and L prolonged the line on the right of 1 Green Howards.

It was now apparent that reinforcements would not arrive in time to prevent the Germans reaching the coast, and the problem was rapidly becoming that of how best to extricate

THE 15TH INFANTRY BRIGADE IN NORWAY

what was left of "Sickleforce" for the inevitable evacuation, preparations for which were now in hand. Any further battles must aim at holding off the enemy long enough for this to be achieved. There was the further disquieting news for General Paget that German ski troops looked like being able to threaten the rear of 15 Inf Bde. On top of all this, the Luftwaffe had practically obliterated Andaalsnes and with it a large proportion of the brigade's reserve ammunition and had halved the ration supply. There appeared to be no answer to this overwhelming air superiority, nor was there any artillery available to counter the enemy's unmolested use of many guns.

The Green Howards at Otta

A further ten miles or so back from Kjörem, the village of Otta, at the junction of the Otta and the Laagen river, was the scene of the third of the brigade's battles. The whole of the German approach could be dominated by two spurs of high ground on either side of the Laagen and about 2,000 yards to the south of Otta. "C" Company manned the eastern and "D" Company (Major C. E. W. Holdsworth) the western spur. H.Q. and "B" Company were disposed on the small peninsula of Otta itself. "Y" Company was on the east bank and was a scratch detachment made up of M.T. drivers, dispatch riders, and odd last minute reinforcements commanded by Captain G. F. P. Worthington, M.C. Behind it was a detachment of Bde H.Q. personnel. Both these parties took the place of "A" Company which had been sent back to strengthen the 148 Inf Bde position at Dombaas. "B" Company, who had fought with Y and L at Kjörem, had been withdrawing throughout the night and did not arrive in Otta until after first light. To start with, once more, there was no artillery support and but five anti-tank guns now remained effective. It was a very large area for such a small and ill-supported force to hold.

Almost to time-table, the German air reconnaissance started at 0700 hrs. on the 29th April, to be followed by light bombers who swept the area effectively, although not quite so effectively as before, as the Green Howards had had more time to conceal and dig their positions—or build them up when the ground was too hard. The first attack arrived up the railway line at 1030 hrs. and consisted of about a company of infantry supported by armoured vehicles and guns. This force was obviously intended to draw small arms fire and this it did very accurately. Follow up infantry, as at Kjörem and Kvam, moved from the road up the slopes, while the tanks rumbled on down the road right into the well-concealed anti-tank guns. One of the latter, alone, knocked out three of the enemy's tanks.

The Germans then made an attempt to cross the river to take Otta from the east, but their rubber boats and their passengers were promptly sunk by accurate rifle fire from "Y" Company. A further attempt was made to cross with a pontoon bridge, but this was also checked with heavy casualties to the German sappers. P.S.M. W. H. B. Askew, who controlled part of "Y" Company at this time, particularly distinguished himself with conspicuous skill and a total disregard of personal danger, bringing his men back in perfect order when the task had been completed and earning the Distinguished Conduct Medal for his fine example to all ranks.

Throughout the rest of the day the enemy hammered away at the Green Howards with heavily supported frontal attacks on the west side of the positions with a few more abortive attempts to turn the left flank. Any Green Howards who moved to reinforce attacked positions were cut by murderous cross fire, and it was not until late afternoon that "C" Company (Captain Armitage) were able to move further up the slope to gain a protected position from which they could master a German force almost double their size and thus put an end to further infiltration. By nightfall, the Germans had exhausted their effort and had to break off the engagement to sort themselves out. At 2230 hrs. they made an unexpected and desperate dusk attack which would have run into "C" Company withdrawing had the latter not failed to receive their orders for the move. As it was, they were able to drive off the attack with further heavy casualties to the enemy. The company then made use of the lull after the battle to withdraw quickly over the difficult rocky high ground, having to proceed often on their hands and knees to avoid further trouble. It was from this high ground nearly 400 years previously that some invaders from Scotland were slaughtered in the valley by boulders and rocks rolled down on to them by the local Norwegians. When "C" Company got down to Otta eventually they found it deserted by the rest of the battalion. They immediately set off to cover the thirty miles to Dombaas on foot, reaching the latter that same day. This withdrawal of "C" Company was a very fine example of good imaginative leadership.

Such was the beating taken by the enemy at Otta that day that they were quite unable to follow up quickly and the battalion were thus able to withdraw without further battle, although the remaining five anti-tank guns were so damaged that they had to be destroyed.

The defence of Otta had been an exemplary one, a great credit to the defenders and a clear demonstration of the ability of the men of 5 Div to absorb heavy punishment and still be able to shoot back coolly and accurately to good effect. Two examples of outstanding individual initiative were displayed by L./Corporal C. F. Headley and Lieutenant Rawson, both of "C" Company. The former went out on his own with a Bren gun to get a devastating enfilade shoot on some attacking Germans and thus forcing them to withdraw. Lieutenant Rawson took out a small party to within effective range of a conference of some thirty German officers which they effectively broke up in disorder. They then tackled to some purpose a party of Germans trying to build a pontoon bridge. Although they were being heavily shelled, Lieutenant Rawson quickly led his men to alternative positions, and finally he volunteered to lead back a fighting patrol, in broad daylight, to try to contact the remainder of the battalion. Neither he nor his party were seen again.

"During the afternoon," wrote the Force Commander, "1 Green Howards fought splendidly. There is no doubt that the enemy suffered many casualties in this battle and in his subsequent action showed little desire or ability to press home an attack."

The Evacuation

The last stand of 15 Inf Bde was to be made at Dombaas. Here 1 KOYLI had prepared a position to the south of the village with three companies forward and two in reserve. The other two battalions organized the defence of Dombaas itself. The ice on the river was now thawing so rapidly that "A" Company of KOYLI were nearly cut off from the rest of the battalion.

The Germans were obviously not expecting this last rearguard position, as they arrived almost casually during the afternoon in infantry formation, dragging their mortar carts, without the customary air, artillery or tank support. On the other hand, for the first time, the brigade was strengthened by the appropriation of four Norwegian guns and crew. They were, however, of such ancient design that they were quite unable to clear the crest and succeeded only in dropping their shells in the forward companies of KOYLI. An effort was then made to dig in the trails of the guns and make use of the upper register, with the result that the shells disappeared into the next valley. This greatly relieved the forward companies, who naturally assumed there were Germans at the receiving end, an assumption that heartened them a great deal.

From well-covered positions 1 KOYLI caused the enemy grievous casualties before they even knew what was happening. Without their normal fire support and helped by a single all-purpose aircraft, which was shot down amongst them, the Germans seemed quite unable to mount a proper attack; and during the evening Brigadier Kent-Lemon was able to order the withdrawal to continue without further contact.

That night, 1 Y and L with 148 Inf Bde and base details embarked for the United Kingdom. The remaining 1,700 or so left of 15 Inf Bde were to have further adventures before following them. At about 2230 hrs., Bde H.Q. and the remnants of 1 KOYLI boarded a train for Dombaas whilst most of 1 Green Howards travelled in Norwegian lorries. The first part of the train journey was uneventful; the passengers were dog tired and extremely cold, huddled up in the windowless carriages. This was a change from the train used by 1 Green Howards on the way down to Otta, which had sleepers reserved for officers with beds made up with clean sheets! At midnight, after travelling about fifteen miles, some Norwegians and the remains of the Bde A Tk Coy were picked up at Lesjaskog. At about 0100 hrs. there was a terrific shock when the two engines and the first carriage were derailed in a bomb crater across the line. Eight were killed and many seriously injured, some by the impact and others by the exploding ammunition. Rescue was made difficult by the deep snow surrounding the scene and it was quite obvious that the train would never start again. Accordingly the survivors set out on foot to try to reach the cover of a long railway tunnel marked on the map as being some eight or nine miles away, at Verma. It turned out to be eighteen miles in all, and a very weary column arrived at the tunnel at 0900 hrs. on the 1st May, after being machine-gunned from the air.

The tunnel at Verma was some 800 yards long with a hairpin bend in the middle so that daylight did not penetrate far. The sides of the tunnel were rough and rocky and thick in sooty slime. There were two trains in the tunnel. The one at the other end was to take them farther on their journey. The whole of that May day was spent in the tunnel in great discomfort waiting for darkness, while the Luftwaffe made desperate attempts to seal the ends with bombs.

It was a greasy, grimy band of singing warriors that eventually arrived at the other end of the tunnel, after completing a particularly difficult obstacle course. Here, however, when the engine got up steam, they were driven into the open by the intense fumes. There was some difficulty then in getting the train, which was on a slope, to move. At this juncture the Norwegian train crew decided to stage an unofficial strike! The train, moreover, had to be reversed manually for which, fortunately, there was no lack of help. Whilst this manœuvre was in progress, news came that the small rearguard detachment of Marines left at the scene of the crash had been overwhelmed, and the Germans were making a great effort to get to Verma. Both 1 Green Howards and 1 KOYLI hastily deployed so effectively that the enemy, when they arrived, declined to press home the attack. The train was finally got under way and took its passengers without further incident to within a mile of Andaalsnes. After another short march, they arrived in the devastated harbour at 2300 hrs. to be embarked, under the light of blazing buildings, within three minutes—about the quickest embarkation on record. There was hardly a man who was unable to resist the time-honoured remark "Thank God we've got a Navy."

And so thanks to the Royal Navy, who had also taken it there, 15 Inf Bde came back to the United Kingdom defeated, but glorious in that defeat. In sixteen days they had travelled from France to Scotland and back to Scotland via Norway, two thousand miles or so in all. They had set a high standard of determined, courageous and skilful defence against tremendous odds for which they lost thirty-two officers and five hundred and fifty-two other ranks. That these figures were not greater is a lasting tribute to the standard of leadership at all levels. It was to be the fate of the Germans, some of them also of the Hermann Goering Regiment, some three years later, themselves to be chased down some other deep valleys in Italy by the same soldiers they had driven out of Norway. The odds were then on the side of the Yorkshiremen, but it is questionable whether the technique was much different.

In the meantime, although fighting was to continue in the north of Norway for a further month, the task of 15 Inf Bde was now completed.

NORWAY.—A driver from 158 Field Ambulance searching the wreckage after a severe bombing attack in Norway.

NORWAY.—The King's Own Yorkshire Light Infantry waiting to embark for England.

The advance into Belgium.

The Belgian peasants get their first taste of German air ferocity.

The air war hits the civilian personally.

The advance towards Bruxelles proceeds as refugees pass on the way back.

An imprest vehicle is destroyed in the retreat.

The Field Ambulance find time to look after a German pilot shot down in their area.

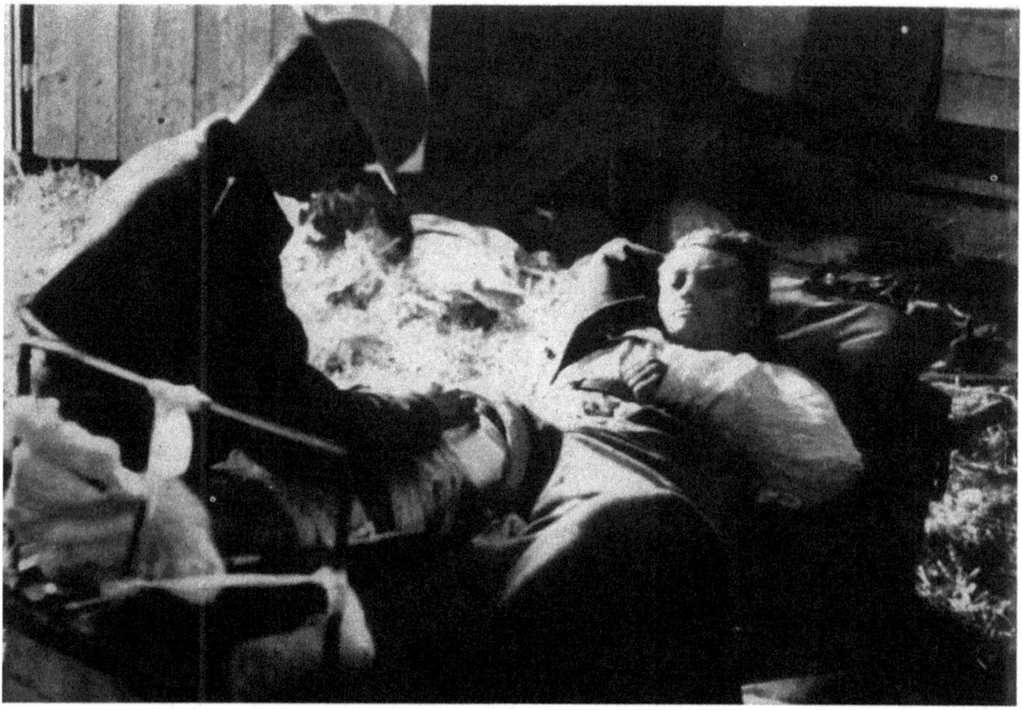

CHAPTER THREE

CAMPAIGN WITH THE BRITISH EXPEDITIONARY FORCE, MAY 1940

In which the German armies of the West invade the Low Countries and France, causing the British Expeditionary Force to move up to the River Dyle: in which the 5th Div as G.H.Q. Reserve moves up behind into the Senne River Line to the south of Bruxelles, from which to protect the right rear flank of the B.E.F.; in which the Division, part of "Frankforce", moves south to cover Arras and hold off the enemy armoured divisions from Dunkirk; in which the Division disengages skilfully and just in time to close another gap between the failing Belgians and the rest of the B.E.F., to the south of Ypres; in which, after a bitter holding struggle, the remnants of the Division evacuate in an orderly manner from Dunkirk.

The Background to Plan "D"

It was the intention of the Higher Command that the remainder of the 5 Inf Div should return to the United Kingdom as a reserve on 9th May 1940. Certain units of the division actually reached the Channel ports. The move was cancelled late on that day. When it was decided that the division would not be leaving the British Expeditionary Force it was drawn back into G.H.Q. Reserve.

It would be difficult to understand how the B.E.F. could have fought the ensuing battles without an adequate reserve, but then nobody could have foreseen the real nature of those battles; in addition, the problems that confronted the Allied commanders in making any plans were made more difficult by the uncertainty as to the military intentions of the Belgians. With undoubted integrity and good intention, the King of the Belgians had steadfastly refused to co-operate with the Allied Command in forming defensive plans against the almost inevitable violation of Belgian neutrality by the Germans. It was too painfully obvious that the French Maginot fortifications ended abruptly at Mézières and that the Belgians had made almost as much of a show against potential attackers from the west as they had on the Albert Canal and the Meuse against those that might come from the east. The equally obstinate convictions of the French that the Wehrmacht could not possibly operate in the wooded hilly country of the Ardennes permitted them to place there two of their most tactically weak armies, both of them under strength. Their two strongest armies, the First and Seventh, with the Cavalry Corps were with the B.E.F. waiting for action in the extreme north.

Having made up their minds that they could in fact use the Ardennes front for a break through, especially against such obviously weak opposition, the German High Command were quite content to see these strong Allied formations drawn well up into Belgium before they were committed to battle; there was, furthermore, always the chance that the strong Panzer drive might reach the Channel ports and thus paralyse the Allied lines of communication. It was this weakness that caused the Allied commanders finally to adopt two separate alternative plans for dealing with the Belgian vacuum.

Plan "E", for the defence of the Line of the River Escaut, envisaged an advance by the B.E.F., in line with the French, to the river to the north and south of Oudenarde. Plan "D", for the defence of the Line of the River Dyle, took the advance farther into Belgium over unreconnoitred routes, to a much shorter front, nearer the enemy. The former plan entailed an advance of but a few hours, whereas the latter involved a march of some sixty miles. It was to be a race between the two main protagonists, the Allies having little doubt but that the Germans would pay scant heed to Belgium neutrality, especially as King Leopold had, by his neutral unpreparedness, left this way so open. Furthermore, the alternative was the difficult wooded and hilly terrain of the Ardennes or the much vaunted steel barrier of the Maginot forts farther to the south; a barrier which no foe was permitted to pass. Whether plan "E" or "D" was adopted by the Allied High Command depended entirely on the weight of the German attack and the degree of resistance offered to it by the Belgian Army. It was apparent to all concerned that the latter would benefit more from the operation of plan "D".

A close study of their order of battle, which had fortuitously remained unchanged for some time, should have revealed the

German intentions very clearly. Opposite Belgium and Holland stood Von Bock's Army Group "B", some twenty-eight divisions in all, three of them armoured; farther south, facing the Ardennes, Von Runstedt's Army Group "A" of forty-four divisions of which seven were armoured, was poised against the French 2nd and 9th Armies hardly a third of their strength physically. Von Runstedt, moreover, had the advantage of the comparatively narrow front between the Sambre and Meuse rivers and the northern pivot of the Maginot Line, an advantage which enabled him to attack in some depth.

When the time was ripe the Wehrmacht was able to carry out this plan to the last detail, its opponents moving exactly as they wanted them to move. The break-in on the Southern front gained sufficient momentum quickly enough to cause the B.E.F. to be hemmed in against the Belgian and French armies of the north, with little serious frontal fighting against the enemy.

Preceded by widespread bombing attacks on most of the Allied war installations in the early hours of 10th May, the Germans struck at Holland, Belgium and Luxembourg. General Gamelin ordered Plan "D" to be implemented and reconnaissance units of the B.E.F. reached the Dyle that same night, to the unbridled encouragement of the Belgian population. The Dyle Line was manned from Louvain to Wavre, some seventeen miles, by I and II Corps with 1, 2 and 3 Inf Divs up and 4 and 48 Inf Divs in reserve covering positions. Behind them were 42 and 46 Inf Divs hastily preparing the Escaut Line while 5 and 50 Inf Divs, each of them only two brigade divisions, the latter a motorized division, formed G.H.Q. Reserve.

The early use of airborne troops and Fifth Columnists, particularly in Holland, and a determined thrust down the Meuse, which caught the French before most of them had even manned their forward positions, gave the Belgians little chance to stand for long on either the Meuse or the Albert Canal Lines. It took the Germans barely three days to break-in to the South and this was achieved with so much impetus that the Dyle Line soon became untenable.

I and II Corps were in position on the Dyle, dug in, by the afternoon of the 14th. The Germans attacked on the 15th particularly in the area of Louvain, with little success, but that night 2 Div had to withdraw from Wavre, under heavy shell-fire, to conform with French withdrawals on the right of B.E.F. Behind the Dyle lay an intermediate line on the Senne river. It was to this line that 5 Inf Div now advanced to make contact with the enemy.

The Advance to the River Senne Around Hal

The division was far back around Amiens when Plan "D" was put into effect and all units started next day to march towards concentration areas. Some of the way was made in trucks, but a great deal of marching was carried out in very warm weather. 2 Northamptons, of 17 Inf Bde, for instance, marched twenty-five miles from Camps-en-Amiennois to Bernaville on the 11th, followed by twelve miles to Ligny-sur-Cache on the 12th and a further thirteen miles to Herni-court on the 15th, eventually arriving in the Hal area in the afternoon of the 16th. The battalion had had an exhausting final move against an almost overwhelming flood-tide of homeless Belgian refugees. These pitiable folk cluttered with their household goods, pressed on westwards, persistently driven off the roads into the ditches by frequent machine-gun attacks of the Luftwaffe or by the harassed drivers of the divisional vehicles. All roads were in the same state of chaos as the scared mob fleeing from Bruxelles joined those already on the move from Louvain and the villages in between. And so the impeded move of the division up to the Senne Line was completed only just in time.

13 Inf Bde reconnoitred positions quite near the battlefield of Waterloo where once their predecessors had so distinguished themselves. The brigade finally dug itself in around Hal, 2 INNISKS garrisoning the town itself. 17 Inf Bde were to the north of 13 Inf Bde.

On the 16th it was decided by General Billotte, in command of the Northern Group of Armies, that the B.E.F. must withdraw to the Escaut Line to conform with the French withdrawal to the south. That night the Dyle Divisions were withdrawn and 4 and 5 Divs, manning the Senne Line, now prepared to make contact. At the same time, General Giraud's Seventh Army, after its dashing advance up the sea flank, withdrew round the rear of the B.E.F. leaving the Belgian Army fighting on the left flank of the B.E.F. 48 Div now withdrew through 5 Div who had been dug in by 1000 hrs. on the 17th with 1 Div on their left. Up till then the only contact had been with the Luftwaffe who lost one or two of their planes at least to the intrepid machine-gunners of the various Anti-Aircraft LMG Pls of 5 Div. The village in which Div H.Q. had been established was dive-bombed and the H.Q.R.A. anti-aircraft machine-gunner claimed one victim. Around Hal some German cyclists put in an appearance and Major Butler of 2 R INNISKS with a small detachment crossed the canal to draw first blood for the division.* He came back with three dead and two wounded German cyclists. The main enemy impact came later on in the evening, but they were quite unable to penetrate the Divisional front, partly due to some accurate shooting by the Div Arty from behind the Senne, from which positions they had had time to complete meticulous registration since the previous day. Under command of I Corps Arty, the Div Arty had picked up 97 Fd Regt, in place of 92 Fd Regt now supporting 50 Motorized Division, and was further strengthened by the inclusion of 5 Med Regt, under command.

The Withdrawal from the Senne

The enemy made several determined attacks at dusk sup-

*Actually the first German blood attributed to 5 Div was drawn in the Saar by 15 Inf Bde in February 1940.

ported by artillery fire, but they could still make no headway. On the southern flank of the B.E.F., however, the French were being forced back under considerable pressure and once more the B.E.F. had to withdraw to conform. The next intermediate line before the main Escaut positions was on the Dendre between Alost, Ninove, and Grammont. 5 Div, however, were to pass through both these positions to an area into reserve once more around Seclin. The withdrawal from the Senne was premature enough to cause a certain amount of confusion in the orders for withdrawal. There was also a severe shortage of maps to make things more difficult.

17 Inf Bde moved 2 Northamptons back to the Enghien-Castre road to form a base through which 6 Seaforth and 2 RSF moved back to Paricke to be joined there by 2 Northamptons. Again the move was made partly on foot and partly by truck and was completed without much further incident.

13 Inf Bde had greater difficulties in disengaging and two companies of 2 R INNISKS, in Hal, missed the flank line and had to find their way across country to join the battalion as it crossed the Dendre river two days later, a race before the bridges were blown at Les Deux Acrens. 2 WILTS had a more orderly retreat, but 2 Cameronians temporarily lost their "B" Company which rejoined the battalion some hours later at Scaubecq.

The division had had its first taste of withdrawal, a difficult operation of war, especially when undertaken under air attack among panic-stricken refugees and amid rumours of enemy parachute attacks. The M.T. had to be sent back and Brens, anti-tank rifles, mortars, boxes of ammunition and other equipment all had to be carried on the backs of the walking soldier. Furthermore, at least one company in the division had to double for two miles to get over the bridge at Grammont before it was blown. The day or so most units got for rest at the other end of this withdrawal was more than welcome in the circumstances.

The Task of Frankforce

The French First and Ninth Armies were now being mercilessly hammered by Runstedt's Army Group "A". Von Kleist's Army was ordered, at the time that the Senne Line was being denied, to advance to Cambrai and St. Quentin which threatened the right flank of the B.E.F. Little was known of this by Lord Gort, but although it was outside his responsibility, he took steps to cover his southern flank immediately. The Garrison of Arras, 1 Welsh Guards, was strengthened by scratch troops of all arms and three Territorial divisions, the 12, 23 and 46, all of them training divisions on Lines of Communication duties. The whole was put under the command of Major-General R. L. Petre and became known as "Petreforce".

On the 18th, General Gort realized enough of the situation to the south to worry about the gap made by the Germans. Unless that gap could be closed, the B.E.F. would have to go right back to the Somme or evacuate to the Channel ports. The former course was becoming more remote hourly, for there were ten German divisions making good headway in the space between the Allies. The matter was discussed with the War Office by telephone. Meanwhile the Escaut Line was manned after some bristling rearguard actions and 5 Div was gathering round Seclin. The other reserve division, 50, was moving straight back from the Dendre to the Vimy Ridge area.

Arras itself was now holding out against several German armoured divisions, one of them the 7th, commanded by Major-General Erwin Rommel. It was essential that this important road junction should be held, so 50 Div, together with the 1 Army Tank Brigade, was sent there to stop the pressure. The whole force in the area around Arras was to come under the command of General Franklyn and became known as "Frankforce".

On the same day, the 20th, Lord Gort was ordered by the Chief of the Imperial General Staff to make a counter-attack towards Amiens in the south, being assured that the French would be making a similar attack to close the gap from the south. It was obvious, however, that should the French be unable to attack, the Germans would soon be on the coast, leaving the B.E.F. no alternative but to withdraw by sea. Lord Gort, however, ordered "Frankforce" to proceed with a localized offensive south of Arras to delay the German armoured thrust as long as possible. That day, tanks of Army Group "A" reached the coast near Abbeville and the Admiralty started thinking about Operation "Dynamo", the evacuation from Dunkirk.

The orders to General Franklyn were to support the garrisons in Arras by occupying the line of the River Scarpe to the east of Arras and establishing contact with the French by patrols and road blocks to the south to hinder the long lines of communication of the Germans. When these orders were given it was not the intention to counter-attack, but, after the orders from the Cabinet were received, an effort was made personally by General Ironside to get General Billotte to co-operate from the south, with the "Frankforce" attack on the 21st. General Franklyn was given no new orders and when asked by General Billotte at General Prioux's H.Q. if he could help them by attacking towards Bapaume and Cambrai, was bound to reply that the forces available to him only permitted the limited local offensive already planned. When, later that day, the French informed him that they could not attack yet, General Franklyn did not alter his orders at all.

Unfortunately, faulty intelligence at a lower level considerably underestimated the number of German divisions operating in the area, and the offensive became more limited than was intended.

Q Battery, 91st Field Regiment, R.A., at dinner, Christmas 1939. (Photo taken in normal mess lighting.)

Sunset on the Western Front.

"A" Company 7 Cheshire at Monchicourt.

Exhausted men recover lost sleep back in England.

13 Inf Bde relieved the 23 Inf Div and the French Cavalry, on the Scarpe to the east of Arras.

17 Inf Bde was held in reserve on Vimy Ridge until the first phase of the advance round Arras, to be made by 151 Inf Bde of 50 Div, was completed. The other brigade, 150, was sent to strengthen Arras and that part of the Scarpe between it and 13 Inf Bde.

The plan was for 151 Inf Bde first to sweep round Arras to the Cojeul River. In the second phase, 13 Inf Bde was to advance over the Scarpe and join up with 151 Inf Bde to the south of Arras. The story of the advance does not belong here except to record that it was soon overwhelmed by an immense concentration of the enemy and that artillery support was given by the two batteries of the 92 Fd Regt already mentioned as being away from the 5 Div for this period. The attack, together with the subsequent stand of 5 Div on the Scarpe, did, however, give the Germans considerable thought as well as a fair proportion of casualties. During the battle, 151 Inf Bde took 500 German prisoners. Von Runstedt reckoned there was a serious threat to their lines of communication, a threat which unfortunately neither the B.E.F. nor the French were able to exploit.

During the advance, 13 Inf Bde secured a bridgehead over the Scarpe for the second phase advance that never started. General Franklyn cancelled the offensive and decided to inflict the longest possible delay on the Germans, by holding on to the line of the Scarpe and the high ground north-west of Arras, so memorable in the first World War as Vimy Ridge.

The Defensive Battles of Arras, 22nd–23rd May

The 13 Inf Bde front was some 5,000 yards long with the R INNISKS on the left, from Plouvain ("C" Company) to St. Vaast ("A" Company). 2 WILTS on their right, stretched to Roeux, and 2 Cameronians were in reserve, two miles to the north, around Fresnes. Bde H.Q. and the 91 Fd Regt were around Gavrelle. The 9 Fd Regt was at Oppy and the 97 Fd Regt at Neuvireul. 17 Inf Bde were to the west of the Arras Road, around Maroeuil, with a few game tanks of the 1st French Light Mechanized Division farther over to the west on Mont St. Eloi.

Quite a few of 17 Inf Bde positions were dug or scraped

without the help of the picks and shovels that had to be left on the MT. On the 21st May, a patrol of "D" Company the Cameronians, led by 2nd Lieutenant A. R. Kettles, made an assault crossing of the Scarpe to draw enemy fire and came back with the division's first unwounded prisoner—a greatly surprised German dispatch rider.

In the early hours of the 22nd May, the enemy, on the left front, forced a way over the river between 13 and 150 Inf Bdes and penetrated quite deeply between 2 R INNISKS and 2 WILTS and between "C" and "B" Companies of the former. The break through between companies of the two battalions was promptly and skilfully dealt with by the Cameronians, who later on in the day moved under command of 50 Motorized Div and took up positions on Vimy Ridge. The breach between "B" Company (Captain Shaw) and "C" Company (Captain Nugent) of 2 R INNISKS was gallantly fought off with grenades and Captain Shaw and Lieutenant Foulkes gained M.C.s before they had to withdraw to "A" Company position. Some of them were, as 17 Inf Bde had been, in the old trenches of the first World War preserved as part of the Canadian Memorial. On the memorial itself the 92 Fd Regt had established an Artillery Observation Post in support of 50 Motorized Div.

The enemy did not press heavily against 17 Inf Bde until early on the 23rd May when Brigadier Stopford (later General Sir M. G. N. Stopford, G.C.B., K.B.E., D.S.O., M.C.), out on reconnaissance, saw German tanks and about 200 infantry moving up towards Mont St. Eloi. At the same time, shelling increased and culminated in an attack against the Northamptons on the extreme right. The first German tank was knocked out by the guns of the Bde Anti-Tank Company on the edge of Maroueil Wood. At this moment the French 75 mm. Field Gun Regiment at Ecurie announced dramatically that they were wanted elsewhere and proceeded to give a flawless demonstration of an extremely rapid withdrawal, and the French tanks with the Northamptons on Mont St. Eloi announced that they also could do their job better elsewhere although they were still willing to counter-attack Mont St. Eloi should this be necessary. At 1415 hrs. Brigadier Stopford learned that the French on his left had gone off to attack some enemy in Souchez.

The Germans got into Maroueil Wood and amongst the

Northamptons. They were immediately driven out again by a counter-attack from a platoon of each of "D" and "A" Companies. Again the enemy attacked and one of their tanks got near enough to shell Bde H.Q. very effectively. "C" Company (Captain Norman) were shortly afterwards overrun. After a very gallant defence, the battalion was ordered to withdraw at 1800 hrs., as there were no French left on their right flank, to Neuville St. Vaast, where they were very heavily bombed. The two days had cost them 352 casualties, including the C.O., the second in command, the Adjutant and the R.S.M. Major R. M. E. Wetherall took command as the battalion moved farther back at 2200 hrs. that night.

That evening the enemy again penetrated deeply on the left of 2 WILTS, and 2 R INNISKS were divided into two groups with orders to get to Raches and there form a Brigade Reserve. The second in command of the latter, Major Vining, performed a miraculous extraction of the whole of the Regimental Transport by night, under fire, harassed by enemy patrols, he safely led them over fields of stubble until they ran into a German machine-gun nest. L/Corporal Quigg took this on alone and systematically destroyed it by good shooting for which he earned a Military Medal.

The gunners fired a great deal of ammunition to some effect in the defence of the division and 91 Fd Regt, after producing a good regimental concentration on to a German Bridging Train as it moved from Moncroy over open ground down to the river, became involved in heavy hand-to-hand fighting, before the situation on 13 Inf Bde front was restored by the Cameronians' counter-attack.

The divisional front that evening was now sorely pressed. On the right 17 Inf Bde had been forced back to the line from Berthonnal Farm to Ste. Catherine, whilst the French, as already reported, had fallen back to Souchez. The remainder of the tanks, of the 1st Tank Brigade, had fallen back even farther, behind the Canal Line. Between Souchez and Vimy, 150 Inf Bde were still holding, in some disorder, whilst to the east of Arras, 151 and 13 Inf Bdes were only just keeping their ground against a superior enemy. The latter were still denied Biache, however. The remains of "Petreforce" were still besieged in Arras itself where they were almost entirely surrounded.

Lord Gort now had no option but to try to extricate "Frankforce" and rely on the Canal Line to guard his right and right rear flanks. A gallant defence had gained valuable hours and it would be useless to lose the reserve for the sake of a few hours more. That night, 23rd–24th, saw one of the miracles of the campaign as the remainder of the 5 and 50 Divisions made an orderly withdrawal from the Arras Salient under the most difficult circumstances. There was only one road then known to be clear, save for refugees, for this move back into the perimeter of the B.E.F. and that road was threatened by the rapidly closing in German forces. Yet they never fully followed up their advantage and were probably too tired themselves to make the best of the opportunity. The Luftwaffe were heard in the air above almost continuously, but they never bombed this slender route through Henin Lietard, cluttered with wrecked vehicles, abandoned farm carts, some of them with dead horses still in the shafts and often partly blocked by the bricks and rubble of bombed walls. Slowly and silently this phantom column wound its way through these obstacles, and against the restless sea of refugees moving in all directions with no apparent aim other than that of just keeping on the move.

The holding of Arras for those vital days had held off a

great number of German divisions to whom it had indeed been a thorn in the side. The German High Command acknowledged this and admitted that the offensive caught them in a very tired and stretched position. Although they were not prevented from reaching the Channel ports, their rate of advance was slowed down by their anxiety for the security of their lines of communication. It was unfortunate that the Allies were unable to turn this into an advantage by closing the gap between their armies. The B.E.F. was now facing the enemy on two main fronts; I and II Corps were facing east and III Corps with 5 Div were facing south-west on what was known as the Canal Line. An attempt was being made to mount another attack southwards, this time on a much bigger scale in conjunction with the French in the south. This counter-attack had been first planned by General Georges on 18th May, "proposed" by General Gamelin on the 19th, discussed by General Weygand, who had now taken over supreme command, on the 21st and cancelled on the 25th, a day before it was due, when it was realized at last that it was a sheer physical impossibility. This muddling amongst the French commanders was just one more of the unnecessary difficulties manufactured for the B.E.F. which undoubtedly owes its salvation to the fact that Lord Gort courageously rode above them and made his own clear-cut decisions, well ahead of events.

When the counter-attack was cancelled, 5 and 50 Divs were ordered to close the gap now widening between the B.E.F. and the Belgians in the area of Ypres. And so after barely two days' rest, the division was rushed to new positions along the line of the Ypres–Comines Canal.

The Ypres–Comines Canal Line

After the nightmare withdrawal from Vimy, 5 Div had some respite on the 24th and the 25th, whilst preparing for the Weygand attack southwards, that never materialized. On Sunday the 26th the situation of the B.E.F. altered for the worse. It was now being attacked, together with the French First Army, on two separate fronts of almost a hundred continuous miles.

To the north the Belgian Army was quickly disintegrating and it was only a matter of hours before it would vanish altogether. Between it, to the south of Ypres, was an ominous gap on the left flank of the British II Corps. It was in this gap that 5 Div was to fight a very great and critical defensive battle. II Corps front stretched along the Lys to Halluin and thence to join 1 Corps north-east of Roubaix. The latter extended to Pont-a-Marcq, the junction point with the French First Army, who held a salient as far south as Marchiennes and Raches. The British III Corps took over from there north-westwards to Dunkirk.

General Brooke, commanding II Corps, first filled in the Ypres–Comines gap, with 143 Inf Bde from the 48 Inf Div. This Brigade came under command of 5 Div when the latter arrived in the area, later on the 26th, only minutes ahead of the three divisions of the German Sixth Army of Army Group "B", and under their shell-fire. The division came in on the left of 143 Inf Bde, on a wide front from the bend in the canal north of Hollebeke, to Zillebeke, a village three miles south-east of Ypres. Although this front was mostly close country, facing the north-east, the defensive positions had to be sited mostly on forward slopes in full view of the enemy and open to heavy and accurate mortar-and shell-fire. The canal

would normally have been an anti-tank obstacle, but, being unfinished, was quite dry.

12 Lancers had found Ypres to be undefended. It was not attacked until 50 Div was brought up the next night to extend the II Corps front well to the north of it. The French 1st Light Armoured Division claimed to be holding Zillebeke, but when Brigadier Stopford went to see them, he found only a few tanks and these were on their way to Ypres. At Zillebeke, 17 Inf Bde formed the left flank until 50 Motorized Div arrived. 2 RSF were on the right and the 6 Seaforth on the left, along the railway line, with 2 Northamptons in reserve on the west bank of the canal in thickly wooded country. On the right of 17 Inf Bde, 13 Inf Bde stretched to Houtham, where 2 Cameronians joined the 7 R Warwick of 143 Inf Bde. On their left were 2 R INNISKS and, in reserve, 2 WILTS on the high ground nearly a thousand yards to the east of the St. Eloi–Warneton road.

Div H.Q. was in the basement of a large house in Ploegsteert Wood; the Cheshires and the Div Arty were also deployed around the Ploegsteert–Wytschaete–St. Eloi area. The latter were the first to arrive and were able to complete some effective registration during that Sunday afternoon. In their reports on the battle, the Germans complain bitterly of the good use made by the gunners of their observation posts. It was as well that good O.P.s were available, for there was such a shortage of maps that each regiment had to rely on one 1 : 100,000 map of the area until the Commander I Corps Medium Artillery personally brought a further supply in his staff car.

The German plan for the following day was that Army Group "B" should take Kemmel and Poperinghe. The former was to be the objective of the Sixth Army of Von Reichenau, which consisted of the 18th, 31st and 61st Divisions. Against them stood the strengthened 5 Div. By the evening of the 27th, General Franklyn had the following additional troops under Command: I Corps Artillery, 18 Fd Regt, three other batteries and Chestnut troop of the Royal Horse Artillery for the Div Arty; some spare 18-pounders to stiffen up the anti-tank guns of the 52nd Anti-Tank Regiment; the 143 Inf Bde; 13/18th Hussars; 10 and 11 Inf Bdes and the RE from 4 Inf Div; and later on were added 3 GREN GDS, 2 N STAFFS and the 2 Foresters all from 1 Inf Div. All these extra units and sub-units under command of the division played their great part in this vital defensive action, which enabled the rest of the B.E.F. to withdraw into the Dunkirk Perimeter.

During the night of the 26th–27th, 2 Northamptons were moved slightly forward to the line of the railway, to conform with the right-hand brigade, 150, of 50 Div, which had moved up on the left of 5 Div. There was no contact during that night except for the odd patrol.

At daybreak on the 27th, after their patrols had crossed the railway line, the enemy attacked along the whole of the divisional front. These attacks were supported by heavy artillery and mortar fire and accurate dive bombing. The augmented Divisional Artillery immediately opened up with strong defensive fire which caused the enemy grievous casualties, and this fine support was kept up throughout the day.

On the right, 143 Inf Bde were soon slowly forced back and this, together with a strong attack on Houtham, another between 2 Cameronians and 2 R INNISKS and a third at Hollebeke, put 13 Inf Bde in a difficult position by early afternoon. On top of this both Bn H.Q. were harassed by direct attacks and both suffered heavy casualties. It was soon obvious that the canal positions were untenable and at 1600 hrs., Brigadier Dempsey (later General Sir M. C. Dempsey, G.B.E., K.C.B., D.S.O., M.C.) ordered the forward battalions to withdraw to the position of 2 WILTS on the high ground around the Eloi–Warneton road.

This withdrawal was carried out by 1730 hrs. in difficult circumstances as nearly all communications forward of battalions had been cut by shell-fire, and enemy patrols were active.

A similar situation had occurred farther to the north on 17 Inf Bde front. Here, enemy pressure forced back 6 Seaforth from the railway line and almost surrounded 2 RSF. Both battalions were drawn back to the south of 2 Northamptons' reserve position by the early afternoon. The latter quickly had two of its forward positions overrun on the left flank, in "A" Company area, and lost touch with 150 Inf Bde of 50 Div which had come up to the north of Zillebeke. A section of Carriers was swiftly put out to protect the division's left flank. The remainder of the battalion was then seriously attacked and "B" and "D" Companies had to give ground

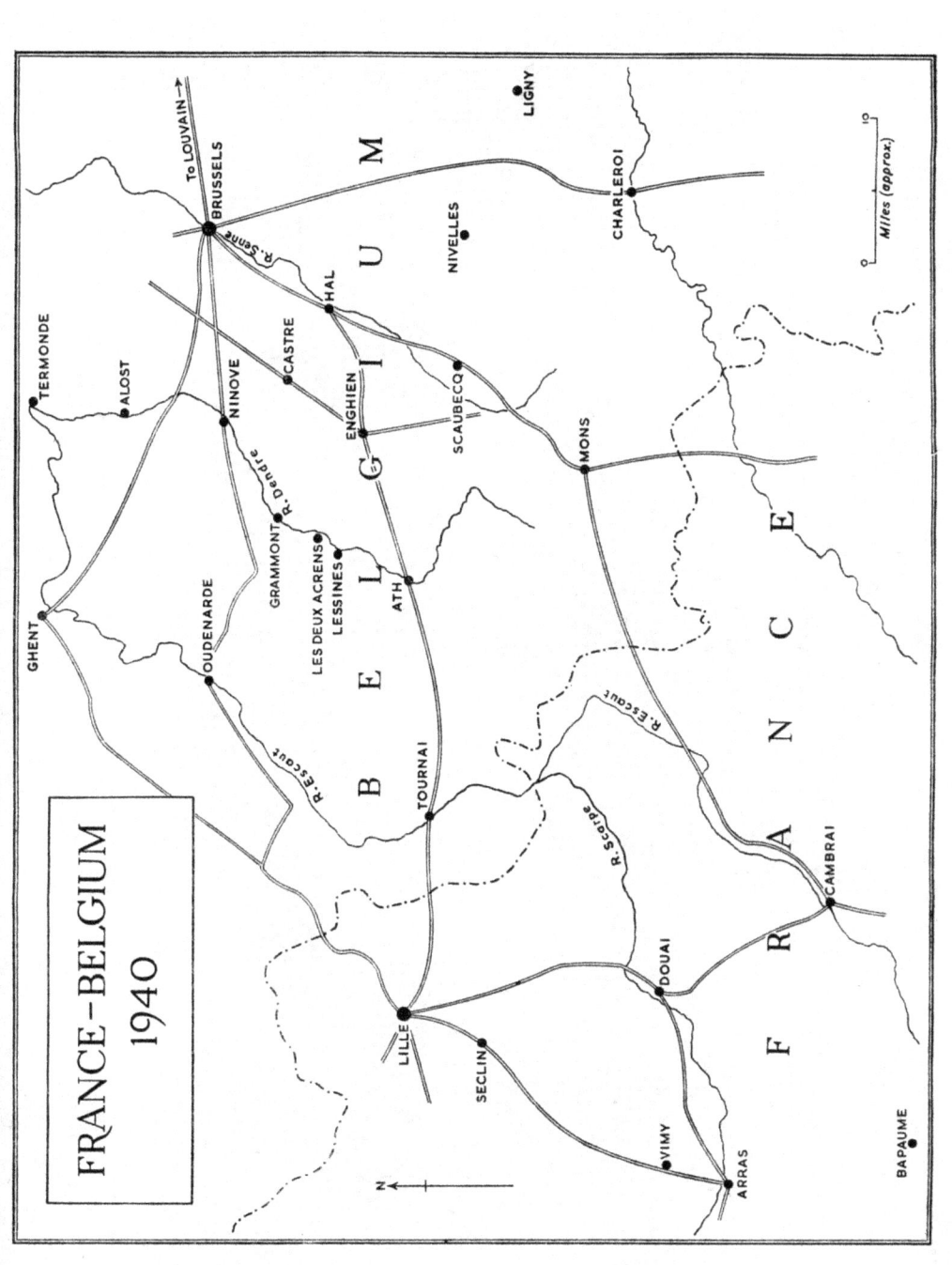

almost as far as Bn HQ where the second-in-command (Major Watts) had organized forty men to dig in alongside them.

Some gallant local counter-attacks were put in during the late afternoon and evening. At 1900 hrs. the 6 Black Watch supported by 13/18 Hussars and some Engineers on 143 Inf Bde front, managed to drive back the enemy to the Kortekeer river line at heavy cost; and in the half light, 3 GREN GDS and 2 N STAFFS carried out a most successful counter-attack. These two battalions had marched 20 miles on 27th May and had had no food since breakfast time. Their fine effort did much to ease the German pressure on the right of 5 Div. On 13 Inf Bde front at 1830 hrs., the situation was relieved by a gallant bayonet charge led by the Commanding Officer of the Cameronians (Lieut.-Colonel Gilmore) supported by the whole weight of the Artillery and his own Carriers under 2nd Lieutenant C. A. Weir performing a cavalry charge. This was also a costly affair in which the commanding officer, the adjutant and two company commanders were among the wounded. For this action Lieut.-Colonel Gilmore was awarded a bar to the D.S.O. he received in the first World War.

By late evening the divisional front had stabilized around St. Eloi on the Warneton–Ypres road. To the north of 17 Inf Bde, 10 Inf Bde of 4 Div came into the line between the former and 50 Div which stretched through Ypres with the 12 Lancers in contact with the Belgians around Roulers. The latter were retreating away from the B.E.F. all the time and by midnight had ceased to offer any further resistance to the enemy. After a day of rumour, the King of the Belgians had decided that his army could no longer serve any useful purpose and asked for an armistice. There was some delay before news of this reached Lord Gort and when it did, it was obvious that the gap between II Corps and the coast must be filled before the Wehrmacht was able to pass through enough troops to turn the northern flank of the B.E.F. 3 Div were moved to the north of 50 Div and south of Noordschote. It was now even more vital than ever that the Comines–Ypres line should be held as long as possible by 5 Div Group, to enable the remainder of the B.E.F. to get safely into the Dunkirk Perimeter.

The night of the 27th/28th came as a timely relief. Contact was kept by patrols, but the Germans, on the whole, stuck to their familiar routine of breaking off the engagement by night.

The remainder of II Corps, however, had wheeled back to the line of the Lys, prepared to hold an "L" shaped front for yet another day whilst 13 Inf Bde made a difficult move across the front about a mile northwards. At 0400 hrs. the whole front woke to gunfire as the German Sixth Army renewed the attack. On the right of the Divisional Front, at the junction with 4 Div, 3 GREN GDS, 2 N STAFFS, and 2 Foresters withstood sharp assaults which were to continue throughout the day. 13 Inf Bde on their left had all three battalions committed. 2 WILTS now on the right, with 2 Cameronians in the centre about a mile to the east of Wytschaete, 2 R INNISKS being further to the north. Two battalions of 4 Div, the Bedfordshire and Hertfordshire and the Duke of Cornwall's Light Infantry, were placed between 13 and 17 Inf Bdes. The latter was on the extreme left of the front with 2 RSF on the left of the DCLI, 2 Northamptons in the centre and to the north of them 6 Seaforth. The line held, and spirited counter-attacks were mounted locally, but the strength of all battalions was draining away rapidly. By 2030 hrs., 2 Northamptons and 6 Seaforth had so few men left that it was only a matter of time before the sheer weight of the German attack must tell; of the former battalion, only forty N.C.O.s and men managed to get away at the end of the day. Every battalion had to reorganize and few of them could muster more than a headquarters and two rifle companies throughout the day. Senior officers became casualties in every battalion, but always junior officers stepped unflinchingly into the breach and filled it well. The R.S.M. of the Cameronians took over as Adjutant and 2 R INNISKS lost every one of their senior officers.

At about 1100 hrs., a particularly vicious bombardment, which mercifully failed to do much damage, so small were the battalion localities, proclaimed a renewed main effort from the Germans. Fortunately, artillery and infantry O.P.s were able to spot their forming up manœuvres and great and effective measure was dealt out! To such effect that it deterred them from trying to mount another attack for some hours. Many were the acts of heroism displayed by all ranks of the division and its temporary attached units during this magnificent stand on the Warneton–St. Eloi road. By the end of the day neither brigade could muster more than 600 all ranks and it was necessary to form a battalion from each of them. All of them paid tribute to the magnificent work of the divisional and I Corps Artillery whose guns fired continuously, until their ammunition was completely expended. The latter were full of admiration for the magnificent personal leadership of the two brigade commanders throughout the day. At one time both of them, shelled out of their own Headquarters, found refuge in the Regimental Headquarters of 91 Fd Regt.—and ate their dinner.

Mention has already been made of the good observation available to the gunners; there were many disadvantages other than a lack of maps; signal cable was continually breaking under shell-fire and radio became jammed. News of the infantry was intermittent and, at times, stragglers had to be organized for the defence of the guns. What news that did get through almost inevitably came through gunner channels, themselves often shaky. Communication got so bad that observed fire became almost impossible. This did not deter the Forward Observation Officers from going right forward in a supreme effort to support the battalions. One such officer from 91 Fd Regt, after his N.C.O. assistant had been wounded, went forward alone on foot for a mile and a half until he eventually found the drive leading to the château that was occupied by 2 RSF. The latter, a company strong, were practically surrounded, so the gunner made his way back to the wireless set in his carrier, now under heavy fire from three sides, where he called for fire from his battery. Very few of the RSF came out of that château, despite effective artillery support.

During the afternoon, 3 GREN GDS carried out a successful counter-attack at Warneton, which eased the German pressure once more.

The enemy came back to attack strongly just after nightfall. Hardly a man in any of the battalions was not completely exhausted, if he had not already become a casualty, and there could be no mistaking the signs that they would be unable to withstand a further heavy attack. Gradually the Germans worked their way towards the gun lines where every spare man was armed and ready to defend the guns.

On the extreme left at this stage one had a masterly example of co-operation between Gunner and Infanteer.

One of the forward O.P's of 91st Fd. Regt. on this flank had been withdrawn at dusk, and a young M.G. officer of the Manchester's who was siting his guns forward of the ridge in front of the guns, was tapped in to the O.P. line to the Bty. Command Post.

As dusk fell, this young officer came through with the news that the enemy were forming up in strength in the front edge of a certain wood, and from his description the Battery was able to bring down heavy and accurate fire on them.

The Battery Captain and the C.P.O. had a map between them on a table and as the description of the target came through on the phone, the Battery Captain drew the position on the map and it was quickly plotted by the C.P.O. and passed to the guns.

This happened with increasing frequency as the hours went by, the excitement and tension mounting rapidly, particularly after the Battery was told that they were to hang on at all costs.

The enemy were obviously suffering heavy casualties, for as they came forward they ran into the zone of the M.G.'s and when they fell back to reform they came under heavy fire from the 25 pounders.

Conversations such as follows were taking place on the 'phone.

M.G. officer, shouting with excitement: "They're coming on again from that wood on the left—I don't think we shall be able to hold them this time."

Gunner: "Hold on, old boy, and let us know when they get back to the wood."

M.G. officer: "We've done it, we've done it—they're going back again—to the same wood."

Gunner: "Good show—leave 'em to us now."

Some light relief was afforded the people in the Command Post when, at a particularly tense moment, the B.C.'s batman appeared at the top of the cellar steps and said in a thick Cockney voice—"Could you gennelmen eat a plate o' sossidge an' mesh?"

In such a spirit was the defence maintained by all arms of the division. Many a time the Germans came to within a few hundred yards of the gun positions only to be driven off by point-blank fire from guns and all available small arms as well.

From 2200 hrs. onwards, the infantry withdrew through Wytschaete. 2 Cameronians were so depleted that they were all able to get in or on to the normal battalion transport. The other battalions were in no better state, they had paid dearly for their glory. The gunners moved out last at three o'clock in the morning into positions near Kemmel. They were again attacked in the process.

Captain Bassett, commanding "D" Troop of 363 Battery, 91 Fd Regt, had great difficulty with the boggy ground that compelled him to winch out his guns one by one. In the middle of this operation some of the infantry arrived in the gun area hotly pursued by the enemy. Quick action had to be taken to destroy two of the guns, for which the Detachment Commander, Sergeant Dowley, was awarded the Distinguished Conduct Medal. He was left behind severely wounded for two hours and was rescued by a local counter-attack. The Troop Commander was wounded and later captured in a casualty clearing station.

During this hard day, all officers of Company Commander level learned of the immediate evacuation of the B.E.F., and although the fighting had been bitter and the divisional losses severe, it had not been realized how much the safety of the whole B.E.F. had depended on the defence of the Ypres–Comines Canal.

While this difficult disengagement of 5 Div was being effected, 3 and 50 Divs, who had not been so seriously attacked during the day, swung back and northwards on the pivot of Noordschote, to form an Intermediate Line from Noordschote to Poperinghe by way of Lizerne.

By 0500 hrs. on the 29th, the division, now virtually reduced to two battalions, had withdrawn through this Intermediate Line to man yet another defensive position alongside 42 Inf Div on the Line of the River Yser.

There was to be no more fighting on that line and then during the night, 29th–30th, all vehicles and equipment were destroyed at Houtham, whilst the men marched into the final perimeter in the sandhills around Moeres and Adinkerque. The remnants of the battalions of 13 Inf Bde took up one more defensive position in the early hours of the 29th to cover a bridge being used for the withdrawal of the 4 Div over the Furnes Canal. The bridge was blown, after its garrison had been very accurately shelled, in the early hours of the 30th. The 91 Fd Regt, however, remained to continue shooting, now alongside their sister regiment, 92, at Adinkerque.

After a silent trudge along the dunes the last members of the division joined the patient queue of British and French that slowly shuffled its way along the beaches to embark in destroyers, pleasure steamers or whatever vessel turned up, from the Mole at Dunkirk, in the early hours of the "Glorious First of June". Few will forget those poignant last hours of the B.E.F. that have been so much better described elsewhere. Up to the last minute many of the men, who had suffered the onslaughts on the Scarpe, and on the Ypres–Comines Canal; who had ducked and dodged bombs, shells and bullets for the last two weeks, died in this defenceless queue.

It will probably never be known exactly how much the miracle of Dunkirk owed to the great stand of General Franklyn's 5 Div with its attached troops. It should certainly not be underestimated when the full story comes to be told, and was not underestimated by either the Corps Commander or the Divisional Commander at the time, as this Special Order of the Day confirms.

Special Order

"The Commander II Corps has asked me to convey his warm congratulations and thanks to the 5th Division and to other troops who fought so gallantly in co-operation with the 5th Division on 27th and 28th May. It is his opinion that it was entirely due to our action that the whole Corps was able to effect a withdrawal and that unless we had held the Ypres–Comines Canal so successfully the safety of the whole B.E.F. might have been put in serious danger. I am confident that this fact will be confirmed by history.

"It is a matter of great satisfaction to all of us that we were able to carry out such a vitally important task with complete success. It was not done without heavy loss; this must be so when troops are asked to hold wide frontages to the last.

"It is sad to see such fine units reduced by casualties to their present small numbers but it would be much worse if they had not achieved a vital task and inflicted far heavier losses on the enemy.

"I am indeed proud to have under my command such a splendid body of troops and to all Commanders and Troops I offer my sincere congratulations and thanks.

        (Sgd.) H. E. FRANKLYN,
Field,   Major-General.
29th May, 1940.   Commander 5th Division."

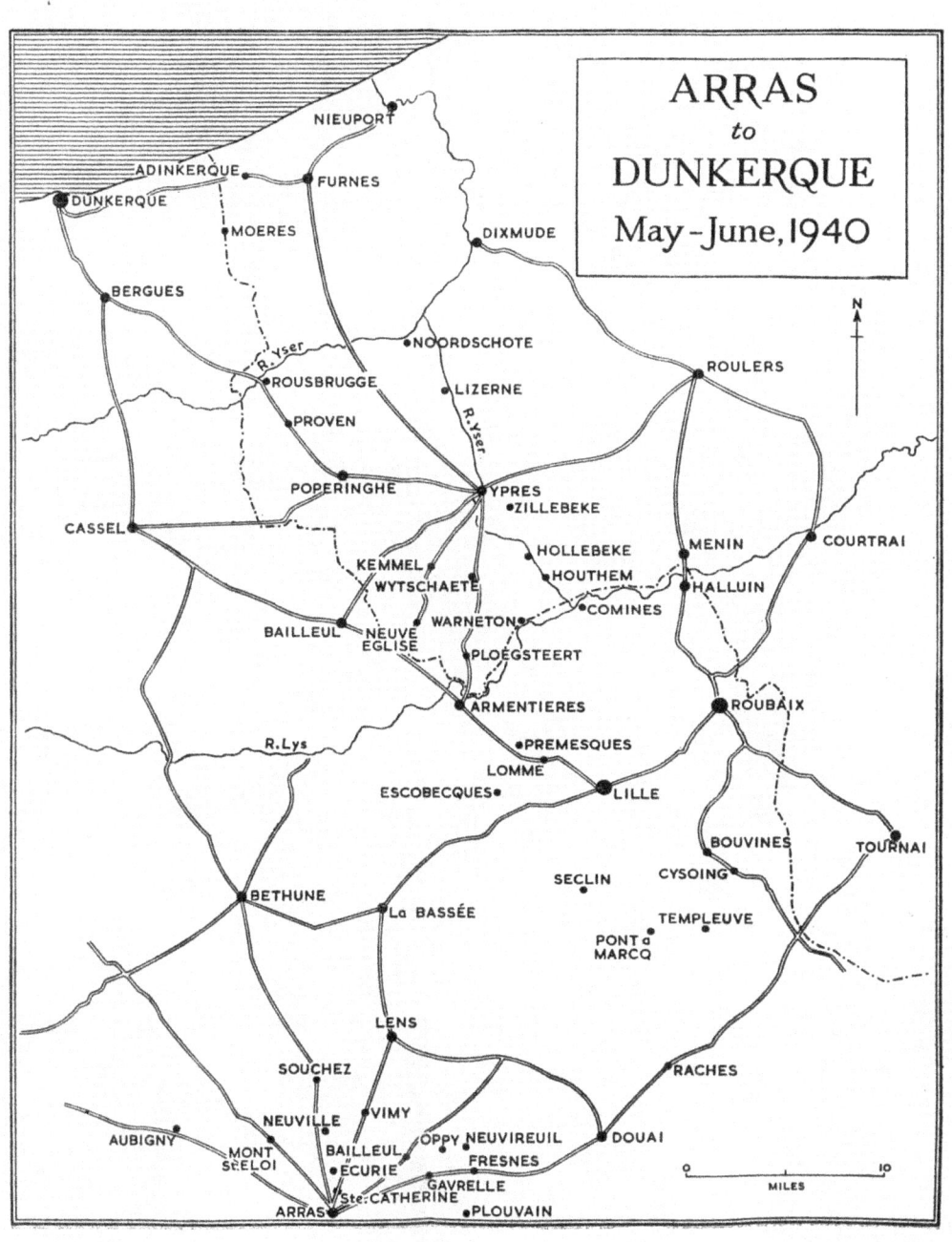

CHAPTER FOUR

TRAINING IN THE UNITED KINGDOM

In which the 5th Division concentrates in North-East Scotland in an anti-invasion rôle; in which training starts again in North-West England and is intensified in Northern Ireland. In which the Division moves back to South-Eastern England and prepares for a long sea voyage.

Concentration Again in Scotland

All three brigades of the Division were fortunate in their alternative escapes from Andaalsnes and Dunkirk. The first round had not gone well for the Allies, but the Division certainly had no reason to be dispirited. There was to be a long interval, three years, before the next round was to be fought. It was to be an interval crammed with training and travel; in itself the subject of a volume. Here, unfortunately, it is only possible to touch on some of the highlights.

After the evacuation from Dunkirk, the torn remnants of Div H.Q. and troops of 13 and 17 Inf Bdes found themselves entangled with other formations scattered the width and breadth of the United Kingdom. The urge to unite again was realized by kind permission of a friendly, if bewildered, movement control. The Divisional Standard was raised once more on 4th June in Scotland, at Inverurie, Aberdeenshire. This was just about as far from Adinkerque as it was possible to go in the circumstances, but only a short trip compared with those to come. Here, in two's and three's, the men of the Division rallied around General Franklyn and his staff.

Gone now were many familiar faces; there were new commanders and new sergeant-majors to be faced; there was only a meagre collection of weapons and vehicles, but there was no lessening of the spirit that had recently risen to such great heights.

This depleted division mounted in motor buses was to be prepared to defend almost all of the north-eastern seaboard of Scotland, particularly that in the Stonehaven-Inverurie area.

Another task was to defend most of the interior against the much-vaunted parachutists, which the Germans had employed so adroitly in Belgium and Holland.

Gradually stores, equipment and reinforcements began to trickle in and the mobile columns were strengthened. As yet there were few field guns available; these were reserved to the privileged few in the Div Arty whilst the remainder formed a comparable formation of infantry battalions with their full share of defence responsibilities. 92 rejoined 9 and 91 Fd Regts and Lieut.-Col. Howard Greene (later Brigadier Howard Greene, C.B.E., D.S.O., M.C.) who had been commanding 9 Fd Regt took over command from Brigadier Barry.

Further changes in command were to follow. On 21st June Major-General Franklyn handed over the Division to Major-General H. P. M. Berney-Ficklin now recovered from the air crash which had kept him out of Norway.

Brigadier Gammell (later Lieut.-Gen. Sir James Gammell, K.C.B., D.S.O., M.C.) had taken over 15 Inf Bde but soon handed it over to Brigadier H. R. H. Greenfield (later Brigadier H. R. H. Greenfield, C.B.E.), after it had moved up to the Huntly area in the middle of August. Here the whole of the brigade was to act as a mobile reserve to the newly reconstituted 51 Highland Div, who were defending the rest of the coast line.

17 and 13 Inf Bdes had assembled in the Huntly-Turriff area immediately after Dunkirk. The latter moved down to Crieff at the end of June. Here Brigadier D. N. Wimberley (later Major-General D. N. Wimberley, C.B., D.S.O., M.C.), took over from Brigadier M. C. Dempsey. At the end of September a further short move was made into billets from canvas.

The whole of the Division was to be prepared to attack as quickly as possible any air or sea landing that might occur in north-east Scotland. Schemes for all eventualities in this rôle were worked out and rehearsed; a particularly memorable one being that operation designed for the relief and restoration of Dundee by Lieut.-Colonel Jordan and his Y and L Flying Column.

Many were the various march tables worked out by harassed staff officers, only to be calamitously disproved a few minutes after passing the start point on the trial run. It was

Major-General H. P. M. Berney-Ficklin, C.B., M.C.

this early grounding in the mechanics of military movement that was to enable the Division to move so freely and smoothly, under any conditions, in almost any part of the world, at future dates.

Early in September the Div Arty was provided with some French 75 mm. guns by American emergency aid. They were the famous Puteaux "soixante-quinze" that had been the background of a very efficient French artillery since 1870. Although they made an undistinguished and hardly inspiring entry into battle inside the back of a three-tonner, they were, at least, better than no guns at all and certainly were steady in action. It proved possible to balance a full glass of water on the metal tyre of the gun wheel and it would not spill when the piece fired. Immediately these guns arrived some recently infantry-converted gunners, reverted to their normal rôle with delight.

On 7th September, the famous national false alarm of "Cromwell" was given. Some returning fishing vessels in the West Country had been mistaken for an invading force. Fully expecting a shower of parachutists to descend all over Scotland, the Division stood to and some units had to return hurriedly from an exercise then being held.

Such an occasion had been rehearsed previously and repeatedly. Motor transport, mainly commandeered coaches and single decker buses, reported and hurried units to pre-arranged assembly areas, from which points they were to deal with the enemy. All possible avenues of approach to each problem in any area had been thoroughly explored, or so it seemed. Landings by sea were also similarly covered.

On 7th/8th October an Inter-Brigade battle was "fought" between 15 Inf Bde and 154 Inf Bde of 51 Highland Div representing German forces that had landed at Peterhead. Some intensely cunning movement by the Green Howards upset the battle almost before it had commenced. They captured the enemy Artillery Regimental Commander and his headquarters. The much baffled umpire had to call an armistice whilst the balance of fire power was restored. This exercise was repeated a week later to test the lessons learned the first time.

A few days later, H.R.H. the Duke of Gloucester paid the second of his several visits to the Division. By now it was mid-October and the wet weather had set in with a vengeance. He visited some units in the Huntly area whose tents, pitched under trees to deceive enemy airmen, were continuously dripping with damp. As the rain persisted so these miserable residences sank lower and lower into the mud.

North-West England

By the end of October the Highland Division was nearly returned to strength and well able to take care of any enemies in the north-east. Accordingly, 5 Div was withdrawn into reserve again to Lancashire and Cheshire. As before, the move was by Brigade Groups; 13 Inf Bde group to the Liverpool–Ormskirk–Southport area, 15 Inf Bde group to the Rochdale–Bury–Middleton area and 17 Inf Bde group to Cheshire.

5 Div with HQ at Knutsford, Cheshire, came under Western Command, as the latter's operational reserve and under General Anderson's III Corps for training and administration.

Exercises on a Brigade Group basis were resumed around a great deal of the West Midlands and Lancashire, and air raid warnings now became familiar. All units were practised in the various rescue drills although it was not anticipated that they would be called on to help the Civil Defence and Fire Services. When raids came in Manchester and Liverpool just before Christmas, units had to stand by and watch the disastrous fires without being able to help. This was a serious strain, particularly for those whose families were at that time undergoing similar raids in other parts of the country. Full co-operation was permitted with the Home Guard, however, and the latter were brought into many exercises.

The Gunners went to fire their new guns, (they had now got a complete establishment of the new 25-pounders,) in North Wales at Trawsfynydd and later on in South Wales, at Sennybridge.

Christmas, the second of the war, was not quite the gay party it had been in France, particularly as the N.A.A.F.I. plum puddings had all been burnt out in the heavy raid on Manchester on the night before Christmas Eve. But as ever, a good face was put on it all and nobody went short of food or amusement.

Early in January General Anderson held a III Corps Study Week for senior officers at Shrewsbury and the weather became very cold. On the 15th/16th, 13 and 15 Inf Bdes had a battle around Formby which involved a moonlight crossing of the Leigh–Liverpool Canal at Appleby. This was one of the many river crossings both exercise and operational that were to show the real worth of the Div RE at bridging. The very next day the Div Arty adopted the new organization which gave them three batteries instead of two, each of them now consisting of two troops. This meant that each Battalion in a Brigade Group would have its affiliated Battery in the Fd Regt. These affiliations remained throughout the war and their constant practice became one of the greatest match-winning factors available to the Divisional Commander as it indeed did for most other Divisional Commanders. It is worth mentioning these affiliations at this stage:—

13 *Inf Bde Group*	91 *Fd Regt*
2 WILTS	466 Bty
2 Cameronians	361 Bty
2 R INNISKS/5 Essex	363 Bty
15 *Inf Bde Group*	92 *Fd Regt*
1 Green Howards	365 Bty
1 KOYLI	368 Bty
1 Y and L	467 Bty
17 *Inf Bde Group*	9 *Fd*/156 *Fd Regt*
2 RSF	593 Bty
6 Seaforth	591 Bty
2 Northamptons	592 Bty

So close they became that they lived in each other's messes at times, and certainly regarded themselves as families within the Divisional community.

On the 5th/6th February 5 Div set out on its first exercise as a complete division fully re-equipped and remanned. Through heavy snow, using well tried marching techniques, the Divisional columns marched to the area of Stoke-on-Trent, acting in their main rôle against a landing by the enemy, represented on this occasion by 47 Div. Concentration was hardly completed when another false alarm cancelled the exercise and sent units flying back to billets. Several minor deployment exercises were staged on the way back and at least by now the Divisional Staff had gained enough confidence to know that units could move and concentrate into a Divisional area efficiently and quickly.

The weather remained hard and cold but that did not prevent units from continuing training and moving about the countryside. Towards the end of February the weather became much milder and a thaw set in. Now it was mud alone that slowed things down, got into the hair, the rifle and machine gun and showed the soldier who wore the "Y" a little of what central Italy was going to be like in the winter of 1943-4.

There were further Corps, Divisional and Brigade exercises and it was during one of the latter that it was learned that the Division was to go over to Northern Ireland. Very hastily, 15 Inf Bde abandoned a river-crossing exercise in the Blackburn area, and made ready to leave England.

Northern Ireland

For some time now it had been known that Hitler thought he could secure a good footing in Southern Ireland from which to spread into Ulster. Thence he could springboard into Northern England, in an area less heavily defended, than that which he then faced across the channel in the form of the redoubtable defences of the south coast of England. German infiltration, under the guise of strict neutrality, was already notorious and many were the stories of unseen power controlled by the German Embassy in Dublin. It was thought that much lay behind the multitudinous but perfectly legitimate visits of German "U" boats into Cork, for refits lasting only forty-eight hours at a time. It was rumoured that the Southern Irish might be winking an eye at this German infiltration with the hopes that it might be going to do themselves a little bit of good. Who was to know?

To prevent such a wild outlandish manœuvre and to protect the loyal Ulstermen of the six counties, Northern Ireland district was to be enlarged to embrace General Anderson's III Corps, with the 5 Div joining later. III Corps before long was to grow into three divisions.

The decision was made very quickly, a fact which by now the Division was beginning to take in its stride. Much new equipment hitherto not available was issued to units and customary rumour became rife.

Advance parties left early in April followed by several other parties a few days later. These latter went up through the main Carlisle road to Stranraer in the south-west corner of Scotland. Here was the nearest point to Ulster and vehicles and guns could be driven on to the ferry boats that, before the war, had operated between Dover and Dunkirk. Short though the journey was in mileage it is a notorious stretch of treacherous water and every member of the road parties had more of it than he bargained for before landing at Larne.

The Division was concentrated in Northern Ireland by Easter Sunday, 13th April, 1941, and quickly settled down in its new area. Div H.Q. was at Armagh with 13 Inf Bde in the Armagh–Cookstown–Portadown area. 15 Inf Bde were across the other side in the further frontier county of Tyrone around Omagh and Newton Stewart. The latter housed Bde H.Q., two battalions and the Fd Regt. The battalions were in tents in the grounds at "Baronscourt" the home of the Governor General, the Duke of Abercorn, who made them most welcome. 17 Inf Bde were also on the border, but further to the south around Enniskillen where they owed much to the hospitality of the Prime Minister, then Sir Basil Brooke.

Before long training started again, an intensive period of training which was to cement the foundations of the machinery that was to function so well in Sicily and Italy.

Speed of movement was now practised assiduously and the Div Arty particularly taught itself to come in and out of action at great speed to give controlled continuous support at whatever speed the infantry should choose to lead.

The Gunners shot their guns in the field rôle up in the Sperrin Mountains, near Tobermore, and in the anti-tank rôle at targets on the edge of the lake at Hog Park Point on Lough Neagh. The Engineers practised bridging, as river crossings had again become prominent. Almost all exercises included long concentration marches. Wireless technique and procedure became more fluent; the services started to function as part of the fighting machine and all units became aware of each other's capabilities to a most beneficial degree.

The weather improved into brilliant sunshine; good visibility, cold nights and dusty roads were normal and 1st May was the first really warm day of the year.

But perhaps the greatest feature of training in Northern

Ireland was the large-scale exercises of which only the beginning had been experienced in Western Command. For the first time since France, the Division was able to practise all its various parts and functions in series spread over several days and at a speed far greater than likely to be encountered in conditions of normal warfare. The first of these was held towards the end of June and rejoiced in the name of "Rudolph"; the part of the "Hessian" invaders from the south was taken by 5 Div. This was a tribute to the recent arrival in Scotland of a now famous Rudolph by less orthodox means. This exercise raged over most of the six counties and had few dull moments. The whole of the Division was to sweep down from the west to perform some nefarious deeds in Belfast. The east was to be held by the rest of the United Kingdom Forces in Northern Ireland. To do this, long advances had to be made either round the northern end of Lough Neagh or to the south of it. The Division hoped to draw the enemy, who were not nearly enough in numbers to hold both approaches at once, to the south, and then perform an overwhelming sweep round to the north. 15 Inf Bde moved to secure a bridgehead in the Dungannon area whilst 13 Inf Bde held another bridgehead at Agivey, west of Ballymoney. During the night of 24th/25th June the Sappers built a pontoon bridge at Agivey, and 13 Inf Bde passed over it early next morning. 2 R INNISKS formed the advanced guard and were considerably hampered by the constant contact with enemy rearguards that had to be eliminated. The enemy left special parties behind and captured quite a few Divisional personalities including the General himself; however, they all soon got away to fight again. The enemy did much harassing by road cratering and Ballymena had to be by-passed. This gave some valuable training to the Pioneers and the Sappers whose problems were then certainly prolific. June 26th was a day of glorious confusion, with 13 and 17 Inf Bdes pinned down to the north of the lake as much by umpires as by the enemy. A long flanking advance on foot and in MT to Ballyclaire by 15 Inf Bde was planned. This went well and got as far as a line just north of the lake when it was pulled up at midnight 26th/27th. 1 Y and L and 1 KOYLI were ahead now. Early next morning a hastily improvised mobile column, consisting of the 1 Green Howards and Gunners, gave the slip to the umpires and were tearing into Belfast, when the cease fire was sounded. Unperturbed they proceeded to capture the headquarters of the exercise Directing staff. A great many valuable lessons were learned from this and the exercises that followed it. The technique of command and control facilitated now by a really excellent standard of wireless procedure, was becoming alive and real. The Divisional Staff could now feel that it was possible to order moves that would be accurately and quickly carried out and that march tables now needed only last-minute minor adjustments, if any at all.

Nor was the social side neglected; a very important factor from the point of view of morale. Units at all levels mixed at each other's cocktail parties, in each other's Sergeants' Messes, and by umpiring each other's exercises. The local inhabitants were particularly generous in their hospitality, it being possible to borrow their guns for shooting, their rods for fishing, or their horses to ride, their courts for tennis, and even their gear for cricket and other games. Tennis matches, cricket matches, association and rugby football matches were fitted in at every odd moment between the vigorous spells of training. E.N.S.A. sent their age-worn but none the less welcome concert parties to brighten the dingiest of "Orange" Halls. Units' own concert parties developed, and unit dance bands played at local dances which were always well attended on Saturday nights. One unit, which shall remain anonymous, opened its own night club, called "Hellzapoppin" in a small market town, to the bewilderment of the simple local folk. Needless to say it was a one night performance. To return civilian hospitality, brigades and battalions ran cocktail parties for the local worthies and 15 Inf Bde went further with an Officers' Ball at Omagh. Neither Belfast nor Londonderry were ever particularly bright spots but certain members of the Division soon put that right. They were aided and abetted by the Royal Navy, particularly in Londonderry, where the first United States troops in Europe added their contribution at the end of the year. 5 Div was always particularly friendly with the Royal Navy and was to have much to thank the Senior Service for in the next few years. It was appropriate that games of football between the two should be played and visits of all sorts exchanged.

Administration got a great deal of necessary attention and a special week was held in mid-August wherein so many tried so desperately to administer to each other. About a month earlier, there had been a concentrated Gas Week, all training being done in gas respirators. As a result of this, the training not unnaturally lost some of its strenuousness.

In early August, 5 Div took part in another inter-Division exercise called "Summit". In early September, III Corps exercise "Greenland" had to be called off before it had run its course. The Army Staff had hoped that 5 Div would have to deploy completely before attacking another division. The enemy was so speedily dealt with and tied in knots by 15 Bde Gp as advance guard that there was no point in proceeding further. Early in October, III Corps exercise "Harvest" was held in the Portadown-Newry area. This was a good exercise which enabled the Div Arty to be concentrated under its Commander for the first time for many months. For the first time, on this exercise, it became necessary to decentralize Forward Observation Officers to battalions and companies together with their No. 18 sets and were thus forced to depend less on transport. On the last day some excellent weather broke into a steady downpour of torrential rain.

Training on these lines continued at a lower level until Christmas, the third of the war. It was a good Christmas for all of the Division in Ireland, but nobody was really disappointed when news was received, on 9th January, that the Division would move to England at once to join General Montgomery's South-Eastern Command. Advance parties left three days later and rail parties crossed on the 17th/18th. The road parties were held up by very bad weather until 21st/22nd, the roads being dangerous with severe frosts and some snow lying about. Eventually, by means of a very rough Larne-Stranraer crossing and after quite a hazardous journey through South-West Scotland, Carlisle over Shap Fell to the football ground of Preston North End, the convoys got under way. The next stage brought the convoys to Lutterworth in Leicestershire, and the last day, a long one indeed, brought them down to the Surrey and Kent outskirts of London by way of Windsor, thus avoiding the metropolis.

THE MOVE TO NORTHERN ENGLAND.—15th Infantry Brigade Commander's staff car arrives at Larne on the 10th April, 1941.

H.R.H. the Duke of Gloucester inspects the Royal Inniskilling Fusiliers at Armagh on the 24th April, 1941. Major-General Berney-Ficklin can be seen to the left of the picture.

Lieut.-General H. E. Franklyn, late G.O.C. 5th Division and then Commander-in-Chief Northern Ireland, inspects "B" Company of the Green Howards at Omagh on the 15th October, 1941.

Two famous England cricketers, Lieutenant N. W. B. Yardley and Captain H. W. Verity, both of the Green Howards, seen on one of the many exercises involving 15th Infantry Brigade.

Viscount Trenchard, Colonel of the Royal Scots Fusiliers, inspecting the 2nd Battalion before it left for overseas on 23rd February, 1942.

The carriers of the recently formed 5th Divisional Reconnaissance Regiment training at Armagh on 18th October, 1941.

H.M. KING GEORGE VI – Inspecting men of the Divisional Artillery before they left on the long sea journey. With him is Lieut.-Colonel Buffey commanding 91st Field Regiment and behind them can be seen Brigadier Greene, the C.R.A.

CHAPTER FIVE

A LONG SEA VOYAGE—13TH AND 17TH INFANTRY BRIGADES IN MADAGASCAR

In which the 5th Division sails from the Clyde round the Cape. In which, at the last moment, the 13th and 17th Brigades are diverted to help in the occupation of Madagascar, whilst the remainder of the Division sail on to India.

A Voyage to the Indian Ocean

The Division was now concentrated on the south-eastern outskirts of London, in Surrey and Kent. Divisional Headquarters was near Redhill and units stretched from Oxted to Hayes Common. On 1st February all units received mobilization instructions. These were put into effect immediately and completed by the 26th of February. The vehicles were to go ahead on slower convoy and the drivers, who were to accompany them, completed their embarkation leave by 20th February. Special issues of stores, equipment and clothing had been completed by the 14th so that, where necessary, they could be stowed non-tactically in the vehicles. The guns of the Divisional Artillery were calibrated at Sennybridge, in South Wales and at Lydd in Kent; in both cases, in extremely cold weather.

The vehicle parties left for ports of embarkation on 2nd March, the vehicles having been cut down in size for shipping stowage; the carriers left the following day. Neither party had any idea of where they were going and this was to be the first of many times when the vehicle parties were to be separated from the rest of the Division for weeks, sometimes months on end.

On 4th March rumour was narrowed by the issue of tropical khaki drill. It was pretty certain now that India was the destination, there being few other tropical countries left in the field. It was assumed that the Division was to reinforce General Alexander's great battle in Burma and the cover plan put out for security purposes was that the Division and other troops were going to Colombo from which port they were to re-take Rangoon that had recently fallen to the Japanese. This would account for the commando and other combined operation elements that were obviously part of the convoy.

Preparations went on without ceasing. All ranks completed embarkation leave and as many specialists as possible from surveyors to cooks had been rushed through special last minute courses organized at the various training centres. Many articles of personal equipment were purchased although later they were mostly found to be useless or to be obtainable much more cheaply abroad. On 12th March H.M. The King visited units by brigades and created a great inspirational impression. When late at one point he showed obvious concern to the C.R.A. (Brigadier Greene) that he was behind schedule, hoping that the parade had not been kept too long on such a cold day. Whilst inspecting Div H Q and Divisional Troops, His Majesty asked the R.S.M. of the 5 Reconnaissance Regt if he were a Territorial. The R.S.M. squeezed another inch upwards and outwards and replied, "A regular soldier, Your Majesty, with over twenty years service." The King smiled and moved on. He was quick to notice that the second-in-command of the Regiment, Major Goldie, was wearing Royal Scots Fusiliers buttons and Reconnaissance Corps headdress.

On 15th March, at midnight, Div HQ closed in the United Kingdom never to reopen there again, it being disbanded in Germany some five years later. The following day parties left to get the baggage stowed and ships generally prepared for the embarkation of personnel. The next few days were spent in anxious last-minute dashes to London on leave, or to telephone kiosks; it was a difficult period as there were no stores left for training and the troops had to be kept mentally alert at all costs. The last few hours ticked over slowly and then, on the 19th March, the various trains started on a two-day run to the port of embarkation, Gourock on the Clyde. Embarkation started immediately on arrival.

Just before embarkation it was learned from the War Office that 17 Bde Gp had been earmarked for Operation "Ironclad"—the occupation of Madagascar by a mixed force, known as Force 121 and commanded by Major-General Sturges of the Royal Marines. This was disconcerting news as the ships were not tactically loaded and the men could hardly be expected to be fit and acclimatized immediately after disembarkation. Furthermore the Division had not, as yet, done any amphibious training and it would not be possible to pass on the necessary information required at that stage for reasons of security. To add further difficulty, the units of the Brigade Group were spread over many ships unlike those of 13 Inf Bde who were all in the same vessel. However, manuals and reports of landing techniques were put on the ships concerned together with one or two specialized instructors. This was one of the first of many headaches for the Divisional staffs who took them all in their easy stride during the coming years and miles of travel in and out of battle.

The days of 20th–23rd March were spent on the Clyde, where the convoy, which was the largest so far to leave England, was making final preparations before putting to sea. All ranks were instructed in boat drill and in finding their way around the ships and in a little of the mysteries of seafaring terminology. Short cruises, down river, were made in order to calibrate the various wireless equipments of the vessels. At long last on the 23rd March as dusk was falling, at 2000 hrs., the convoy sailed down the Clyde to the strains of lusty singing of the old familiar sentimental and raucous songs so well loved by the soldier. For many it was to be their last view of the British Isles as the blackout mass of Glasgow and the hills to the north slowly receded.

The convoy was an impressive one. Amongst the protector ships of the Royal Navy were the Aircraft Carrier *Illustrious*, the Battleship *Malaya*, the Cruiser *Devonshire*, and many destroyers and corvettes. Among the Merchant ships carrying personnel—all of them great liners—were such as the *Nieuw Amsterdam, The Windsor Castle, Winchester Castle, Duchess of Atholl, Almanzora, Franconia*, and the Polish *Sobieski*.

All ships flew barrage balloons and manned Anti-Aircraft guns in defence against enemy aircraft. The destroyer screen continually weaved in and out ever alert for submarine attack. The whole convoy turned this way to port and then that way to starboard at the command of the siren on the Commodore's ship.

The weather was fine and calm for the time of year, although the Bay of Biscay claimed many *mal de mer* victims. Below decks, however, it was becoming very hot, for troops were packed very tightly together and any movement had to be highly organized. Soon it became too warm for battledress and, on 2nd April, ten days after sailing, Khaki Drill was worn for the first time and many a good laugh was had at the immediate results. Pink, hairy and knobbly-kneed legs stuck out of shorts which were either so short as to be almost indecent or so long as to be embarrassing. Bush jackets were also an ill assortment of fittings, but much was put right by judicious swapping. The ensemble, particularly when surmounted by the ridiculously outdated Wolseley pith-helmet, was more suited to the stage of Drury Lane.

The days were getting long and officers were hard pressed to keep training going, but a lot of useful work was put in backed by a miscellany of entertainment. Ships' concerts, radio programmes, games of "crown and anchor", ships' news sheets, boxing, wrestling, physical training, ships' libraries, all helped to while away the intervals between boat drill, alarums and excursions and periods of training. Fish spotting, aircraft spotting, bird watching, and "sailors-at-work" watching, all had their ardent devotees, whilst some lucky ones with the necessary qualifications manned the ships' Anti-Aircraft guns and took over signal watches.

On Easter Monday, 5th April, the great convoy steamed into the harbour of Freetown, the notorious "white man's grave", which seemed harmless enough to those in the ships. Nobody was permitted to go ashore and the only movement between ships during this three days refuelling stop, were those of the General and the Brigade Commanders who were allowed to visit their units. Whatever plans for Madagascar that could be made were made and Company Commanders were informed accordingly. A little extra training could be done during the second part of the voyage and indeed one battalion succeeded in route marching round and round the decks of its ship in boots, much to the horror of an irate Captain, for boots on boat deck were absolutely forbidden.

A torrential downpour of tropical rain was a great relief whilst at anchor. It was the first of many more to be experienced later on. Much amusement was caused by the native boys who dived naked for anything the troops could throw in and by the bum-boat merchants who offered for sale bananas, coconuts and some other quite useless paraphernalia.

Most whiled away the time studying the jungle background to the town from the deck rail and many imagined they could see some Hollywood vision, in a sarong, flitting among the dark trees; those with less imagination noted the monkeys at least.

A LONG SEA VOYAGE

The convoy was now split into two portions. The first was to go on ahead and make for Durban. This included the "Ironclad" ships carrying 17 Inf Bde, 29 Inf Bde and 5 Commando with supporting troops. The remainder, the slower part with the rest of the Division was to proceed to Captetown. The convoy sailed on the 9th April, and on the 13th crossed the Equator. On most ships the traditional Crossing of the Line Ceremony was carried out with its full peacetime trappings. The Kings Neptune were husky individuals who mostly wore the "Y" somewhere on themselves. But when this frolicsome interlude was finished everybody went back to the routine of troopship life. In view of possible operations for some, renewed efforts were made to keep the men fit, and what training was possible was carried out religiously. There were many later who congratulated themselves that the day of the "dry" troopship was not then on hand.

The Cape was rounded on the 21st April and could be seen quite plainly from all ships. It was fortunate that most of the troops by now had got their sea legs as the famous Cape swell was in great form. Here the convoy split into those going into Capetown, mostly Divisional troops, and those going on to Durban. The latter next day reached the port whose skyscraper outline they had seen from some miles off. 17 Inf Bde had arrived several days earlier and had been very busy reloading their ships into some sort of tactical order. On arrival in Durban the 13 Inf Bde Group, who were all in "Franconia", received orders to take part in "Ironclad". The expedition was to sail within 48 hours and as 13 Inf Bde Bns might, and in fact did, have to land on the assault beaches and march across the peninsular, it was necessary to sort out in the hold the individual arms and equipment of the three Bns. As these were all mixed up with those of the Gunners, Sappers, and Services, the situation became chaotic. However, before the convoy reached Madagascar the Bns had sorted out what they wanted and the units remaining on the ship had to be satisfied with what was left. 15 Inf Bde was the most fortunate of the three as they were not to be concerned in the landing at all, except if the worst were to happen to the initial assault. They were able to relax a little in the wonderful city of Durban where the most hospitable and attractive citizens were so generous to all ranks. Who can forget the gallant lady who sang to the ships as they came alongside the quay, the monkeys on the hill, and the many lovely houses and clubs that welcomed all and any rank of soldier to come in and feel at home. It was most fitting that a Ceremonial March should be arranged to pass the Town Hall where the Lord Mayor took the salute. Every morning battalions marched far along the promenade towards the Country Club and back with pipes and drums in several cases. Some had time to swim, if they could brave the sharks, others to play golf or tennis or to dance at the night clubs, or at the most attractive Ball organized in a local Drill Hall.

Meanwhile warlike preparations gathered apace. To the roll of warships present were added *Ramillies* and, later, the Aircraft Carrier *Indomitable*. On the 28th this convoy sailed headed by *Winchester Castle*, the H.Q. ship which also carried the Commando. It made a brave sight as it passed out of harbour and very particularly the Carrier *Illustrious* with decks lined by ratings, her band playing and flags flying. There was a faint tinge of regret in the farewells from ships manned by those left behind, part of 15 Inf Bde. The remainder left in the early hours of the 1st of May and joining with the Capetown Convoy steamed slowly up the Mozambique Channel waiting for news of operation "Ironclad".

The Setting for Operation "Ironclad"

Whilst in Northern Ireland, on 7th December, 1941, the Division heard of the Japanese attack on Pearl Harbour that brought war into the Pacific Ocean. Malaya and the base of Singapore, the Dutch East Indies and the Andaman Islands in the Indian Ocean later all fell into Japanese hands. By March, 1942, India and Ceylon were threatened by Japanese armies moving northwards through Burma and by Japanese aircraft, submarines and surface raiders operating against the main British supply route to the Middle East and Burma, that lay round the Cape. Allied convoys used the shelter of the Mozambique Channel on the east coast of Africa, but this last lane would soon be closed to them, if the Vichy French Garrison were to permit Japanese raiders to operate from bases in Madagascar, the third largest island in the world, and particularly from its main deep water harbour of Diego Suarez.

This port was well defended by coastal batteries and although mostly the defenders were colonial troops with only thirty-five aircraft in support it was apparent that it would not be an easy nut to crack. The Garrison of the island actually consisted of 2,500 troops of which 500 were Senegalese and the remainder metropolitan and coloured troops of the Régiment Mixte de Madagascar.

Even before the Pearl Harbour incident an expedition had been planned. But this plan had had to be considerably modified for Force 121 in view of possible Japanese augmentation of the Garrison. The original Force 121 consisted of 29 Indep Bde commanded by Brigadier F. W. Festing, 5 Commando, a few tanks, a light battery of four 3.7-in. Howitzers, two 25 pounders and a LAA Troop. All these units had been trained for amphibious operations. To them was now added Brigadier G. W. B. Tarleton's 17 Inf Bde Gp backed up by Brigadier V. C. Russell's 13 Inf Bde Gp, neither of which had had the necessary training for sea landing.

It was essential that the enemy should have no suspicion of the intention to invade Madagascar, and this was why the cover plan of an invasion of Rangoon from Colombo, already mentioned had been put about. As General Alexander's fighting withdrawal from Burma was now getting near Assam and Bengal, it was decided to limit the Madagascar Operation to the Capture of Diego Suarez and its dockyard of Antsirane, a mile across the water. There were a number of good beaches on the northernmost peninsula of the island in Courier Bay. Here the Commando would land with 29 Indep Bde a little farther to the south of it. Having disposed of what was confidently expected to be a nuisance operation, the Force would set off for Diego Suarez and Antsirane in two column thrusts. When both of these objectives were secured the next phase was to launch all Forces, including the 17 Inf Bde, against the headland of Orangea where there was known to be a garrison, probably well dug in.

The whole operation was to be supported by naval aviation from the Carriers *Illustrious* and *Indomitable*. Before dropping bombs these aircraft were to drop leaflets proclaiming the Anti-Japanese object of the expedition.

The Initial Landings were to be quickly followed up by 17 Inf Bde in support who, in their turn, were to pass through 29 Inf Bde and exploit to Antsirane and the Orangea peninsula to the east of it. 13 Inf Bde were to be landed in the captured harbour as a further reserve, to be deployed as and when required.

The Assault on Madagascar

At 0530 hrs. on 5th May, the Commando assaulted Courier Bay after an extremely hazardous approach through a narrow entrance, covered by extensive minefields which had been efficiently cleared by the Royal Navy. This surprised the Coastal Defence gun crews in their beds and all objectives were carried by 1600 hrs. on the same day, with little difficulty.

Meanwhile the three main landings had taken place in Ambararata Bay. There was only minor beach opposition but a heavy swell caused considerable difficulty to those trying to get tanks and guns ashore. One landing craft turned completely over, and the vessels waiting outside with 17 Inf Bde troops on board dragged their anchors for half a mile.

The bombing of the airfield six miles or so to the south of Antsirane was effective enough to prevent any significant interference by enemy aircraft. A pre-"H" hour bombardment of likely landing places south-east of Antsirane by the guns of the warships had had a similarly restraining effect, and distracted the enemy's attention from the main landings.

The Assault Brigade wasted no time in advancing on a single road led by tanks who quickly destroyed some lorry-borne infantry sent against them. When they reached the main position covering an anti-tank ditch, they met heavy fire from well concealed and dug-in Vichy 75 mm. guns. This was at 1700 hrs. on the 5th and up until then they had marched some eighteen miles along a rough and dusty track in tropical heat, since they landed in the early hours of the morning. It was soon clear that a full Brigade attack would have to be mounted against such a position. This latter consisted of a mile and a quarter of trench system stretching across the peninsula of Antsirane with a formidable fort at either end of it; Fort Caimans in the west and Fort Bellevue in the east. In front of this line was the anti-tank ditch already mentioned and beyond the forts on each flank steep bushy slopes ran down into the mangrove swamps at the edge of the sea. What roads there were were well covered by pill-boxes mounting field and machine guns. It was a veritable little "Maginot Minor"

On board s.s. *Dominion Monarch*.

Crossing the line.

MADAGASCAR.
Training resumed by men of 9th Field Regiment after the campaign.

The guns of 9th Field Regiment march past at Tananarive on the 3rd October, 1942.

and it would have to be cracked by dawn of the next day, at the latest, if surprise was to be maintained.

Back on the beaches the landing of 29 Inf Bde vehicles and of 17 Inf Bde itself was going slowly, owing to the persistently powerful swell, but four of the 3.7-in. Howitzers were got ashore to support the attack which went in on a three-battalion front (29 Inf Bde had four battalions). It soon ran into difficulties through lack of preparation and support against a well organized and conducted defence. The right flank battalion nearly succeeded in penetrating the defence and collected several hundred prisoners. The fire power available to 29 Inf Bde was quite inadequate for such a task and what shooting was done only set fire to the bush and hindered progress. A further difficulty lay in controlling the battle owing to the erratic behaviour of wireless sets, which was not peculiar to that Brigade. Many casualties were suffered and it was decided to call off the attack and await the arrival of 17 Inf Bde who were beginning their march from the coast.

The plan for 17 Inf Bde was that they should attack at 2030 hrs. on the 6th with all possible help from the artillery that could be got up in time, from destroyers firing offshore and from the Swordfish aircraft of naval aviation. As a diversion, a very successful one as it turned out to be, some fifty Marines were to be taken right into Antsirane harbour to land on the jetty and attack the town from the rear. As much softening up as was possible throughout the rest of the day, proved a tremendous help.

Apart from this, the conditions under which 17 Inf Bde were to enter this battle were scarcely favourable. They had taken some time to negotiate a rough landing and were not concentrated until 0100 hrs. on the 6th. They were immediately ordered south for this attack which was to be mounted some eighteen miles away the same evening. This was a long and dusty march for which their sea voyage had hardly helped to fit them and during most of it they were persistently eaten by insects, which were later to take their feverish toll. They arrived on the scene of the battle less than an hour before the attack with little or no knowledge of the enemy. Their objectives were hard to pick out on the ground, maps were inadequate and there were no air photos to study. The approach from the forming up place was over rough ground which was quite unfamiliar to them. They were working among strangers after two years without battle experience and yet they gave excellent account of themselves.

The Battle for Antsirane

The attack began at 2030 hrs. on the 6th May, with 6 Seaforth on the left and 2 Northamptons on the right. The former with the more difficult task had under command a company of the Royal Welch Fusiliers sent by 29 Inf Bde.

The task of 6 Seaforth was to clean up a pill-box area bristling with machine guns and 75 mm. field guns about 600 yards ahead of their start line. During the hour between finishing the approach march and crossing the start line they revived themselves with special "pep" tablets and cups of tea. It was a very dark night when they set off over rough ground.

With "A" Company (Major A. M. Low) and "B" Company (Major J. Marnham) leading to left and right, "C" Company (Major F. Waylen) were in between the other two and slightly behind supported by "D" Company (Major G. Smith). So little time was there for preparation that the platoon commanders were briefed on the march from the forming up place to the start line—this was to the effect that either they took the "adjectival town" or they didn't "adjectivally well come back". In the event of the former they were to put up a green light as a success signal, in the unlikely event of the latter it would be considered that no known signal was necessary. They encountered a little sniping on the way up at a track junction near a particularly memorable dead cow. Here the ground became open, with long grass and a few bushes. The objective, a railway line on the far side of a native village, now became discernible. To their right they heard much firing in front of where 2 Northamptons should be and the troops could not avoid making a lot of crunching noise as they pushed through a crop of maize. Suddenly they came upon the anti-tank ditch, about which they had not been warned, and the enemy fire covering it opened up at no more than twenty yards range. In an instant, with the regimental cry of "Cabar Feidh" they went into a rough and tumble with the bayonet until the French resistance petered out. They went on to take another native village and then became very doubtful about the direction of their next objective. It was now 2300 hrs. and the map did not help them very much, but almost immediately success signals went up to the right and the left of them so they took up a defensive position where they were. They had not been without casualties in the advance among them, the Adjutant, Captain McCall, and the Intelligence Officer, Captain Black, were both killed.

Meantime 2 Northamptons had fared well on the right. Their first objective was a radio station south of the village of Anatanambao, about a mile and a half beyond the start line. Major Houchin ("C" Company) put in a very lively attack on a pill-box, similar to that encountered by 6 Seaforth on the left. For this he was awarded a Military Cross, the first to be won in the Division since Dunkirk. "B" Company, after an unscheduled detour, passed through Anatanambao with little incident. Both Companies put up success signals at 2300 hrs. and on this the 2 RSF proceeded straight into Antsirane led by the pipers of both the 1st and 2nd Battalions of the Regiment, the former being part of 29 Inf Bde. Antsirane was now well on fire which helped the RSF considerably in their mopping up. There were but small local incidents but one of these entailed a brilliant personal attack on a resisting pill-box by Corporal Lyle who was for this awarded the Distinguished Conduct Medal, again the first since Dunkirk. The pipes played all the way to the Governor's Residence and undoubtedly contributed their bit to the end of all resistance in Antsirane.

By 0330 hrs. on the 7th May, HQ 2 Northamptons was established on its original objective of the wireless station, and at 0600 hrs. a battery of 75 mm. field guns on the right of the position was surrounded by Captain Hickson and "B" Company. The harbour was completely cleared by 2 RSF by first light, but the two forts of Caimans and Bellevue and the coast defence guns on the Orangea peninsula held out until midnight on the same day.

Although the Frenchmen's hearts were undoubtedly not always in the battle they had fought at times with their traditional brilliance. The surprise achieved by the battalions of the 17 Inf Bde when they came up between the forts quite unsuspected, threw them out of their stride and the determined and courageous leadership shown throughout by all three battalions never allowed them to recover.

It was a great achievement for 17 Inf Bde to march for so long and then to successfully tackle such a formidable position with inadequate preparation.

On the Defensive

As already mentioned it was not intended that the invasion should go beyond the objectives by now achieved. 17 Inf Bde took up defensive positions on the Orangea peninsula for some six weeks. These six weeks were not without incident. There was some difficulty about completing the delicacies of the French surrender. It appeared that the Royal Navy had fired on the French whilst an Armistice was in force during the preliminary negotiations. The French were very touchy about this and refused to complete the surrender until they were assured that the Royal Navy would not repeat the incident and that their wives could remain unmolested at the camp of D'Ankarika. Quite a few small pockets of French diehards nobly refused to recognize the armistice and had to be "mopped up" to satisfy their honour. On Friday, 8th May, 6 Seaforth formed a guard of Honour on the main road out of Antsirane for the surrendering army. They found themselves presenting arms to a column of native troops who appeared to be fully armed and who went on advancing for another thirty-one days!

The main object of the defensive position on the Orangea peninsula, however, was against Japanese landings which were quite possible at this stage. There was indeed one minor invasion when a Japanese two-man submarine got among the shipping in the harbour and causing a few casualties, notably to H.M.S. *Ramillies,* which was seen to be listing sharply as a result of this foray. The two men got out of the harbour and made their way to the shore where they were expecting to be picked up by a seaplane; instead, to their dismay, they were picked up by Commandos.

During this time the 9 Fd Regt (Lieut.-Colonel Lupton) had managed to get their guns ashore although they were too late to contribute greatly to the battle. Their finest shooting was undoubtedly against a high ranking French officer who was trying to escape across the Bay in a sloop. With no hesitation a gun in action on the beach swivelled round and sank the sloop with one shot! Although they did not then know it, this was to be the Regiment's last appearance with 5 Div. The

A LONG SEA VOYAGE

only regular unit in the Div Arty, they had served it magnificently during the Battle of 1940 and in the intensive training ever since, where they set a good workmanlike example to other gunners. They were to remain behind in Madagascar and later found their way to Burma.

13 Inf Bde had had no part in the battle. They landed as planned and spent about a week in Madagascar before sailing on to Bombay. They remained long enough, however, to pick up malaria and sandfly fever from which they suffered considerably and intensely when they arrived in India, to the extent of some fatal casualties. They completed the eighteen-mile march and took up defensive positions before it was certain that they would have no fighting to do. The Bde Gp re-embarked on the *Franconia* on the 19th May.

17 Inf Bde were relieved by a brigade of the King's African Rifles and sailed for India more than a month after landing in Madagascar. They too had their toll from fever and learned to take precautions the hard way.

It is interesting to note that the occupation of Madagascar was not completed before November, 1942, although as Mr. Churchill put it, the resistance after 17 Inf Bde left the island, was "mainly symbolic".

CHAPTER SIX

ACROSS INDIA

In which the 5th Division, without two of its brigades, sails on to India later to be joined by them there. Where, after sweltering journeys by road and by railway and jungle training in torrential monsoons, it is soon decided to move them back across India to Iraq and Persia.

The Gateway to India

The convoy that was not involved in the Madagascar landings now sailed on past the Mozambique Channel, the Divisional Commander assured that the task of 17 Inf Bde had been well and truly done and that it would only be a matter of weeks before the Division would be complete once more in India. It was calm and hot weather now and the air was charged with the ever near possibility of attack from Japanese surface raiders known to be operating in the Indian Ocean. Actually nothing disturbed a peaceful ten days' voyage and the convoy steamed into Bombay in impressive line ahead formation, on the afternoon of 16th May. The peace was ruffled at the last minute by a quite impolite exchange of signals between the Commodore, now in *Windsor Castle*, and the commander of the naval escort in his flagship. It concerned a small matter of precedence and professional etiquette but was quickly forgotten.

Troops disembarked that same night and marched through the hot streets of Bombay. They almost had to pick their way among the recumbent white shrouded figures that know no other dormitory than the streets of Bombay. They marched to Victoria station where they boarded smart new electric trains completely devoid of windows. It was but a short journey up to Kirkee, Poona and Ahmednagar which were to be the concentration areas of 15 Inf Bde Gp and Div Tps. Here they went into Kiplingesque Barracks where the punkahs were rhythmically pulled by small boys; where the books fell apart in the hand when taken from their shelves, so great was the appetite of the ant; where the stone barrack rooms were unbelievably cool in the heat of the day and almost stifling by night.

Those officers and other ranks who had served in India before the war were on familiar ground. But for many in the Division, this was their first visit to the Indian sub-continent. This was the first time an English division as such, mobilized for war, had landed in India and the respectable inhabitants did not take kindly to these invaders, who only wore khaki drill and had no "whites" for evening wear. A north country regular battalion not yet embodied, was stationed in Poona. Their band, immaculately attired, played at the Saturday night Ball at the Gymkhana Club. Those of the Division who tried to gain admission had short shrift from the residents who openly forbade their daughters to dance with them. There were exceptions of course, but not many. At the Yacht Club in Bombay, furthermore, officers of the Division were welcome but had to eat behind screens in the dining room so that members should not be pained by the sight they presented. Those of the Division who went on the road journeys found the same attitude almost everywhere. One officer of a Divisional Field Regiment, in sheer exuberant exasperation leaped up to grab an enormous chandelier which graced the bar of a well-known station club in Central India, and the lot came down, ceiling and all. It seemed symbolic somehow. It was all very strange after the basically severe economy just left behind in the United Kingdom and a little sad to experience such an obvious decline.

But the Indians themselves welcomed fresh British soldiers to their bazaars and barracks, and the soldier soon discovered that India had its compensations. He could wear clean clothes, beautifully laundered twice a day at a very modest cost; he could have nice pairs of shoes and desert bootees made from real leather or suede, again at a very modest cost; he could lie in bed whilst an efficient barber came round and shaved him so delicately that some soldiers swore they were not woken whilst it was being done; he could get well-tailored clothes, copied for a mere song, within the space of an hour or so and, by and large, he regretted the money wasted on such in England.

Quartermasters and their staffs were no longer in any doubt as to their importance, now that Indian contractors came to them on their bended knees for the privilege of being able to do the dirty work and chores so much a part of the British soldier's life. To be allowed to clear away the swill; to peel the potatoes, clean the equipment, provide vegetables and ice and almost anything from an elephant to a toothbrush, these gentlemen were prepared to give the quartermaster, and his staff, unheard of riches and luxuries.

There were a lot of things that could be achieved if only one knew one's way about local regulations and there were a lot of strange angles to Indian administration that had to be mastered. Native Babu clerks took over the Orderly Room, or so it seemed, to organize the pay, for which they used many long and complicated volumes even more voluminous than those used in more civilized stations. Many were the additions and subtractions that could be made from one's pay if only one knew how to encourage the former and divert the latter. Such was the "closed shop" angle of this babu system that all detail had to be left to them as only they could understand the superior type of babu that resided in higher places such as records and pay offices. Officers found their pay quite beyond their comprehension but, as it mostly appeared to be on the generous side, they let it take its own course, until it caught up with them. There was the occasion, for instance, when the Pay Office in England thought it had to pay officers up to the time of disembarkation in India, whereas the India Office were equally sure they were committed to pay them from the moment the officer stepped on board ship at Glasgow. Wives and dependants benefited enormously—at least temporarily.

The Urdu language had to be mastered and for this purpose the Munshi, or teacher, came to pester units. The customs of the nations had to be respected, as the captain in the Royal Army Service Corps on a road convoy discovered when he shot a peacock in the state of Gwalior. It was not a good thing, for instance, to run over cows or to gape at some of the things one couldn't help seeing.

The food, which contained a high proportion of goat meat, had to be gently introduced to English stomachs; anti-mosquito veils had to cover the sleeper at nights, boots had to be emptied of snakes, particularly, the deadly little krait, before putting them on in the morning; alcohol needed to be avoided in the noonday sun, as did any exertions for that matter. Parades for this reason, had to be held at an unearthly early hour of

CROSSING INDIA.—The rail party halt for some food, some char, and a stretch.

The road party halt for a rest. A Don R. finds some shade and time for a sleep.

The 15th Infantry Brigade Company R.A.S.C. camp at Gutua near Ranchi and a near-by pool which was gladly shared with the water buffaloes for a cool swim.

INDIA

Planting rice.

Neighbours at Ranchi.

Tom-tom wallah.

Timber merchant.

The women carried the hay.

Captain Howard Naish, R.A.S.C., takes a tonga in Poona.

Sergeants Dee and Corton, R.A.S.C., take a rickshaw whilst on leave in Calcutta and visit the Queen Victoria Memorial.

In Kermanshah the local public transport was the garry.

An appendicitis case is put ashore at Karachi, and (left) the Shat-el-Arab.

An Arab at Asha.   The road to Basra.

Time off to visit Babylon.   A familiar sight.

the morning; armistice being declared from noon until five in the afternoon, when work was feverishly resumed. The head had to be covered at all times and much liquid to be consumed. In connection with this a well, if a little prehistorically, decorated senior officer, on visiting a unit in the Division said, "There is only one thing to do as far as the men are concerned out here— keep their mouths shut and their bowels open."

Inoculations had to be frequent and close study made of the many poisonous snakes that abounded; one had to get used to the noise of jackals and wild birds at night and to the vultures and pi dogs that emptied your plate for you if you were foolish enough to leave it unattended.

Yes, perhaps after all it was quite easy to understand the queer attitude of the residents to whom such things had become second nature.

After the troops of 15 Inf Bde Gp had been in the Ahmednagar and Poona area for a week, taking in all these new angles on life, Brigadier H. R. H. Greenfield went round units to tell them that the rest of the Division was on its way to India but that the Bde Gp must go on ahead to the eastern side of India to prepare for a possible Japanese invasion of Bengal.

The Divisional area was to be around Ranchi, a small town in the Native State of Bihar, the base area for what was then described as Eastern Army. This entailed a journey of some 1,200 miles by train for the personnel parties, and by road for the vehicles and their drivers. The road companies were to leave on a daily Divisional basis from Bombay, as units reported there, starting on 31st May.

13 Inf Bde arrived from Madagascar and were concentrated around Ahmednagar when 15 Inf Bde started out on their journey. The rail journey took four days via Nagpur and was a novel experience. Stops were made at selected places for meals and the trains appeared to move in easy stages at the whim of the babus who ran the railway. It was very trying in the heat of an Indian summer and most of the troops were glad to get to Barkakhana, the station for Ranchi, even if, when they got there, they found it was just a bare stretch of semi-jungle and paddy fields. Upon this they had to build their camps with coolie assistance and a minimum of stores, due to scarcity of transport, and the long distances involved.

Across India by Road

Meanwhile the road parties were assembling in Colabar Camp at Bombay where the DA and QMG of Div HQ, Major John Waldron, was sorting out the chaos in his usual masterly way, helped by Major Hunter and Major Lascelles, 2nd in Command of the Div RASC. The journey was to be quite an undertaking; never before had a division attempted to cross India by road in the heat of summer. The vehicles were not designed for tropical heat and many modifications, where possible, had to be made. Each vehicle was issued with two chaghals, canvas water bottles, which were to be very much in demand. It would take a book in itself to describe the many adventures of the different convoys, but the following notes are extracted from the diary of one of the convoy commanders and is typical of them all:—

June 7th

Left Colabar 0630 hrs., escorted by Div Provost and route picketed by Div Signals. Few minor temporary breakdowns, Bullocks and Carts a damned nuisance. Pools full of Water Buffalo steaming away. 1053 gets very hot—radio report from rear of column that all is well,—horrible smells in some of these villages. 1545 hours reports of petrol pump trouble on quite a few vehicles. Head of column arrives Nasik (very holy City and full of Crocodiles) at 1715 hours; last vehicle in by 0030 hours June 8th!

June 8th

Start 0640 hours. Ration lorry mislaid. 0650 hours, ferocious looking dog chases us—small girls, not a stitch between them, grin in a friendly way. 0845 hours crossed river Majau—dried up—then river Saie, a couple of Wild Wart Hogs dash across our path—lorry of Native drivers come straight at us on a steep hill with a good view! We play gramophone at Lunch Halt (Strauss, Sibelius and Noel Coward) to small posse of intrigued boys and shrivelled up old men, who giggle monotonously.

June 9th

Now petrol trouble—grit gets in easily—first Heat casualty evacuated by ambulance—people fairer skinned in these parts. 0810 hours Old lady just spat at my Motor Cycle Orderly.

Advancing Steam Roller of ancient design challenges us; seems to be out of control. It is out of control. 1150 hrs. Funeral procession passed us, Corpse sits in chair has his face painted red and his feet green. Rather revolting.

June 10th
Left Khaleitat 0640 hours. Women washing in river by a lovely temple—Turtles and Crocodiles scared Water Cart driver as he stopped to fill up in the river. 0900 a Modern factory, but can't make out what it makes. Bad signposting in the State of Indore. Indian official of some sort stops us,— something about Man-Eating Tiger Ahead—have we knives?— only for eating? no good—. 0835. Into Dhow State—couple of large monkeys jump on to the truck take one look and jump off again. Arrived Mhow 0900 hours.

June 11th
Passed Indian OCTU on Bicycle T.E.W.T. 0720 hours large "V" Sign cut in hill on left—curious notice in a field "Field cultivated by voluntary labour for the poor man's Spitfire fund"—0910 hours Pass GUNA H.Q. of 1st Gwalior Lancers. Night spent surrounded by howling Jackals. Headlights kept them away.

June 12th
Fantastic Shivpuri—State Shooting Box of Maharajah of Gwalior—Steamer on the Lake. Victorian type Hotel and natives do roaring trade selling earthen pots to keep the water cool.

June 13th
Jhansi—very very hot, but comfortable barracks for night. Across plain strewn with large boulders and dead trees. Somewhat desolate and eerie. Vultures picking at the remains of a Water Buffalo. Probably died of lack of water.

June 14th
Signals driver swallowed some Sulphuric Acid, but appears to be none the worse for it.

June 15th
Country now flat (with small thin trees) coloured in pastel shades. Sky grey with heat—0900 hours cross the Jumna at Kalp—in one small village a bungalow proudly displays

notice "War Office". *Cawnpore*—Modern Factories—Vile smells—the Wolverhampton of the East! Each man received 10 cigarettes from the ladies of Cawnpore—what a nice gesture—about 30 men now very ill from heat exhaustion. Doctors work overtime.

June 16th
Down the Ganges Valley on a good road—now exotic vegetation. Allahabad for the night—not a great welcome—met an officer of 16th/5th Mahrattas—who told us he'd served in the Division with the Cameronians in Ireland—News of rain in Calcutta—could do with it here. On and on, in perspiration and dust, reddish dust.

June 17th
Peahen and guinea fowl observed here—coming to Benares. Wonderful city a mixture of Balmoral and Rangoon alternately. All getting very listless now but sum up enough energy to go round the burning ghats—horrible sights. Thousands upon thousands of people bathing in water—corpses half burned floating by, not enough wood to do the job properly—floating down Ganges to the Crocodiles and turtles—saw a lovely Temple door solid silver with rubies and emeralds studded into it—utter poverty, filth and mire all round and a cow wandering inside—two members of previous convoy died yesterday and now buried at Benares.

June 18th
Hottest place of all—Aurangabad—most of us very ill now but struggle on—one of our best Officers died here—temperature 138° in the shade and there is none.

June 19th
Welcome relief—climb to Hazaribagh—Tiger shooting country. Nearly there now and almost delirious with extremes. —Green grass and luscious shrubbery.

June 20th
Arrived Ranchi with all the vehicles intact—I don't know how the drivers did it!

The first of the road convoys arrived in Ranchi on 11th June after nearly a fortnight on the road. By now the rail parties had got the camps fairly well organized but a lot of road making had yet to be done.

The rôle of 5 Div in Bihar was to repel any Japanese invasion of the north-east coast of India, or through the Assam Jungle. 70 Div, not a very strong one numerically, was also stationed in the Ranchi area for this purpose. The special task of 5 Div was to defend the valuable Tata Steel Works at Jamshedpur and no time was to be lost in reconnoitring all possible means of doing this should it prove necessary. The Div Recce Regt made very detailed and exhaustive surveys of all the possible routes involved in a march into Assam, and various commanders and staff officers made similar excursions. It will probably never be known who in the Division got farthest east, for Ranchi was the turning point in the Division's long journey.

Training at Ranchi

The rains began to fall with a vengeance almost as soon as the concentration in Ranchi started. As in France and Scotland two years back, a torrential downpour greeted H.R.H. the Duke of Gloucester when he made his third visit to the Division. But the monsoon was not allowed to interfere with training. The Division now had quite a leeway to make up. Training in jungle tactics, endurance tests, and shooting were the order of the day for the Infantry, whilst the Sappers explored the use of local materials for bridges, building and other machinations. The Gunners organized practice camps; at the village of Mandar they carried out field firing and at Opa they constructed an anti-tank range to practise what was only just their secondary rôle at that time. At Mandar when the Compensation Officer went round a village in the centre of the ranges to meet claims, he was horrified to find some old people bound hand and foot in the deserted houses waiting for the 25-pounder shells to qualify their families for compensation. The Gunners had to send in patrols to stop this. The Infantry of the Division brought the 6-pounder anti-tank gun into India for the first time. The Indians had had to be content with a few 2-pounder anti-tank guns and the Boyes Anti-Tank Rifle. Everybody put in as much marching as possible and got themselves pack minded; an experience which was to stand them in good stead later. After a few days of the rains, walking and manhandling of equipment became almost a necessity as, one by one, the ill-founded roads began to cave in from the continual strain of army traffic; much repair was effected by the Sappers and local labour and, in some cases, by the nearest units themselves. The use of roads had, of necessity, to be severely restricted with subsequent loss of training time, particularly for the Gunners.

Leave was soon organized in Calcutta and courses were well subscribed. Much time was spent in Camp improvement, in mastering the rations, and how best to prepare them. The natives, magnificent specimens of Dravidian Indians, were very shy yet friendly. They were not used to seeing many white soldiers, and their own weapons were confined to the bow and arrow at which they were masters. Quite a few units attended tribal ram-samis (parties) and their quaint chromatic Indian music became a customary camp background, particularly in the evening. The natives instantly responded to the bagpipes and grinned from ear to ear when the pipers paraded past their villages. The soldiers' peculiar games now included contests between centipedes and scorpions. The excitement over these contests, more interesting than the more hackneyed contests between snakes and mongoose which they had been introduced to in the Bombay area, never flagged.

The Threat to the Middle East

The rains at least helped General Alexander in his withdrawal through Burma and it looked as though the Japanese would have little chance of reaching East Bengal before Eastern Army could be built up. It was at this moment that the more serious threat was seen to be in the heart of the Middle East, the area around the River Tigris and Euphrates, known today as Iraq. This was the cradle of civilization, the traditional site of the Garden of Eden and for centuries it dominated the world. Its natural wealth was coveted by ambitious neighbours and it finally sucumbed to a succession of invasions mainly by Persians from the north, and by Mongols from the east. Alexander the Great from Greece, after he had disposed of Egypt, came to Babylon, and from there he advanced to the North-West Frontier of India. The Emperor Trajan, from Rome, used these two great rivers to get as far as possible down the Persian Gulf, the natural way to the East. It was logical that Hitler, in his turn, should feel the urge to go the same way. He wanted *Lebensraum* for his increasing population; he wanted the oil in the Persian Gulf now denied to him by allied encirclement and at the same time, he wanted to deny it to his own enemies. The Persian supply of oil to the Middle East was a vital life blood without which they would lose their mobility.

Some years before the war Hitler dreamed and prepared for his *drang nach ost*; he sent German engineers to improve and build new Persian railways, evidence of which is in the Terminal Station at Teheran, completely devoid of any oriental atmosphere at all. He had infiltrated engineers and scientists and had encouraged Raschid Ali in Iraq to plan a revolt against the English when the time was ripe. He had just such an expansion in his mind when he launched his armies against Stalingrad and the Caucasus. His armies would gather momentum and sweep on, virtually unopposed, to India, "liberating" the Arabs and their neighbours, and welcoming them to his beloved Reich.

In 1941, before the battles of Stalingrad had started, his plans had been set back by the defeat of the Vichy French in Syria and the cost of the Greek Campaign. Furthermore, his supporters in Iraq, under Raschid Ali, were forced to make their insurrection before the Germans could go to their aid, although by then Hitler had mastered Crete, at great cost, and was rapidly approaching Egypt from the west. All plans were upset by a scratch British Force of two Brigade Groups and the R.A.F. garrison of Habbaniya who, augmented by loyal Iraqui levies, put down the rising and captured Baghdad. This put the people more on the side of the Allies, and did much to harm the German cause.

This felicitous warning forced the Allied High Command to build up the Tenth Army based on Basra, at the head of the Persian Gulf, to keep enough troops in the Middle East to forestall any possible further German advance, and to protect the vital Allied lines, and communications in that area. At first only Indian troops were to be available and from them, the Command, known as Paiforce, took its sign of the Elephants' Head, familiar to readers of *The Trunk Call*. It was a very slow build up, depending entirely on the ability of the Eighth Army to keep the Germans at bay in the desert and of the Russians to contain other Germans around Stalingrad and in the

Caucasus. At that time neither of these provisos was in the least bit assured; the Battle of Alamein had not yet been fought out, the Battle of Stalingrad was not beginning favourably for the Russians.

In between these two fronts the Germans were already in Bessarabia, between the Black Sea and the Caspian. The Army Commander, General Sir Edward Quinan, was thus faced with a potential front in Northern Iraq, on the borders of Turkey; a Turkey that was at that time much under the spell of Franz Von Papen. This front would entail lengthy lines of communication back to Basra, and it was soon appreciated that the original concept of three divisions was not going to be enough to cover this vast field; a further target of ten Divisions was set for Paiforce.

Furthermore, impressed by the revolt in Iraq, the Persians started to become defiant. They then possessed a strange army, small but well equipped by the Germans and Czechs, although very limited in its tactical possibilities. All the same, if not dealt with, it could be of great nuisance value as it had been openly trained and partially led by the Germans as part of Hitler's plan, before the war. German influence was noticeable and particularly in the cut of the Persian officers' uniform. Persia had to be dominated if Paiforce was to secure its eastern flank and if supplies now promised to Russia were to get through unmolested. It is of interest to note that the U.K.C.C. organization eventually carried 5 million tons of stores to Russia by lorry over the 1,000-mile line of communication.

Based on Khaniquin, a small town and railhead to the north of Baghdad, a small British and Indian force commanded by General Slim set off up the tortuous Paitak Pass to seize the Persian garrison town of Kermanshah. After a few desperate and bloody excursions, the Persians, sensing that the Germans were still too far away to influence the campaign, decided that they had no quarrel with the British and ordered the garrison of Kermanshah to surrender.

Again the writing was on the wall although it was not easy to see from where the extra divisions were to come. The more favourable situation in Burma, created by General Alexander, aided by the monsoon, had stopped the Japanese advance enough to permit the initiative to be taken, when the time came, with the minimum of British reinforcements. The jungle was no place for a multiplicity of divisions; its very density precluded manœuvre on the grand scale. It was probably for this reason that General Wavell was able to spare one of the two divisions recently arrived from the United Kingdom. The question was which one of these two divisions should go, 2 or 5?

It was said that General Wavell was about to direct 2 Div from Bombay and Karachi when Major-General Berney-Ficklin went to see him and asked outright if 5 Div could go to Persia. It was pointed out by him that two-thirds of his Div was across the eastern side of India whereas 2 Div was still concentrating near the western ports, and therefore much better placed for a quick move. After much discussion General Wavell agreed that, should they be able to be clear of India within ten days, 5 Div should be allowed to go. The splendidly trained officers of the Div Staff and the experience of their units would alone make this possible and General Berney-Ficklin was perfectly confident about the outcome. Naturally it entailed great personal speed on the part of all concerned to ensure that men in hospital and on courses were got out quickly, also for vehicles to be retrieved from workshops and made ready for a long journey. The fact that the Div was still the British Reserve Div must also have played its part in the decision and in its subsequent realization.

The Move to Persia

The most ambitious movement of all was now prepared and put into effect. It involved movement of the road parties across India by the North West Frontier across the Baluchistan Desert and thence into the heart of Persia from the south. The rail movement of the personnel was to be just as complicated, including much chopping and changing, but the projected desert approaches held a great element of excitement.

Every effort was made to ensure that this little-used trail was as secure as possible for the convoy. Navigational centres linked by radio were set up at frequent intervals as any system of roadways was non-existent. Refuelling and feeding both had their complex problems but, with the help of the Indian staffs, they were soon resolved and the series of expeditions, as the convoys were, set off eventually in the first week of August in pouring rain. This rain caused a day or two's delay to the road parties in the early stages.

F.D.–G

The route retraced the previous journey for most of the way. At Benares there was civilian trouble led by the Vice Chancellor of the University, but the convoys kept out of the trouble except for a bit of brick and mud slinging. At Delhi where the carrier parties were concentrating, the disturbances were more serious and Div Carrier Parties were used to help the civil power. A few brickbats were thrown at the road parties at Allahabad and Div Officers now openly carried revolvers. Cawnpore was relatively quiet and the sun was shining again as if to confirm it. Here the convoy left the outward route for Agra and then to Quetta. A day of refitting was spent in Agra and here were met the first Americans in India setting up one of their vast dumps near by. Here Noel Coward's description of the Taj Mahal by moonlight was confirmed as being exactly like a "Biscuit Box". But closer inspection was fascinating, particularly as the River Jumna was now in full spate and reflected the moonlight intensely. The contrast to the large and impressive Red Fort of Agra was most noticeable. Here there were civilized hotels manned by barmen straight from Hollywood. At Agra the convoys were directed back to Bombay. At the crucial moment the Indus had flooded and taken away the bridges at Quetta. Much to the disappointment of all concerned the great Desert Epic was not to take place, there being not enough time to wait while the bridges were rebuilt. The next day's run out of Agra was a very beautiful one through the magnificent wild jungles of the State of Gwalior that now had got back a little of the colour lacking a few weeks previously before the magic touch of the rains. Gwalior itself appeared, at a short glimpse, to be a very go-ahead city with a large, rambling fort perched on a rocky promontory and its citizens looking clean, colourful and busy. At Shivpuri and Biaora the outward route was taken back into Bombay without further incident. The warning order reached convoy commanders that vehicles would have to be prepared for embarkation again and as much preliminary work as possible was done on another day's rest in Mhow. The residents seemed a little less hostile as the Division pointed the other way. It was interesting to note, since the outward journeys, how much the staging arrangements had improved. Even the Station Staff Officers, a peculiar breed of English Babu, mostly were alert and helpful, in contrast to the one on the outward journey who had solemnly refused one convoy commander his supply of fresh vegetables and ice, as, according to his typewritten instructions, that particular convoy had passed through his station the day before. He was eventually persuaded, after he had had his afternoon siesta, that the convoy was actually there; that he had been the victim of a typist's error, and all was well.

The convoys went down the western ghats into the humid heat of Bombay once more. Here arrangements were being hurriedly made to effect the switch over of routes and, Colabar Camp being full, some of the convoys had to sleep in the Brabourne Stadium under a large expanse of leaky roof. Work on the vehicles was immediately started so that embarkation and disembarkation straight into the Iraq desert would go smoothly and quietly. Desert tyres were put on, sand channels fitted, heights cut down and after much checking of measurements, the vehicles were hoisted into creaky old tramp steamers and set off ahead of the personnel.

Brigadier G. W. B. Tarleton, Commander, 17th Brigade was now in control of all Divisional movement through Bombay, and Major Waldron and his staff were performing the same series of miracles. A few final days were spent enjoyably in Bombay and in Karachi, before the personnel convoys sailed only partially escorted.

CHAPTER SEVEN

AUTUMN AND WINTER IN PERSIA, 1942-3

In which the 5th Division continues the move from India, up the Persian Gulf, through Iraq, over the Paitak Pass to Kermanshah in Persia. In which, after concentration again, the Division moves on to Qum, due south of Teheran, where a cold and sterile winter is spent in tented camps.

The voyage up to the Persian Gulf was a comparatively restful period, the climate getting hotter every day and the troops having to take salt water on parades to replace lost energy. One gunner of 91 Fd Regt has cause to be grateful to the destroyer that took him off and quickly got him to Karachi for an acute appendicitis operation. The journey lasted some ten days in all, due to various delays. Off the oil refinery of Abadan, the convoy was halted by a dense sand fog, but proceeding up the Tigris, the port of Basra at Maghil was reached. From here the troops were taken over flat hot desert to Shaiba, the camp where they were to meet the vehicles again. Some three days were spent in the most intense heat of all; the "cold" water was almost boiling and the hot wind continually whipped up the sand into thick fog, as off Abadan. There was nothing to do but get the vehicles roadworthy and go to the N.A.A.F.I. in the coolest parts of the day and night. Basra, the hometown of Sinbad the Sailor, was too far away for a visit, even had there been time.

It was at Shaiba that 156 Fd Regt, the Lanarkshire Yeomanry, joined the Div from Karachi. They were to replace 9 Fd Regt, left behind at Madagascar and were to give supreme support to 17 Inf Bde until the end of the war, in the best traditions of the Royal Regiment.

The road parties set off for the next stage through the desert of Mesopotamia to the First Staging Camp at a mound that was once better known as Ur of the Chaldees. This city, the birthplace of Abraham, was once the centre of all the tracks to Egypt, where Nebuchadnezzar, last King of Babylon, built a temple

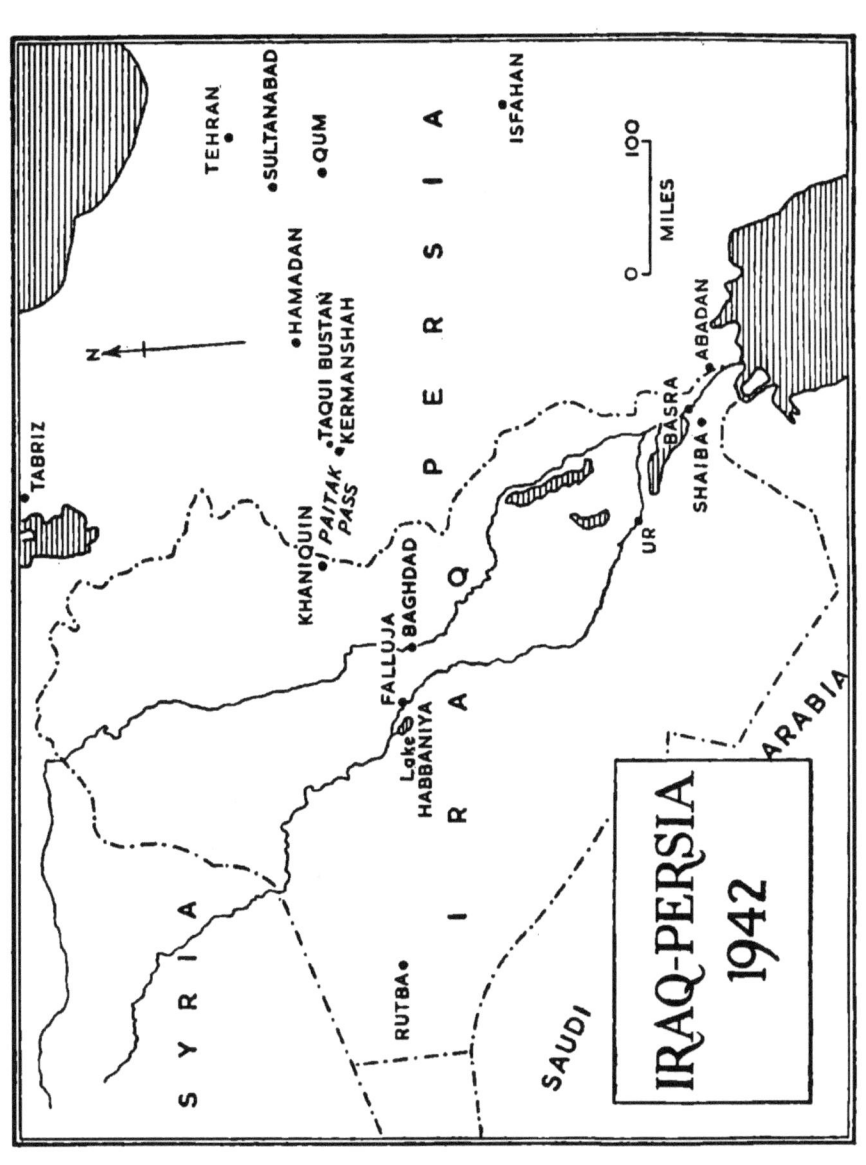

and where the last traces of the flood were found. This run was over untracked stony desert and each convoy commander had with him a guide who knew the way. When the guide left, the Basra-Baghdad Railway acted as an indication of the right side of the still nebulous route. Mirages were now seen frequently and ranged from mountains and lakes to English Public Houses. Except for a little camel thorn scrub there was not a vestige of vegetation.

A short pause *en route* enabled the enthusiasts to spend some minutes in the remains of Babylon.

Arab caravans were met as the convoys moved nearer Baghdad. The landscape became much more restful than the more vivid one of India. Vegetation became more noticeable and lonely Police posts were encountered. A night was spent at Khanjadwal near a battalion of Gurkhas in camp. These were guarding the lines of communication against a violent local tribal clash then in progress.

Baghdad, city of minarets, mosques, magic carpets, thieves, and particularly the latter, was reached without incident and all units passed through on their way north, staying at Lancer Camp to the south of the city. The rail parties passed through here as well, after tedious but generally uneventful journeys across India and longer stays in Shaiba and the western ports of India. Members of the Division found that a day in Baghdad cost as much as a week in Bombay, with the cheapest form of drink at 5s. a glass. Like Benares it was a violent clash of splendour and poverty but unlike Benares it had suffered from a ghastly cheap form of western modernization. It is a comparatively young city but during its twelve hundred years it has been the seat of a civilization, a Mongol capital, battleground between Turkoman and Persian, a Turkish colonial possession, an outpost of the British Empire and the centre of a young Arab state: small wonder it is now an unfortunate mixture of strange contrasts.

The convoys moved on after a few days refit to Khaniquin, only a day's run to the north. Khaniquin, entered by tarmac road, was railhead for all troops of Paiforce going north to the Iraq Frontier or into Persia. It was here that the rail parties finally detrained and proceeded for the rest of the way in road transport. Here were miles and miles of Polish refugee camps that were built up into the Polish Corps that was to fight so well for the Allies in Italy. At Khaniquin, 5 Div had set up one of its reporting centres manned by Div staff and convoys received orders and information from Major Colville of the Cameronians.

The Persian border was crossed the next day and there was an immediate noticeable change of landscape and people. A distinct Khurdish flavour, Cossack hats and long frock coats at the Customs Post, a French atmosphere accentuated by the long, straight, poplar-lined roads and the cloth caps of the many peasants who were not wearing the white egg-shaped felt caps, underlined this abrupt change of background.

The drive up the steep winding Paitak Pass was a terrifying experience for the Div's drivers who had to compete with African convoys, taking personnel parties up to Persia and now returning empty. These African drivers drove like demons possessed, with little fear of the steep ravines that lay beyond the barrierless roadsides. A glance over the edge revealed quite a few that had shot over the side. It was nerve-racking for those who had to be their passengers.

The weather was lovely and revealed fully the delicate pastel shading of the countryside, as in parts of dried-up India.

The journey crossed a series of plains and minor passes through verdant oases and queer villages down to the garrison town of Kermanshah. Here in a camp at the foot of rugged tall mountains near the well of Taqui Bustan, the whole Division was reunited by 5th October, 1942, after their various journeys from India, of which it is not possible to record details here but the road parties varied little from the experiences already described and the rail journeys were mostly uneventful. During the last three months, however, the Div had crossed India twice and passed up into Persia across the plains of Iraq. There had been casualties of course but that these were infinitesimal was a source of pride to the Div Comd whose staff had organized and controlled this extremely complex series of moves in the most efficient and friendly manner, for which they were now famed. Mention must be made of Lieut.-Colonel R. C. H. Kirwan the G.S.O.1 and his G.S.O.2 Major J. M. Sinclair, of Lieut.-Colonel P. F. Shakerley the A.Q.M.G. and his D.A.Q.M.G. Major Waldron already noticed. Operation "Character", as this move was known, had certainly been aptly titled!

Kermanshah, about the size of Winchester, had a mixed poor population of Persians and Assyrians and was the garrison town headquarters of a Persian Division then much under strength. It was an indescribably filthy town with no drainage, the centre of the Persian hide industry with a few carpet looms. Disease was rife, accentuated by the bestial habits of the inhabitants who were now paying for it by a visitation of the plague whilst the Division was near by. Nevertheless the crowd was interesting and cosmopolitan with here and there the mustard coloured uniform of the powdered and scented Persian officer, and the sky blue musical comedy garb of the policeman.

Everywhere the sheep lined yellow poshteen, short and long, dirty and clean, was worn as protection against the cold winds that swept across the plain of Kermanshah. Soon many members of the Div had bought poshteens, a uniform acceptable almost all over the Middle East in winter or at night. Taqui Bustan was about ten miles or so to the north of Kermanshah and between the two on the long straight road was the little oasis of the British Colony of the oil company's pumping station. Here was hospitality indeed from a pleasant little outpost of empire. At the well of Taqui Bustan, a small market centre, was the rock which Moses is alleged to have struck and from which, so it is said, water has poured ever since. The camp was a long line of unit tents sheltered either side of the road that ran along the foot of the mountains. No time was wasted in shaking off the dust of recent journeys and in getting back to training which took the usual pattern of marching and Company schemes, of anti-tank and other weapon shooting, of instruction in the many specialist rôles. Brigade exercises were soon under way. While at Kermanshah the Colonel-in-Chief of the RSF, Marshal of the Air Force Lord Trenchard, visited the 2 Bn.

Winter at Kermanshah, however, was to be avoided for its severity, and within a month the Division was moving on further into Central Persia to the Holy City of Qum, a hundred miles or so south of Teheran. Two routes were used for this journey and one, the most northerly, entailed negotiating the Shah Pass which is one of the highest passes in the world. Over this pass the Divisional Artillery managed to get their guns in order to show the flag in Hamadan, a town noted for

The Pipers of the Royal Inniskilling Fusiliers lead back the Battalion to camp after an exercise near Qum.

The Northamptons marching through Teheran with the white-clad Elburz mountains as a background.

Paitak Pass.

TRANSPORT IN PERSIA.

Above: The R.A.S.C. dug-in near Qum—a train in the background returns from Teheran along "the life-line to Russia".

Left: Laagered for the night.

The Seaforth Highlanders preparing the Caber for their New Year's Games at Qum.

The Golden Dome of the Mosque at Qum.

Company Office and Staff
15th Infantry Brigade, R.A.S.C.

Keeping warm in poshteens.

QUM

"Doc" Wainwright.

A game of football.

being the oldest in Persia, one of the great centres of the carpet industry, and for being openly anti-British. Persian officers solemnly turned their backs as the convoys passed through its streets, and there was a distinctly teutonic smell in the air.

Winter at Qum

The camp at Qum was astride a road fork a few miles west of Qum in a sandy plain between two lines of hills much lower than the mountains at Kermanshah. Here tents were pitched in groups of three, some 200 yards apart which made recognition difficult. Under the canvas tops the interiors of the tents were dug down to six or more feet and "furnished" with carpets and trappings bought in the local bazaar. The by now automatic adaptability of the man who wore the "Y" had enabled him to be comparatively comfortable in the middle of a Persian plain some 5,000 feet above sea level during a particularly severe winter.

Qum was about the size of Kermanshah but architecturally much more beautiful and less dependent on the use of flattened petrol containers. It was destroyed by Tamurlane who marched through Persia several times between 1384 and 1439. It was rebuilt by the kings of the Safavid Dynasty in the next two centuries as a centre of pilgrimage and royal burial places. Twelve kings and 400 princes, numerous saints and the daughter of the prophet Mahommed are all buried in this Holy City which, as a result, was mostly out of bounds to British soldiers. It will be chiefly remembered for the gold-leaf-covered dome of the large mosque which shone brightly in the sun and could be seen for many many miles, an object for which, as an aiming point, the Div Arty were eternally grateful. It could be seen from practice camp, north of the city and from almost everywhere where gunners were to be exercised.

The great battle for the Division, now a real long-stop for Eighth Army in the Western Desert and for the Russian Armies in the Caucasus, was to keep the men fit, in high state of training and morale. The latter was by now well recognized in the Division as being the key to the two former. Entertainment was not easy but at least one E.N.S.A. party, that of Terry Thomas in "You're Welcome" got as far as Qum, although not until after Christmas. Leave in Teheran was permitted but, after having been in Qum for a short time, disorders broke out in Teheran and 5 Div was ordered to send up battalions to help the civil power once more. Early in December, 6 Seaforth camped for a month on Teheran Racecourse, to safeguard British interests and to ensure that no more British citizens were shot. There they shared guard and duties with two Russian battalions already in Teheran. The latter kept smartly aloof but were as susceptible to the Highlanders Pipe Band as were the Persians. The most effective soother of the latter were the frequent route marches of the battalion headed by their pipes, and on one occasion a platoon of the Persian Army attached itself to the column! Much was done to make life bearable for these battalions in Teheran. The cinemas were opened so that the marching troops could halt, see a film and take refreshments before continuing their march. The Highlanders celebrated Hogmanay in fine style by holding a dance in the hall of the totalisator of the racecourse for which they borrowed 120 Polish A.T.S. girls as partners.

2 Northamptons moved to Teheran before 6 Seaforth and camped in similar circumstances. Here they took part in the famous "Bank Incident" and were probably the only official safe breakers in the British Army! On this occasion, the Persian authorities had refused to sanction an increased issue of paper money by the State Bank to pay the inrush of troops into the country, and particularly those of the 5 Div. The Northamptons and a troop of 25 pounders from 156 Fd Regt, a squadron of armoured cars from the 5 Recce Regt and a section of Sappers from 38 Fd Company planned to surround the bank, enter it and remove the required number of notes to another bank. If necessary the Sappers were to blow the safes open, but, at the last minute, probably to the disappointment of those concerned, the Persian Government relented.

2 WILTS, of 13 Inf Bde, spent a less eventful and shorter period in Teheran in early January. Certain staff officers made long reconnoitring visits to the shores of the Caspian Sea, but, by and large, there was no movement north of Teheran where the Russian Army, centred on Tabriz, had its base area. As already mentioned the lorries of U.K.C.C. were continually plying backwards and forwards from Kermanshah to Tabriz with supplies for Russia. A great deal of stores also

went by train and on some of these trains detachments from the Division were placed as guards. It was strange to see German locomotives manned by Russian crews, guarded by British troops, hauling carriages of all nationalities and labelled still "Tunbridge Wells" or "Bloemfontein". Teheran must have been one of the most cosmopolitan cities of the war. Here East was linked with West and North with South. Here was international gaiety in the most sophisticated nightclubs next door to the ancient wrestling booths and massed Turkish baths. The architecture is again mixed, a great deal of the Teuton mixed with the florid Italianate style, the Byzantine with the Mongol simplicity. Almost every language could be heard in the buses and in the street. Brightly painted kiosks and urinals adorned the streets as in France against a background of plane trees and open drains. Behind it all rose the peaked, shapely Mount Demavend, a snow-covered cone of 18,549 feet which could be seen from Qum on clear days. It dominates not only Teheran but the thousands of miles of salt desert that lie to its south-east. (There were good winter sports to be had in the Elburz mountains and there were members of the Division who benefited from this.)

The Div had detachments spread as far as Baghdad where G.H.Q. was guarded and at Tenth Army H.Q. at Sultanabad. Duties of a special nature also took them to the south— to the lovely city of Isfahan, where the authorities wished to capture a certain Persian General who was not being as co-operative as he might be. A platoon of 6 Seaforth, commanded by Lieutenant Robertson, was trained specially for this cloak and dagger operation. For some time, troops of the Division from the Gunners and other units had been sent on special short leave to Isfahan to give the impression that it was to become a leave centre and to arouse no suspicion when the special platoon arrived. The English Colony here were particularly hospitable and the troops were instructed to enjoy themselves and to be seen enjoying themselves. The General was caught at tea and taken by road to an airfield whence he was flown out of Persia with Lieutenant Robertson as escort.

There were many other small incidents during that winter but on the whole the Division did its somewhat negative job efficiently and effectively. It was a trying job with apparently no object in view except to sit and wait for the war to catch up.

Ever since Dunkirk the Division had been waiting, in Scotland, in North-West England, in Northern Ireland, in India, and now in Persia they sat in far from comfortable circumstances and waited whilst others did the real fighting, or at least that was the way they saw it at the time. But now can be appreciated the importance of the rôle of the Reserve Division—a task not lightly undertaken by less experienced formations.

But this was now to end and the much awaited Mediterranean offensive was already being planned in Cairo. The Eighth Army had won the battle of Alamein and was pushing on to Tunis. The Russian defences of Stalingrad had brought disaster to the German Armies that were to have swept down through the Caucasus into Persia. There was no longer need to keep a division sitting in Central Persia; there was work for the highly trained and experienced Division elsewhere where it would no longer be in reserve.

Div H.Q. left Qum on 31st January, 1943, and there followed another period of Bde Gp control widely spread over the Middle East, a period of intensive preparation for the start of the homeward journey.

CHAPTER EIGHT

PREPARATIONS FOR THE MEDITERRANEAN OFFENSIVE

In which the 5th Division moves by various means from Persia to the Lebanon and Egypt, where 13th Infantry Brigade undergoes specialized training at the Middle East School of Mountain Warfare. Where 17th and 15th Infantry Brigades, in that order, complete another specialized course at the Middle East School of Combined Operations on the Bitter Lakes in Egypt. In which the Division concentrates again in Syria for further training in Amphibious Warfare and finally moves by stages to the Suez Canal, from which it sails for Sicily.

From the Defensive to Planning the Offensive

After the slow and somewhat monotonous Persian winter the next phase of Divisional history comes as a short, sharp staccato period of intensive training in fields new to the brigades followed by the final preparation for at last turning to the offensive.

Div H.Q. left Qum at the end of January and went in the direction of Egypt for the planning period of Operation "Husky".

They mostly disappeared into the mysterious George House H.Q. of the Task Force in Cairo and sat with ice packs on their heads working out the thousand and one problems involved in landing an assault division on a hostile coast. A certain number of ships were allotted to carry the Division with its vehicles and equipment, and since only a pint will go into a pint pot, each unit was rationed so far as vehicles were concerned by the amount of shipping available.

Loading tables were compiled for the assaulting brigades with their gunners and sappers in such a way that the last vehicle loaded was the one required out first. By taking benzedrine tablets and working day and night without sleep the Staff produced the answer, only to be told that on the way out some ships had been sunk and the numbers of vehicles must be cut down still further. All the calculations had then to be started again from scratch. After five days and nights without sleep, the final tables were compiled and despatched to the loading ports.

Unfortunately the embarkation staff—largely recruited from shipping companies—were more concerned with cramming as many vehicles as possible into every ship than with the tactical loading. The feelings, for instance, of the gunner who expected his armoured O.P. to be the first vehicle out, only to be presented with the cook's lorry, can well be imagined!

The mysteries of amphibious warfare were also studied by the H.Q. Staff on a special course at the Middle East School. Some of the specialists went on further courses and many visits had to be made between the various formations and brigades of the Division which were to be scattered all over the Middle East from Cyrenaica to Syria during the next few months. Orders had to be passed, often by air, and many minor details of the planning at its various stages had to be co-ordinated; units had to be moved from here to there and administrative detail such as the drawing of special equipment, the replacement of personnel not fitted for this new phase, had to be supervised. It was probably the busiest time for Div H.Q. but under the aegis of Lieut-Colonel R. C. H. Kirwan, the G.S.O.I., and the inspiration of General Berney-Ficklin, their experiences of the past year had considerably simplified the task.

The Journey from Persia

The move from Persia bore the familiar stamp of previous moves. Units either moved by road or by a combination of rail and river steamer. The former was one of great contrasts and great interest and the latter, less exciting but none the less interesting. Once again Div H.Q., those of it not learning to plan amphibiously, were posted at various stops oiling the machinery as it passed through. Their pains cannot be praised too much or too often. Never was a request for help refused and if it could not be granted it was not for the want of trying every possible source. Special tribute must also be paid to the Divisional Provost who were unfailingly successful in keeping traffic on the move, a task they performed to such effect in the later days in Italy, little wonder they became renowned as the smartest and most efficient Police in the Eighth Army, a reputation they jealously guarded and even enhanced in other fields. To those of the unit, brigade and divisional workshops who strove continuously to save any vehicle from being left behind in any remote corner of the world, the Division owed a great deal on these and other moves. To those who drew up, issued, and accounted for the many extra stores, equipment, supplies and petrol on these journeys, from Unit Staffs to the Royal Army Ordnance Corps representatives at Brigades and Division, appreciation was always felt albeit it was not often possible to show it as it should have been. Although this move from Persia to Egypt, or from the defensive to the offensive, was not to be the last to be undertaken, it was to be the end of an era of large sweeping movements of strategic value described in pages previous to this; a humble tribute now to all those who made such moves possible is not out of place here. Perhaps the greatest tribute of all, however, should go to the drivers themselves who frequently drove unrelieved for hours on end in perfect convoy, often suffocated by heat and dust, or burned by the tropical sun beating down on the metal or canvas tops of their driving cabs, often numbed by cold at heights well above sea level, often so fatigued by the monotony of it all that it was only by sheer willpower that they remained awake; the motor cyclists who stuck to the saddle through the same conditions with soft sands or icy roads to be fought, yet the number of men and vehicles that fell by the wayside was practically negligible; no tribute too great could be paid to them.

The road from Persia was under snow when most of the convoy left, and lay through Sultanabad, Malaya to Hamadan. From here the great Shah Pass had to be tackled again. At the top it was deep in snow and a way had to be kept clear by bulldozers. The descent the other side was steep and extremely slippery and it was not rare for motor cyclists to be parted from their machines more than a dozen times before they reached the bottom. Some of them had their hands frozen to the handlebars and even then refused to be relieved. The cold rough road continued from the Pass across to Chehar Zebab some 25 miles south of Kermanshah where there was raging a typhus plague. Then on again down familiar roads lined with wispy poplar and here and there a small oasis of a village down to the Paitak Pass where there was not so much snow and

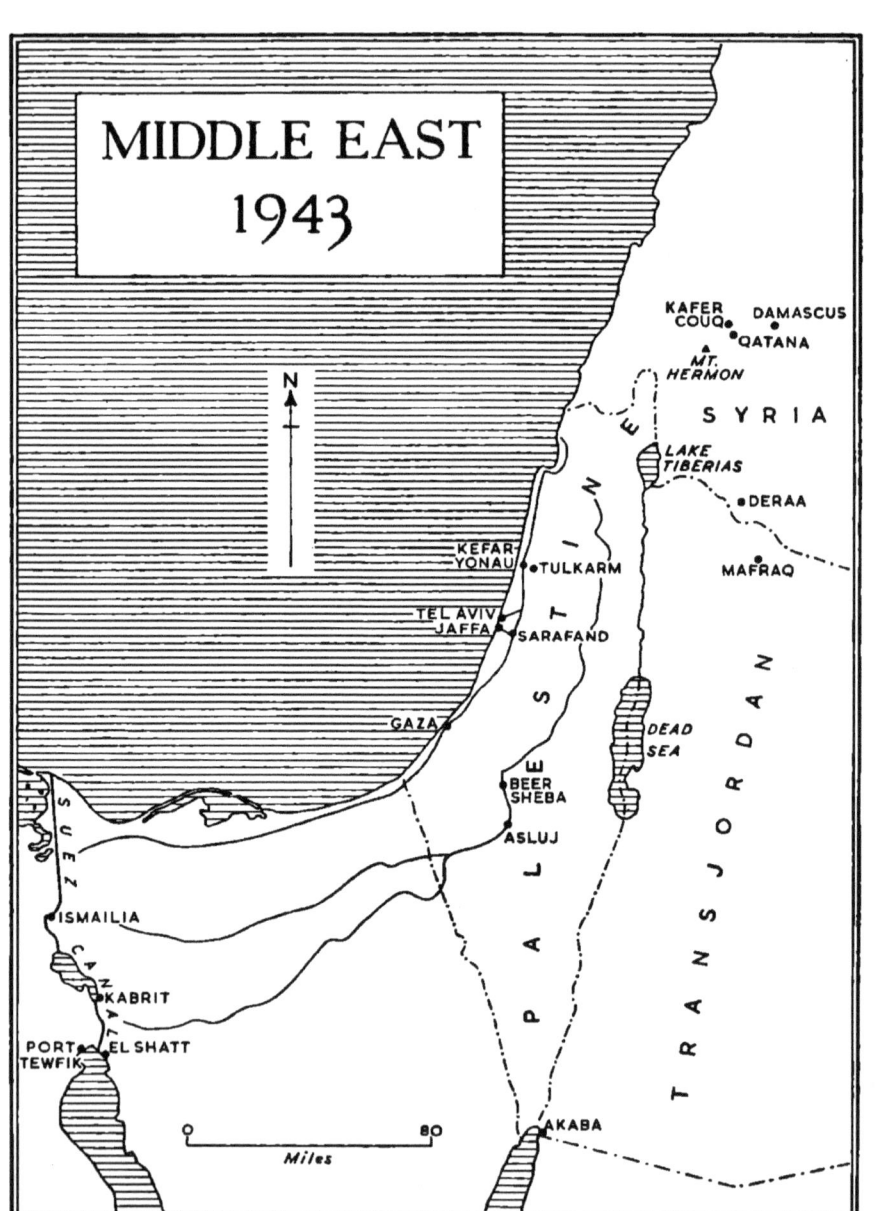

Brigadier G. W. B. Tarleton, commanding 17th Infantry Brigade, with a senior French officer in Damascus when units of the Division marched past Lieut.-General W. G. Holmes, 9th Army Commander, on the 26th April, 1943. Below: The general view of Damascus.

From the sandy waste of Jordan to the green fields and flowers of Palestine. Captain John ("Bert") Barker, R.A.S.C., and L/Cpl. Bob Barrow, R.A.S.C.

Sitting at the feet of the Sphinx.   Roman Triumphal Arch, Jerusalem.

which seemed far less formidable, now that the Shah Pass had been negotiated.

Suddenly it became warmer at the bottom and the layers of winter clothing, leather jerkins and poshteens were hastily discarded as the convoy stopped to gather strength in the little village of Marta near the bottom of the pass. On to Khaniquin, the hot plains of Baghdad were upon them before they realized it and tropical clothing was quickly resumed although the warmer kit was still very necessary at night.

The first stage of the journey, the cold stage, now ended with a much needed day's rest for refitting at the old familiar Lancer Camping Ground in Baghdad. Many pounds of pay accumulated during the winter were spent here in that one day.

At Baghdad also the convoys were sorted out and slightly regrouped where necessary. 13 Inf Bde were to go one way later on and the other brigades a different way still. In one convoy for instance some 214 motor cyclists, mostly of Divisional Troops such as the Recce Regt, were grouped together and made an impressive sight as they swept out of the camp in solid roaring phalanx when the convoy started on the next stage of its journey.

The next stage was the desert crossing from Iraq to Syria by way of Transjordania—a formidable wilderness that had very little highway and even that at times was blotted out by sand storms and a route had to be picked out by oil barrels or the pipeline. Fortunately the pumping stations, at intervals, made good staging points. The first day's run was a straight one to Wadi Muhammadi via Habbaniyah and Falluja. From Wadi Muhammadi to Rutbah, the route was all desert and many carburettors had now to be cleared frequently, to remove the persistent grit and sand. Rutbah was a fort of the "Beau Geste" type with battlements paced by Iraqi troops guarding the gateway into the courtyard. The staging post was alongside and produced petrol and water, rations being carried on vehicles. The next day's run was again a day of nothing but desert to another pumping station unromantically known as H.4. Here there were similar staging facilities and one was really now in the middle of the way beyond, an "abomination of desolation".

The stage that followed between H.4 and Mafraq in Jordan

F.D.–H

was the most interesting. Once out of the dust-fogs, around H.4, the desert gradually acquired features starting with small wisps of camel thorn and small stones, the latter becoming larger and rounder as the miles went by, until, near Mafraq, they became large rounded boulders of lava giving way to green grass, green grass that had not been seen by the drivers for many months.

At Mafraq the convoys of 13 Inf Bde Gp turned north-west towards Kafr Coq, Syria, and then on to the Lebanon to the Mountain School. Those of 15 and 17 Inf Bde Gps turned south to Kefar Yonah in the valley of the River Jordan. As the route wound down into the valley the grass covered slopes became more and more studded with the most wonderful wild flowers. For some very hardened drivers when they halted this was too much, they got down, picked handfuls of these flowers and decorated themselves and their vehicles. At the time it seemed to be a lovely valley, but on reflection it appeared to be very like the many little valleys of South Wales.

At Kefar Yonah, a day's halt after the dust and heat of the desert run, was very welcome. The privileged few managed to get in a quick visit to Tel-Aviv and Jaffa; both places were to be revisited at a later date. The rest of Palestine was covered in the next day's run via Gaza and Beersheba to the desert again at Asluj on the Egyptian border. Asluj sported a good N.A.A.F.I. club which was to become a familiar port of call for many members of the Division on their various journeys during the next few months. The final run into Kabrit was along one of the bumpy tarmac roads across the Sinai desert to Ismailia and then south along the Western bank of the Suez Canal. Kabrit was at that time the centre of spasmodic dust storms of great intensity, but the School of Combined Operations was a comparatively comfortable place with a pleasant Naval and Military staff who made units feel at home. The routine here, as at the Lebanon, will be described later.

The other parties from Qum went by various ways, some to Baghdad by rail and after a short pause at the latter, went on by M.T. across the desert to 'Deraa in Transjordan and then into Syria. Others went to Magil by road, crossed the River Tigris by lighter and then by rail to Baghdad and onwards by road. 2 RSF on their train from Qum were involved in a train smash at Sultanabad with a few casualties—

then to Khurramshah and by river steamer to Shaiba, proceeding from there by the same route as the other parties.

Very early on it was decided that 5 Div would be part of XIII Corps which was to be commanded by Lieut-General M. C. Dempsey, an ex-commander of 13 Inf Bde in 1940. Although he was no stranger there was much liaison to be effected by Commanders and Divisional Staff with the Staff of Headquarters XIII Corps. There was further discussion with the Royal Navy which was working so closely with XIII Corps and Eighth Army under whose command the Division was now to come. Eighth Army at this stage were up in Tunis busily crushing the Afrika Korps against the First Allied Army that had recently landed in North Africa. Both these formations had different ways of doing things and as a result of their vast experiences gained in the Desert Campaign, there were new techniques to be learned, particularly with regard to the handling of massed artillery, as at El Alamein. It was not then generally known that the next move would be to secure Pantellaria and Sicily; it might well have been Greece or Crete, or a combination of all of these places. In any case the flat desert would be replaced by terraced hills and rocky terrain such as the Eighth Army were beginning to experience in Tunisia. This entailed special training in mountain warfare and the mastery of tactics not dissimilar to those practised on the North-West Frontier of India before the war. Then, before reaching any of these countries it was necessary to make a short sea voyage and land on the beaches selected. This required knowledge of further specialized techniques and a certain amount of initiation into the mysteries of the Royal Navy.

Time was all too short for every unit to complete all this training before embarkation which was to be timed to follow up the expected victory in Tunisia just as soon as it was humanly possible to benefit fully from the resultant chaos into which the enemy must be plunged. 5 Div was immediately earmarked as an Assaulting Division and within the Div it was decided to gain the beachhead with 15 and 17 Inf Bdes whilst 13 Inf Bde was to be held in reserve for the follow through. This narrowed the primary training objective to amphibious warfare for the former two Bde Gps and mountain warfare for the latter.

When Div H.Q. left Qum, command of the Div passed

to 15 Inf Bde who were to be the last brigade to undertake these special courses. 13 Inf Bde went to the Middle East School of Mountain Warfare and there studied the problem at first hand. They learned the art of climbing over rocky hills, of "picketing the heights" and of building sangars of rock and stones from which to defend them. They learned of the difficulties of getting supplies and equipment up to troops on these heights and of getting down casualties. This entailed study of the peculiar habits of that military mammal, the mule, a traditionally difficult creature to handle but one upon whose back a very great deal of impedimenta could be loaded if the secret of packing it was mastered. They soon realized the limitations of orthodox artillery methods and the 91 Fd Regt was quick to adapt itself to getting guns into and out of what would be normally considered as unsatisfactory gun positions, and getting used to line ahead positions along a road or track. Communications presented no problem if the wireless worked well but too often it didn't in mountainous country for reasons that were partly geological and partly human. As a secondary means, cable had to be laid and this was a laborious process even in reasonably flat country. In many cases the old heliograph, signalling by flag or lamp as was used on the North-West Frontier, would have been the perfect answer, but this equipment was not on issue currently. The 25 pounder itself was not exactly an ideal weapon, but at least it had some of the characteristics of its effective but obsolete little sister the 3.7-in. Howitzer. Because all these problems, and many more, had to be approached from a different angle and because it was neither possible nor desirable to alter the organization of the Inf Bde Gp to cope with them, the School of Mountain Warfare concentrated into this special course, suggestions for meeting the unorthodox with the orthodox then at disposal. Quite apart from the technical and tactical benefits they gained, the soldiers of 13 Bde Gp who attended this course were soon in very fine physical fettle as a result of their goat-like activities and this was a much desired tonic after the sterile Persian winter, if nothing more than that.

From the mountains to the flat banks of the Suez Canal went 17 Inf Bde. Here they were to learn about amphibious warfare or, as it was then known, combined operations. A very small portion of their course was concerned in rock climbing and cliff scaling, which also acted as a physical tonic after Persia, but most of the training concerned the actual techniques of getting into and out of various types of landing craft, or loading stores and vehicles, guns, carriers and equipment into these crafts, an art which called for considerable knowledge of planning right down to the N.C.O. level. A great deal had to be learned about life afloat in the larger vessels, a life far quicker and more organized than had been experienced by the Division in its various sea voyages up to then. The art of getting down a scaling rope ladder into a small landing craft bobbing up and down in a rough sea, was a tricky one to acquire and, as it happened, it was a good thing that it was mastered when the assault went in on Sicily in just such conditions. The actual organization of the beach area, once it had been secured, was in itself a detailed study. Although this was the responsibility of a special unit formed for the occasion, then known as a "Beach Brick", consisting of a large battalion group with specialized services, it was essential that the assaulting battalions should know something about this organization and what it did. This was a very full course, packed with interest and some good exercises. The school was situated at Kabrit on the edge of the Bitter Lake across which many of the exercises took part. The Division had some very intense training in the precision driving of their vehicles on and off awkward landing craft and the support companies of the brigade actually practised the firing of mortars from craft as they moved in to beach. The gunners experimented with this but it was really a speciality of the Self-Propelled Regiment, 24 Regt, RA, which was attached to the Division for the operations.

15 Inf Bde followed 17 Inf Bde on an exactly similar course and then all three brigades with most of the Div Tps concentrated around Mount Hermon near Damascus in Syria. Here with real mountains and sea represented by the flat grassy plain it was possible to practise the techniques already learned at the two special courses, in "Dryshod" exercises when boat decks were taped off on the ground and troops went over and over the essential drills of getting in and out of boats of all shapes and sizes. In fact this was a series of rehearsals of the real thing in conditions as near to it as it was possible to obtain at the time.

At the same time, training in the normal Infantry Division's rôle was stepped up, and some realistic exercises were carried out. To refresh them on the latest trends of tactical thought, the Middle East School of Tactics at Sarafand organized a special course for all senior officers of the Division at which these gentlemen learned a very great deal that was new and that was to be applied in Syria, and later operationally.

It was inevitable that there should be many changes in personnel and particularly in commanders and their staffs who had served the divisions faithfully for so long and were now due to go on to better things. General Berney-Ficklin himself was due to end his tour as Divisional Commander, but fortunately for all ranks he was permitted by the Army Commander to see the Division through the planning and preparation phase and well and truly launched ashore before being relieved. As he alone knew how to get the best out of the Division at this transition stage, this was a boost to the confidence of all ranks in the success of the operation.

Brigadier L. M. Campbell, V.C., D.S.O., took over 13 Inf Bde from Brigadier V. C. Russell, D.S.O., M.C.; Lieut.-Col. G. S. Rawsthorne, M.C. (later Brigadier G. S. Rawsthorne, C.B.E., M.C.) who had been commanding 6 Seaforth took over command of 15 Inf Bde from Brigadier H. R. H. Greenfield. Brigadier H. Greene now became Commander Corps Royal Artillery, XIII Corps and was succeeded by Lieut.-Col. W. Buffey, D.S.O. (later Brigadier W. Buffey, D.S.O., T.D., D.L.) who had been commanding 91 Fd Regt. All Gunners in the Division's Artillery were pleased that they should continue to serve Brigadier Greene who was never far away from them during the next nine months in Italy and was responsible for some of the fire plans in which they were to take part. He had been a familiar figure to them for so long and his relentless strivings for perfection paid off so frequently and abundantly when the fighting came that there wasn't a Gunner who didn't appreciate it and welcome him in his later visits to the guns.

There were many changes also among the Battalion Commanders and their staffs which will be evident during the coming chapters. To those who were now leaving there could be nothing but gratitude for the staunch work they had done for the Division at the time when its final shape was being moulded. That they had trained their formations and their units is alone self-evident when the next four chapters have been read. There can be no shadow of doubt but that this training and experience were the real factors that kept the Division alert and firmly on both feet after the most exhausting and continuous punishment that was to come. In most cases the influence of former leaders remained imbued in the Division all through the fighting that lay ahead.

Gradually the Division reconcentrated in the area around Quatana and Jebel Mazar near Damascus in Syria. Here under the shadow of Mount Hermon the final touches to training and preparations were painstakingly added. This period consisted of a great deal of dryshod training which culminated in Exercise "Topsail", a three-day exercise on 19–20th and 21st May which was a dryshod full rehearsal of the operation ahead. Ten days later after final titivations, advance parties left for the final concentration area, along the eastern bank of the Suez Canal in tented camps known as El Shatt. Here also were other formations of the Task Force, 50 Div, the Commando and other special troops. About four days later the main bodies left in cattle trucks and other sundry rolling stock on the railway, from Quamna Station to El Shatt Camp, a tiring journey of about eleven hours duration. The very next day after arrival there, advance parties went on to board the liners and transports that were now gathered off Suez, about three days ahead of the embarkation of main bodies.

The next few days were spent in familiarizing troops in their ships and in rehearsing the long and complicated process of getting troops from their mess decks up to the Sally Ports from which they were to climb down into the landing craft a few miles off the invasion beaches. Boat drill and equipment checks together with these rehearsals were continuously practised almost up to the time of disembarkation.

There were two big Exercises held before troops were again disembarked. The first, Exercise "Gooseberry", was an elaborate signals exercise mainly to rehearse the signal control at sea, and only commanders, their staffs and the Royal Corps of Signals were involved. The nerve centre for this exercise and for the later operations was the command ship H.M.S. *Bulolo*, which housed the Senior Naval Officers' H.Q.s and that of General Dempsey's XIII Corps, in which there were also Divisional Representatives.

The next, Exercise "Bromyard", was to be the final rehearsal and a wetshod variation of the dryshod exercise at Quatana. This was to practise the landings and first phase exploitations under conditions as near to the real thing as possible. It exercised the ships and their crews and the Beach Bricks. Divisional troops were at a tactical disadvantage because their guns, vehicles and other heavy equipment had already gone off, direct from Syria to Haifa and other ports from which the vehicle convoys were to sail. Furthermore the assaulting Gunners and other troops who had to land with guns or vehicles were now scattered in the smaller North African ports as far west as Tripoli and their vehicles had to be simulated on the exercise by borrowed equipment which was mostly unsuitable and sank quickly in the soft sand. This exercise went well and a lot of useful last-minute lessons were learned. It was carried out in the Gulf of Aquaba at the small harbour of Aquaba, the junction of Sinai, Palestine, Transjordan and Saudi Arabia and a rather neglected outpost. The ships anchored in the Gulf and the landing craft went ashore in the early hours of the morning. As soon as the value of the initial build-up period had been absorbed the exercise was called off in a blinding sand storm. A conference for officers later in the afternoon was addressed by General Dempsey and Admiral Troubridge, who was commanding Naval Forces. The evening was spent ashore and many were tempted to bathe in the now beautifully clear waters of the Gulf where the fishes and coral were extremely coloured, the latter however had a razor-like sharpness which caused many unkind cuts to the bathers, often in quite embarrassing parts of their anatomy. It was furthermore disconcerting for the bathers to see the most fierce tuna-like fish being yanked out of the very edge of the water by bored-looking crosslegged Arabs. Barracuta were prolific, and from the decks of the ships anchored alongside the rock upon which were the grand ruins of the old Crusader Castle built by Rene de Chatillon, the water at 50 fathoms was so clear that the movement of large fish was clearly visible.

The convoy sailed back to Suez next day and troops disembarked for the last session in sealed camps. On 25th June General Montgomery visited the Division and welcomed all ranks to Eighth Army. This was an impressive little ceremony, at each gathering of troops he would stop his car and summon the troops around him. He would look them over, ask them to remove their caps, make a few choice remarks about the conspicuous absence of baldness, about the fitness of the men, he told them of the battles that Eighth Army had been having, of the need for fresh blood now and a quick follow up to take full advantage of the Tunisian Victory, he would finish by a few remarks that would set the Irishmen making ribald remarks at the Scotsmen or the Welshmen at the Yorkshiremen and would suddenly drive away leaving an endearing and magnetic impression.

This was the finishing touch. Five days later the whole force embarked at Port Tewfik and sailed in line ahead up the Canal, past the school at Kabrit, where the current course, an Indian formation, lined the route to cheer the Task Force on its way. Everyone knew what was afoot but very few people, at this stage, knew where they were going. It was not finally divulged until the ships left Port Said as there was to be yet another day ashore. The journeys up and down the canal, whose banks were then lined with camps, were cheerful and intimate, with much cross chat and rude comments passed between bank and deckrail.

At Port Said there was a day to wait, so long route marches with a welcome bathe, well away from the port, was the order for all units. A long line of well-tanned figures marching jauntily behind the Pipes showed how fit every man was. There was probably no fitter division ever to start out on what was to become almost a year of continuous advancing and fighting a way ahead from Syracuse to Rome. The long months of waiting on the defensive were now certainly finished, but they had left the stamp of experience and stamina on the Division; this engendered a quiet confidence which augured well for the battles that lay ahead.

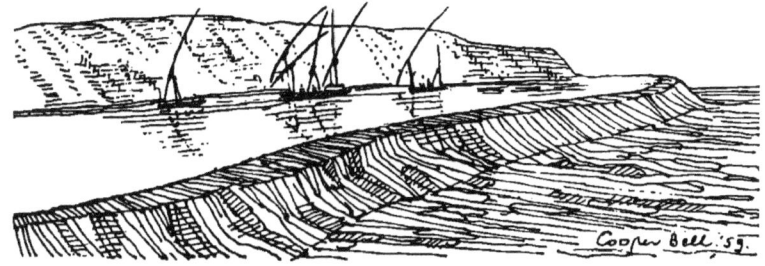

CHAPTER NINE

CAMPAIGN IN SICILY

In which the 5th Division, now part of XIII Corps of the Eighth Army, assaults the island of Sicily and by capturing Syracuse and Augusta, helps to conquer the island as a base for future operations against the mainland of Europe.

The Setting

The convoy carrying 5 Div, part of the Eastern Task Force on Operation Husky, sailed from Port Said on the 5th July in glorious weather, heading north-westward. This task force made up of other convoys from Alexandria, Sfax, Sousse and Malta as well as that from Port Said, carried the British Eighth Army, some two and a half divisions in all, to meet the Western Task Force at a rendezvous off the south-east coast of Sicily. The latter had sailed from Oran, Algiers, Tunis and Bizerta carrying the United States Seventh Army. 3226 vessels of all shapes and sizes sailed in these two task forces.

A deception plan routed the Eastern Task Force in a north-westerly direction, past the enemy held island of Crete, as if to attack Athens. It was to turn westwards at the last possible moment, when it was hoped that enemy reconnaissance aircraft based on Crete would have photographed it and drawn the wrong conclusion. This was carefully explained to all those on board the big ships in the convoy by the senior naval officers in charge of the landings.

It was only then that the troops knew where they were going and it was the explanation of a few maps of Greece carelessly displayed in the briefing rooms at El Shatt Camp. A special order from the Army Commander confirmed this and talked of knocking Italy out of the war for good and all; and if further confirmation was needed it was contained in a little blue book soon issued to all ranks at sea, entitled *The Soldier's Guide to Sicily*.

From this the soldier learned that, "The island has a long

and unhappy history that has left it primitive and undeveloped with many relics and ruins of a civilized past."

The shores of the Mediterranean have probably witnessed more wars than any other part of the world and, at some time or other, almost all of them have had to pass through Sicily. The second World War in 1943, was to be no exception.

Those who remembered their Greek or Latin primers recalled that the gods themselves took a fancy to Sicily and among them Zeus and Hercules. Daedalus the first aeronaut landed there, just about where the 1st Parachute Brigade, or its remnants, were later to touch down, after losing his son to the Sun near Crete. Ulysses came there to slay the Cyclops, the fabulous one-eyed giants who lived along the Etna Riviera. Many were the legends built up around the adventures of these and other mythological heroes in Sicily.

The mortals, however, really accounted for this "unhappy history". Spaniards, some 1,200 years before the birth of Christ, were followed by Greeks from Corinth who founded Syracuse and other colonies. Phoenicians founded similar colonies on the other side of the island having been evicted from Palestine. Then came other Greeks from Athens who tried to dislodge the Greeks from Corinth. Carthaginians invaded from North Africa, under Hamilcar and Hannibal, only to be bustled away by Romans Hannibal was to fight the battle of Cannae in the Foggia Plain, which lay in the path of 5 Div in October 1943, as part of his Punic Campaign.

In the defence of Syracuse, Archimedes contrived some of his most celebrated inventions, before Scipio, the Roman, finally drove Hannibal to North Africa. After more than 1,000 years of Roman looting and misrule, first the Vandals then the Goths attacked Sicily. Over the ninth, tenth and eleventh centuries the Saracens were followed by the Normans, who, after their triumphs in England, tried their hands at colonization; the latter left a lot of typical towns on Sicilian hilltops and were responsible for building the town of Augusta.

Richard Cœur de Lion was the first Englishman to arrive in the island, landing and sacking Messina on his way to the Holy Land; another was Lord Nelson, some 600 years later, but he was part of an English force called in against the Bourbons, and for his services he was given estates near Bronte which are held by his family to this day. In 1860 Garibaldi landed at

Marsala to conquer the dreaded Bourbons and make himself a base from which to unite Italy, whilst sixty years later, Mussolini's Fascism made little or no impression on the backward Sicilian peasants who, in between these various incursions on their privacy, had lapsed into banditry and internal strife.

In 1937 Mussolini made the rash and vain-glorious boast that "Sicily is so well defended on the land, and sea, and in the air, that it would be a nameless folly for anyone to try and invade her. One of the happiest epochs in her 4,000 years of history now begins for her as the geographical centre of the Empire."

The Sicilians, however, were still unimpressed; and when the Germans arrived, whether invited by Mussolini as an afterthought to his 1937 boast or not, the peasants still went about their simple life, with little thought for and much less co-operation with the new champions of the island's defence. Like Scipio, the Wehrmacht used Sicily as a base for their operations in North Africa; unlike Scipio, however, they were driven out of North Africa hotly pursued by their enemy.

Sicily is a triangular island about a third again as large as Wales. The interior is a mountainous mass, some of it highly cultivated with terraced vineyards, olive and almond groves, and most of it just rock and dust. With few good roads, and those mostly around the coastline, its meagre communications are hardly adequate for the quick movement of a modern army. The German Commander General Fridolin von Senger und Etterlin actually used two helicopters to get between Taormina and his regiments. Its small straggling towns are often perched like medieval castles on the hilltops only to be reached by long, tortuous and rutted cart tracks. Sizeable towns are few and far between, most of them being seaports and the whole of the island is dominated by the few thousand feet height of Mount Etna, its wide base overflowing with lava and volcanic rock. This arid setting is more often than not fanned by a sirocco from the south which whips up the black lava dust and the white sand to an unpleasant degree.

Although there are many magnificent buildings in the cities and towns (albeit their walls were "decorated" with suitable Fascist slogans: *Viva il Duce, Vincere*, etc.) and many solid, stylish farmhouses dotted sparsely about the countryside, the average Sicilian lives in a hovel in sheer filth and squalor. Most of the islanders are illiterate and beyond the average power of reasoning. Drinking water and normal sanitation are almost unknown and flies and mosquitoes wallow in the resultant filth. Malaria is rife especially in the Catania Plain. The abundant fruit that can be picked almost anywhere can also be a snare and a delusion to any but the tough Sicilian stomach. These were only some of the problems that the terrain and climate presented to the planners. Baedeker, in his guide book, advises travellers not to visit Sicily between June and September; those who sent the division there in July were certainly not influenced by this. Fortunately by now 5 Div were used to extreme climates at ill-advised and quite unfashionable seasons.

The problems of time and space were unusually complex as well; so much remained dependent on the outcome of the Tunisian campaign, still being fought, when the plans for Operation Husky were being laid in various parts of North Africa. Full advantage had to be taken of a quick follow-up to a North African victory, yet the forces available were abnormally dispersed and their assembly in the correct place at the correct time was to be a very great achievement on the part of the planning staffs. Some of the Americans were to come almost direct from the United States; the Canadians from the United Kingdom; the rest of General Montgomery's Eighth Army was scattered from Tunisia to Central Persia, the winter quarters of 5 Div.

All these troops had to be convoyed, as well as their guns, vehicles and equipment, from scattered ports in merchant shipping, without arousing the suspicions of the enemy, who, despite Allied air superiority, still had enough aircraft available to interfere with the groups of vessels as they closed in on the target area. They did, in fact, only slightly interfere with these concentrations in North African harbours, though the Canadian convoys sailing from England were less fortunate. If his suspicions were aroused, so well were the plan and cover plan conceived and executed, that almost all of the Allied forces did arrive as and where planned in a fit state to fight. This was a masterpiece of combined service organisation.

The number of the enemy in Sicily, moreover, would be changing up to the last moment in accordance with the number they could salvage from the Tunisian débâcle. In fact the Axis powers had the equivalent of eleven Italian and two German divisions on the island when it was assaulted. Six of the former were undermanned and poorly equipped coastal divisions, who, between them, covered the whole of the Sicilian coastline. Here the Italian soldier was mostly a local character with little stomach for organized fighting even in order to defend his homeland. He was not encouraged further by the state and quality of his equipment, being more than content to do his fighting with a rifle from his bedroom window. The more energetic of these coastal soldiers, with bandit background, would take up position in one of the many small concrete pillboxes dotted along the coast and in the hills behind, often draped with a yard or so of barbed wiring accompanied by the indiscreetly placed mine or two. Behind this intrepid marksman, his support came mainly from an odd assortment of Italian field pieces, mostly 75 mm. and anti-tank guns.

These then were the eccentric coastal divisions thinly stretched out, more often than not, remotely controlled by well scented and powdered Italian officers living in comparative luxury and immorality, in the cellars of strongly-built houses not so near by. 206 Coastal Division, facing the landings of the whole of Eighth Army, was no exception. It was quite unable to offer much serious opposition, although the experienced window snipers did cause some casualties with their well-sighted rifles.

Farther inland were four better equipped, and partly motorized, Italian divisions: Napoli, Livorno, Aosta and Assietta; and two first-class German divisions: 15 Panzer Grenadier (until recently known as "The Sicily") Division and the Herman Goering Division, the latter of which had already opposed 15 Inf Bde in Norway in 1940, and was to dog the division's footsteps for some time to come. It is notable that this division only had two of its regiments in Sicily on D-day, the other two being elsewhere on Goering's personal instructions, and that the Commander of the Tiger Tank Regiment was almost useless with lumbago! This group of divisions was placed as centrally as possible in the island with an obvious bias towards the south-east, although the Garrison High Command was expecting a more widely-spread invasion than actually occurred. The cover plan, air attack and otherwise, was also designed to try and draw him as much to the west as possible to gain advantage of the time it would take to concentrate with such poor road facilities. The whole of this mobile reserve could muster about 150 medium tanks with other Italian lightly armoured vehicles, together with their normal complement of self-propelled guns. It was to be seen fighting mainly in the favourite German battle group formation. The Luftwaffe and the Regia Aeronautica, between them, could put about 250–300 fighter and fighter-bomber aircraft into the air, operating mainly from the Gerbini airfields on the Catania Plain.

This, then, was the setting for 5 Div's re-entry into battle after three years. A great deal had happened since Norway and Dunkirk; a great deal of hard and imaginative training, under Major-General Berney-Ficklin, had matured the brief battle experiences of Norway and Flanders. Much travelling and hard living in extremes of climate had seasoned the soldier who wore the coveted "Y" on his arm as, probably, no other soldier had been seasoned before. The long patient wait, made more bearable by frequent moves, had whetted his appetite to get on with the job with the least possible delay. Anxious days and sometimes weeks of waiting for news from home, not always good news when it eventually came, only acted as a further spur to greater things: such was the state of morale. The division had done a magnificent job in reserve; it was now about to do just as magnificent a job in the coming twelve months of almost continual battle.

The Plan

The overall outline plan for "Husky" was a landing of the United States Seventh Army and the British Eighth Army on 10th July almost side by side in the south-eastern corner of Sicily. Then by phases the latter was to take the ports of Syracuse, Augusta and Catania: the former skirting to the west of Etna to take Marsala, Palermo and the northern coast-line. The two armies were to link up and eventually seize Messina.

The outline plan for Eighth Army was to assault with XIII Corps on the right in the Gulf of Noto, to take Syracuse, Augusta and Catania while XXX Corps assaulted the Pachino peninsula to protect the left flank of XIII Corps, contact the

American Seventh Army, and be ready to help capture Catania if necessary.

XIII Corps plan was to land south of Syracuse; firstly an airborne landing to hold open the important Ponte Grande over the River Anapo on the road to Syracuse; followed by a commando landing to silence the major coastal battery at Capo Murro Di Porco; then a two-divisional assault to capture a beachhead. 5 Div on the right, with two brigades up and one in reserve to secure Cassibile and then advance on Syracuse, relieving the airborne force. 50 Div having captured Avola were to secure the plateau overlooking the coast and protect the Corps beachhead from the west. After this, 5 and 50 Divs were to get bridgeheads over the Simeto River and then capture Catania. The three beach sectors allotted were from left to right 50 Div on Jig Sector; 5 Div on How and George Sectors, with 4 Commando landing a little east of the latter.

5 Div plan was to land 15 Inf Bde on How Sector and 17 Inf Bde on George Sector. The latter was to capture Cassibile and advance on Syracuse. 13 Inf Bde in reserve was to pass through the beachhead to cut the main roads leading into Syracuse from the north-west and west after the city had fallen.

15 Inf Bde planned to assault with 1 Y and L and 1 KOYLI, followed through by 1 Green Howards in reserve. Having secured certain given positions the brigade was to protect the immediate beachhead area and the left flank of 17 Inf Bde's advance to Syracuse, by occupying the Hybleau plateau, which dominated the coastal plain. Contact was also to be made with 50 Div on the left.

17 Inf Bde planned to assault with 2 RSF and 6 Seaforth to cross the Cassibile River and capture the town of Cassibile, extending the bridgehead to include Casa Nuove, and then for 2 RSF and 2 Northamptons to advance on Syracuse, relieving Ponte Grande *en route*.

The Beaches

Excellent photographs, models, and accurately overprinted maps were among the aids available for the landing. The beaches in How Sector were small narrow sandy foreshore enclosed by small capes leading up to grassy verges through thicker orchards of almond trees on to the main road. Here

BRIEFING ON BOARD SHIP.—Brigadier G. Rawstorne, commanding 15th Infantry Brigade, holds a final conference on H.M.T. *Reina del Pacifico*.
Major Cooke, O.C. "A" Company, Royal Inniskilling Fusiliers, briefs his men on H.M.T. *Dunera* on the day before the landings.

SICILY: Air photograph of How Sector Beaches.

are some notes on Beach 46 How Sector made at the time of briefing by an infantry Platoon Commander of the first wave, to give some idea of the detailed information available:

"Beach 700 yards long, 100 feet wide. Estimated gradient 1 : 55. Sand. Flanked either end by about 75 yards shingle with sharper slope. Sand probably firm. O.K. for most craft. Exits available for personnel, A.F.V's. and M.T. Whole beach flanked by rocks and cliffs. Track from beach at 050163 meets wider farm road after 300 yards: about 5 feet 6 inches wide; seems to run between earth banks about 18 inches to 24 inches high."

There was some strong wiring and the odd concrete pill-box near to the sea. The sandy bottom of the sea edge was so uneven that one landing soldier might go in up to his neck and another from the craft next to his have an absolutely dry landing, which did, in fact, happen. There appeared to be no underwater obstacles worth noting. Landmarks were easy to pick out and nearly every soldier in the division will remember the cleft in the skyline that resembled the "V" of the backsight on his rifle.

The Approach

For four days the convoys steamed on, unmolested, in a clear blue sea against a clear blue sky only punctuated by the silver lustre of the barrage balloons trailed by some of the shipping and the rare white vapour plume left by aircraft at a high altitude. So in their ships of all sizes from east and from west the Allies closed in on Sicily and its motley garrison. Although outwardly calm, within each ship was a hive of industry, of routine preparation for such an ambitious operation. As already mentioned, the objective was revealed to every man, followed by such careful briefing, that he got to know his little part of Sicily like the back of his hand. There were endless rehearsals of the complicated drill for getting the men, with their correct landing serials from the bowels of the ship, up companionways, along hot dimly lit passages made narrower still by the clattering obtruding equipment they were wearing; routine boat stations drill and the testing of ropeways and other landing gear in the smaller craft to be lowered from the larger vessels. Field cashiers issued special allied military currency; regimental officers issued the little blue guides on

Sicily to their men; ships' staff issued "Mae Wests", and the soldier, in what little spare time was left, packed and repacked his little personal household goods, less those that might establish the identity of his formation, if captured. Many last letters were nonchalantly written, hoping that Mum, Dad, little brother and sister, Cousin Ada and the girl friend were all in the pink as it left him, the soldier. The last condition could hardly now be applicable to anybody; under the hot piercing sun even the pinkest of skins was now fully bronzed. A certain degree of comfort for all ranks was experienced right up to the lowering of the assault craft, and many were the last minute cups of tea and sandwiches made up by the overworked ships' staffs.

On the hot noon of the 9th July, a general rum issue was made to help induce the last pre-battle sleep. Unfortunately, soon after that, the Mediterranean chose to whip up one of its startlingly sudden storms, so that the movement of the sea became very unpleasant, and so rough in the evening that the Garrison Commander in Sicily advised his troops that no landing could possibly be made that night. In fact a postponement was considered, but there was not a man aboard who was not grateful that the assault went in as planned.

The storm abated a little that night to reveal the majestic and awe-inspiring outline of Etna straight ahead. This spectre of the great mountain made a fitting backcloth for the brilliant display of anti-aircraft fireworks spouting up from the foreground of Syracuse and Augusta in the agony of violent air raids, and seemed to bring every man to his toes, poised for the battle. That same mountain, lighted in many different ways, was to serve as a backcloth for the men of 5 Div during the next six weeks or so.

Soon the airborne troops would be touching down; commandos would be leaping ashore to deal with the big coastal guns; and the first waves of 15 and 17 Inf Bdes would be starting their pilgrimage to the landing craft via the hot narrow passages, through the galley ports, and down the scrambling nets. Those in later serials could only wait patiently for news, watching the air raids and the little fleet of small craft manœuvring with difficulty in and out of the swell. Some of the gliders, that had been prematurely cast off on their way to Syracuse, were already floating in the sea; their luckless passengers injured, drowning or drowned already. Little knots of soldiers moved quietly and efficiently about the ships mumbling to themselves the Eighth Army challenge for D-day, "Desert Rats", to make sure that they remembered the bloodcurdling reply, "Kill Italians!"

The Landings and Capture of Syracuse

The air landing troops who were to capture Ponte Grande were mostly glider borne and released from their powered tugs in a thirty-mile-per-hour wind, in a half moon, at 2300 hrs. on the 9th. For various reasons of misfortune only approximately seventy all ranks arrived near enough to be effective in the area of the bridges over the railway and River Anapo. There they very sensibly removed the demolition charges and gallantly hung on under persistent attacks almost until relieved by 17 Inf Bde. Troops of 4 Commando had little difficulty in subduing the coastal battery at Capo Murro Di Porco.

With this pre-"H" hour support added to powerful air and naval bombardment against a morally inferior enemy who was not expecting them that night, 5 Div landings were to be mostly uneventful, save for purely local incidents.

On George Sector, 17 Inf Bde made a good start. 2 RSF and 6 Seaforth were ashore by 0300 hrs. and the latter captured Casa Nuove after the initial bridgehead around Cassibile had been made, and after several clashes with small parties of enemy and sporadic shell fire from field and coastal guns. All three battalions were ready to move by first light. Cassibile was captured by 1000 hrs. when some of the garrison in barracks were actually attacked in bed, and quite a few of them died without their boots on. "A" Company of 2 Northamptons made a slight diversion to help out 6 Seaforth, who were held up by a few stubborn Italians in Casa Nuove, just east of Cassibile, whilst "B" Company put out of action a battery of four field guns. No time was wasted in pushing on to relieve the grimly holding airborne troops at Ponte Grande. The road to Syracuse was a straight one, and open enough to make identification of enemy posts, so clearly and accurately marked on the over-printed maps, comparatively simple.

In the absence of much of the brigade's own transport, local carts, mules, horses and donkeys were impressed, and not a few captured Italian military vehicles. There were not many civilian cars left in the coastal area. For those who had to march it was to be a long day, hampered by the heat of the sun, the flies, and the white dust that penetrated everywhere. Water had to be carried personally, and much additional refreshment was gathered in the form of tomatoes and lemons from the wayside. Here and there a few airborne stragglers were met, but until Ponte Grande was reached there were few incidents. 2 RSF were held up for a time by a well dug-in machine-gun post, and had to send back for a Sherman, which, on arrival, promptly knocked it out with two well-aimed shots. Already the Italian soldier with no further heart for the fight was quietly and unobtrusively disappearing into the civilian background.

In How Sector, divided into Amber and Red beaches, 15 Inf Bde had the same preliminary skirmishes with snipers in the beach area, but their landings did not quite go to plan. The assault went in at 0300 hrs. for 1 KOYLI, but the craft carrying 1 Y and L, after getting off course in the run in, and, at one time, partly grounding, got mixed up with 1 Y and L follow up craft, and were nearly an hour late in landing. The reserve battalion, 1 Green Howards, did not embark until 0400 hrs., and when it did the commanding officer was without any news of the success or otherwise of the landings of the other battalions. No success signals had been seen, and one of his landing craft, having to alter course, landed "A" Company on Jig Sector with 50 Div, which delayed that company and gave them an extra five-mile march before they rejoined their battalion.

Fortunately, apart from some persistent shelling and the expected snipers, the resistance was not very great, and by good local leadership all the objectives given to the brigade were captured. On their way through the KOYLI to their positions on the Hybleau plateau, the Green Howards flushed several small enemy posts in pill-boxes; in one of the latter, among the Italians threatened by one of the platoon commanders, was an American paratrooper who had been captured and objected strongly to being eliminated by his Allies.

15 Inf Bde reported themselves to be on their objectives by 1430 hrs., their H.Q. being in a large mansion lately an Italian Artillery H.Q. 1 Green Howards and 1 KOYLI were

in contact with one another, but not at that time with 50 Div on the left. Later on in the day, the brigade came under temporary command of 50 Div to help them protect the western flank of the advance on Syracuse.

Meanwhile the build up over the beaches, despite the swell and surf, was going to plan, and by 1000 hrs. 13 Inf Bde, in reserve, had landed and started its march inland. 2 R INNISKS landing at 0900 hrs., using the dusty winding tracks north of Cassibile, had reached a defensive position covering the bridge over the Cavadonna River. Here they dug in and awaited further orders. "B" Company set up a road block on the main lateral road, and before long received a succession of visitors; the first was a party of Italian cycle troops, who were so alarmed when the Brens opened up near them that they fell off their cycles. After them, came a dispatch rider leading a column of armoured cars, ammunition lorries and staff cars, in which were six Italian officers in their finest Sunday uniforms. They received the same welcome and, after a skirmish in which Italians were observed diving in and out of ditches, a very fine white flag was displayed. One stubborn Italian, however, undaunted by the many of his comrades lying dead and wounded around him, fired a Breda which caused casualties to the Inniskillings, and refused to be silenced until Sergeant Bogle gallantly dealt with him, at great personal risk, for which he was awarded the Military Medal.

2 Cameronians did not begin to transfer to landing craft until 0830 hrs., by which time the sea was calmer, and the shipping at anchor made an impressive sight. The battalion landed over George beach and was in its assembly area about half a mile from the beach at 0930 hrs. Bombing by now was one of the prices to be paid for this concentration of shipping, and the hardworking beach "brick" battalions suffered some casualties. Both these composite units, based on an Argyll and Sutherland Highlander battalion on George Sector and on a Highland Light Infantry battalion on How Sector, had done and were to do some really first-class work to ensure a steady flow of reinforcements, supplies, guns and vehicles to the division as it advanced farther inland.

During the afternoon 17 Inf Bde continued its march on Syracuse, but the relief of the airborne party at Ponte Grande was only just in time. By 1445 hrs., after successive bitter struggles, the outlying posts had been wiped out. Half an hour later still, only nineteen survivors, almost overpowered in a very open position, and short of ammunition, were forced to abandon the bridge for the cover of the canal bank near the sea. An enemy party was actually in possession when the carriers of 2 RSF arrived only fifteen minutes later. The RSF soon won back what the valiant South Staffordshires had held for so long and the advance of 17 Inf Bde to Syracuse continued.

About four miles from Syracuse, 2 Northamptons met a group of 400 Italians with some guns forming up to counter-attack; they were quietly persuaded to abandon any such idea, although, as they had a few First Airborne Division prisoners with them, the supporting self-propelled 105 mm. guns of 24 Fd Regt could not open fire. By evening, after a fifteen-mile march, 2 RSF and 2 Northamptons were in Syracuse, together with some Sherman tanks of the County of London Yeomanry. Although Syracuse had been severely bombed, the port was found to be comparatively little damaged and was soon to be used by other units in the division. The fall of Syracuse to 5 Div as planned on D-day was the first of many achievements to be proud of, and it was achieved with comparatively little cost. Although this had been a long and eventful day, there was to be no pause yet.

The Advance Continued to Augusta

Several minor incidents occurred in the 13 Inf Bde area whilst Syracuse was being taken, mostly concerning the rounding up of small parties of Italian soldiers amid a sort of benign neutrality on the part of the peasants. On top of the prisoners taken by 2 R INNISKS' road blocks, 2 Cameronians among their battalion transport now boasted an Italian motor tricycle which they captured carrying five Italian soldiers! 13 Inf Bde was ordered to establish itself in Floridia to cut the main possible axis of a counter-attack on Syracuse from the north-west, and advanced, with 2 Cameronians on the right and 2 R INNISKS on the left. The former were to capture Floridia itself supported by a troop of tanks of the County of London Yeomanry, and any available guns of the Div Arty which were in action by then. Floridia was a key road junction about four miles from the area in which 13 Inf Bde had concentrated and shielded from it by a very wooded approach. The battalion attacked on a wide front and met many small pockets of enemy. "C" Company on the lateral road to the west of the town surprised an Italian motorized column who had not expected to find Allied troops as far inland, but who managed to extricate themselves in the darkness. There were many enemy casualties and a few prisoners taken that night, but at dawn, on Sunday the 11th, Floridia was in our hands. For the rest of that day and for most of the 12th, 2 Cameronians were in reserve around Floridia.

2 R INNISKS that evening had a similar battle on the right of 2 Cameronians where they soon ran into a nest of machine guns grouped round an 88-mm. gun, firing at close range, from which the Italians attacked. Although this attack petered out eventually, a great deal of confusion was caused by Italians dashing in and out of the trees making it hard for the battalion to see whether they had surrendered, were about to surrender, or had no intention of surrendering. Some of them gave themselves up in a weeping condition and a large bag of prisoners resulted.

In Syracuse on Sunday morning, the barracks, the last resistance, surrendered to 2 RSF, and already naval experts were working in the docks. After a riotous welcome the evening before, the civilians, when they realized that 17 Inf Bde had not brought a great deal of food for them, became decidedly less affable. That morning saw the first of many dawn and last light air attacks, and from now onwards, the fireworks over Syracuse were to be supplied by our own anti-aircraft guns.

The next task of 5 Div was to capture the port of Augusta, and the coastal road to it passed through Priolo, a small town surrounded by thick woods and only reached by a winding narrow road with stone walls on either side. This was just the setting for the first appearance of German troops from the Herman Goering division, in a typically strong rearguard position. These were troops of the Schmaltz battle group from Misterbianco. The first German blood was drawn by the carriers of 2 Northamptons, in the Priolo woods, when leading 17 Inf Bde on that Sunday morning. The battalion, however, could not make much headway against several well placed and determined Spandau posts. The Shermans supporting them were unable to give much assistance; confined to the narrow banked road, they were to lose three of their tanks to a well sited 88 mm. before the latter was accounted for.

That afternoon a brigade plan was made for an attack at first light on the 12th. This was to include the first full fireplan from the Div Arty most of which was to move through the night to positions between Syracuse and Priolo, to make such a concentration of fire possible. The whole was to be preceded by a dive-bombing programme. The enemy, however, forestalled this plan by evacuating Priolo during the night, and the fireplan was cancelled save for the dive bombing. A platoon of 2 Northamptons quickly advanced and established itself in the north end of the town just as the dive bombing attack came in on the southern end. The platoon went to ground and was amazed to see the Intelligence Officer arrive on a bicycle calling for yellow smoke to be put down as a signal to the planes that friendly troops were in the town; he in turn was being followed by two of the local Carabinieri who were most indignant that he would not take them prisoner.

15 Inf Bde had been released from command of 50 Div in the afternoon of the 11th and started marching towards Priolo to continue on the divisional main axis where 17 Inf Bde were to deviate and capture Augusta. 1 Green Howards passed through the town in contact with 6 Seaforth at 1400 hrs. on the 12th to advance on Melilli, a small hillside town on the north-west of Priolo, and dominating the main road to Lentini. They captured Melilli from an Italian garrison suffering from the effects of a sharp naval bombardment from the gulf of Augusta, which had reduced most of the town, except for the lovely church of San Sebastian, to rubble, cut off the main water supply and caused many civilian casualties. Here 1 Green Howards passed a not too uncomfortable night with a magnificent dress circle view of the Augusta arena, to watch the port virtually taken by a destroyer which boldly sailed into the harbour on the 12th. The Royal Army Medical Corps was later to make good use of Melilli as a hospital centre.

Tuesday, 13th July, was to be another eventful day. At 0100 hrs. 6 Seaforth and 2 RSF on the left entered and occupied the port of Augusta, while commandos landed direct from assault craft into the harbour itself. 2 Northamptons then started to clean up the town and were kept busy mopping up the many pockets of resistance that sprang up. These harassing

Some Italian prisoners taken by 2 Cameronians during their fierce battle at Floridia.

1 KOYLI marching between Cassibile and Priolo.

The King's Own Yorkshire Light Infantry advancing towards Villasamundo after the Battle of the Gorge.

CATANIA PLAIN.—The Royal Inniskilling Fusiliers come under heavy shell fire as they advance across the Catania Plain.

Anti-tank gunners of 2 Cameronians have a quick snack after camouflaging their guns on the Simeto river.

After the capture of Sferro railway station, Corporals McAfee and Graham of the Royal Inniskilling Fusiliers packed their Bren Carrier with bags of grain taken from a railway wagon on the 3rd of August.

A detachment of 467 Battery of the 92nd Field Regiment support the advance of the York and Lancaster Regiment.

tactics from a few fanatical Fascists and odd German paratroopers were to continue for the next two days or so, but control of the port was in our hands on the 13th and so was the second objective planned for the division. After three days of fighting, 17 Inf Bde had taken two major ports and captured more than 1,000 prisoners. Their own losses were not unduly high but 2 RSF alone had lost all three of their field officers.

The advance of 15 Inf Bde beyond Priolo had now cut off the Augusta peninsula from reinforcement from the northwest, but there were still some three or four hundred Italian defenders in positions in the cliffs between the two brigades and these had to be cleaned up by 13 Inf Bde following behind.

On the 13th Y and L led 15 Inf Bde down the road to Lentini when they came up against the next position of the determined Schmaltz Battle Group, very skilfully sited, covering a deep ravine a few miles south of Villasamundo. Again a well sited enemy anti-tank gun took toll of several armoured vehicles of the brigade and of Shermans of the County of London Yeomanry. The tanks, not yet used to the acute confinement dictated by the orchards, terraces and walled roads of Sicily, were still thinking in terms of desert warfare on broad, almost naval tactical lines. The best form of support they could give was to follow the infantry carriers and add their fire power to that of the infantry and gunners when and where they could. They were to have better opportunities on the Catania Plain.

For the whole of that day 1 Y and L and 1 KOYLI tried every means of attack across the ravine, but the small party of enemy was well placed with excellently controlled fire power. Two self-propelled guns were used most effectively by firing and quickly moving to alternative positions, doing a great deal of damage and creating the impression of a much larger defending force. The inevitable Spandau posts and mortars were also mobile and the anti-tank guns stopped armoured and carrier O.P.s belonging to the gunners and a headquarters white scout car in addition to the tanks. 92 Fd Regt supporting 15 Inf Bde put out almost every available O.P. and had two of them badly shot up. The armoured car of one of the Battery Commanders was actually run over by one of the Shermans in the heat of the battle!

In the late afternoon a very gallant attack was put in by 1

KOYLI commanded now by Major A. F. McRiggs who had just taken over from Lieut.-Colonel J. T. Douglas, wounded in the arm and shoulder. An unfortunate misunderstanding caused the infantry to cross the start line without the barrage planned by the Gunners. Fortunately it was to prove very effective when it eventually arrived some ten minutes late but this was only because 1 KOYLI was held up unduly, and it might have been disastrous. This was one of the many lessons learned the hard way that day and one which was not to recur. Major-General Berney-Ficklin himself came up to conduct an on-the-spot inquiry with Brigadier Rawstorne, Major McRiggs and the Gunner. It was then decided that no further frontal attacks could or would be put in by the two battalions, both having had severe casualties.

During the afternoon 13 Inf Bde had been following up and 2 WILTS relieved 1 Green Howards in Melilli who immediately set out to march towards the battle south of Villasamundo. The Commanding Officer, Lieut.-Colonel Shaw, arrived ahead, in time to do a reconnaissance with the Brigade Commander and his Gunner, conducted by one of the Gunner Troop Commanders whose carrier had been knocked out by the anti-tank gun earlier on. The party solemnly walked down the road into the ravine as though the enemy had departed, as someone had suggested they had, and almost immediately returned in full and undignified retreat chased by tracer shot from the anti-tank gun, accompanied by Spandau and rifle music. It was there and then decided that the Green Howards should outflank this formidable position making full use of the high ground to the south-west; a long and wearying trek seemed inevitable. At 1900 hrs. a KOYLI patrol discovered that the enemy had pulled out; at midnight 1 Green Howards continued the advance past the corpses of several enemy victims of shell fire, and entered Villasamundo at 0200 hrs. on the 14th. The "Battle of the Gorge", as it was called, caused 15 Inf Bde many anxious moments but such was the morale and stamina of the troops that it was able to weather this "bloody nose" and profit from its lessons.

15 Inf Bde concentrated in the Villasamundo area for several days, losing 92 Fd Regt who were temporarily loaned to 50 Div to add weight to the support of their artillery in the Prima Sole battles. Back on the beaches, and in Syracuse

harbour, despite intermittent tip and run air raids, the build-up of divisional personnel, vehicles, guns and equipment was proceeding well. Among those follow up units that had arrived was 156 Fd Regt affiliated to 17 Inf Bde who had been until now supported by 24 (self-propelled) Fd Regt. Three squadrons of the 5 Recce Regt had also arrived and undertook their first operational role on the 14th July by mopping up enemy left behind south of Augusta. In one instance about a hundred Italians refused to come out of hiding in a cave until a single round from a Breda 47-mm. gun mounted on one of the regiment's armoured cars made them think otherwise. 7 Cheshire (less one company) also arrived on 13 July.

In Augusta itself on the night of the 13th, the Germans made a determined counter-attack on the harbour and drove a wedge between 15 and 17 Inf Bdes. This was straightened out by 13 Inf Bde who continued a "demonstrative advance" to help ease the pressure on 15 Inf Bde in the "Battle of the Gorge". All through the night of the 14th/15th civilian snipers continued to make life uncomfortable for 17 Inf Bde.

By now most of the Italians had lost what little stomach they had for the fight and were at great pains to avoid being mistaken for "enemies" like the "dreadful Tedesci".* Allied Military Government was busy trying to relieve divisional troops of the care of civilians and areas and sub-areas sprouted miraculously behind the advancing brigades. One such sub-area set up its sign and magnificent staff car by the gun areas just south of Priolo before that town had been captured. It quickly realized its mistake and gracefully retreated.

The Battles on the Catania Plain

On the main road 13 Inf Bde took up the divisional advance and, skirting the towns of Carlentini and Lentini, proceeded up the axis of 50 Div and 4 Armd Bde to the high ground overlooking the Catania Plain from the south. This first sight of the plain was a magnificent panorama: quite unlike the rest of Sicily, and resembling more the flat country of Lincolnshire. The plain stretched from as far as one could see inland to the left, down to the Gulf of Catania. A plain rich in vegetation, of the familiar cactus bushes or "Prickly

---

*"Tedesci", Italian word for Germans.

Pears", of olive trees and almond groves dotted here and there with more prosperous-looking white farmhouses and other buildings. About fifteen miles or so from its foothills Etna rose in lava rock to its full height with the slightly active vapour from its crater easily visible on a clear day—the backcloth once more set for some lively fighting already going on around the bridgehead of 50 Div down to the right front. Here at the Prima Sole bridge over the Simeto River a fierce battle was being waged inch by inch to enlarge the bridgehead so valiantly gained by the survivors of the 1 Para Bde when they dropped on to the bridge and removed the German demolition charges on the night of the 13th/14th. The bridge was the last big bridge before Catania and to hold it open was vital for the future operations of XIII Corps: it spanned the Simeto River with its tributaries, the Gornalunga, forking towards the south above the bridge and the Dittaino also forking to the south from the Simeto farther up, making three rivers in all cutting across any advance inland of the long, straight and exposed coastal road. Almost pointing the direction of such an advance was the embanked main line railway from Lentini to Catania crossing the rivers by ugly iron girder bridges. Straight ahead along the lava foothills of Etna, ran the main road out of Catania to Paterno and farther inland, the main German position to be held at all costs, and the natural objective. From this line the German Artillery of all calibres was hammering against 50 Div and putting loud airbursts accurately over the Prima Sole bridge at monotonously regular intervals.

Successive attacks supported by more and more guns as other regiments arrived, failed to enlarge the bridgehead appreciably, although incredible German carnage piled higher and higher each time. In one of these desperate attacks across the river upstream of the bridge, a battalion of the Durham Light Infantry was supported by one of the Battery Commanders of 92 Fd Regt, Major B. G. Bonallack, who was awarded the M.C. and two of his O.P. parties received M.Ms. This small party although nearly up to their chests in water that was flayed by Spandau fire, brought down accurate fire which accounted for the heavy German casualties and kept communications intact at a tricky time.

It was obvious that a bigger effort would be necessary to

force a way up this exposed coastal road and the Corps Commander ordered 5 Div to attack immediately across the River Simeto on the left of 50 Div to relieve the pressure on Prima Sole bridge. On 16th July 2 Northamptons in Augusta were suddenly warned for a sea landing to be made ahead of 50 Div from their flank on the sea. This plan however was rejected almost at once as being too costly. It was decided that 13 Inf Bde followed by 15 Inf Bde should push on across the plain while the rest of the division was concentrating in the Carlentini and Lentini area. The Div Arty, now with its three normal regiments, was concentrated in the Santa Demetri Valley near 92 Fd Regt who were already in action. On the 16th also, most units of the division received their first regular delivery of mail in Sicily.

Santa Demetri Valley was known as "Messerschmitt Valley" when it became the resting place of several fighter aircraft built by a famous German of that name; they were the victims of 18 LAA Regt of the Div Arty who, by the time Catania Plain was reached by the division, had shot down no less than thirty-two enemy planes. This regiment had done some particularly magnificent shooting since landing in Sicily which it is appropriate to mention here, if only because the capture of the German airfields on the Catania Plain meant that fewer targets would present themselves for the regiment's accurate shooting until the Anzio beachhead of 1944. On the night of the 15th July, three enemy hedge-hopping planes machine-gunned 2 Cameronians near Villasamundo and all three were disposed of by the Bofors guns. In "Messerschmitt Valley" the same guns of 18 LAA Regt shot down five 109 G's out of one sortie. Quite a few of these planes actually fell into the gun areas of the Div Arty and did unintended damage to guns and personnel. The Bofors 40-mm. guns were often sited on the ridges in front of the gun positions and shot down straight on to the field guns, when tackling German fighters flying at zero feet. The tracer they were using also had the disconcerting effect of setting alight the highly inflammable olive trees. In the very high gun positions near Cassibile several serious fires were started by this and by similar residue from the Navy's more powerful *flak* gun which certainly poured "rain on the just" as well as "on the unjust"! Fire was to be a Gunner's nightmare in Sicily; 92 Fd Regt lost a gun through an ignited camouflage net outside Priolo and 156 Fd Regt had a gun knocked out as a result of a bomb in its first gun positions near Villasamundo.

Despite, and because of these incidents, the efforts of 18 LAA Regt were greatly admired and respected by the division and its enemies alike. When there was no enemy air around, the regiment always turned its hand to any task, that came its way, however menial, and made an extremely good job of it.

By the morning of the 18th July, 13 Inf Bde were on the ridge ready to advance across the plain to relieve the pressure on Prima Sole as ordered. In the afternoon, with 2 WILTS on the right, 2 R INNISKS on the left and 2 Cameronians following in reserve with the machine gunners of "B" Company, 7 Cheshire (Major K. Tolchard), the brigade started to move northwards. The rest of the division was either moving up or already concentrated in the Carlentini-Lentini area. 1 Green Howards, ahead of the rest of 15 Inf Bde, were following closely, ready to form a base under command of 13 Inf Bde, in the area of the Gornalunga River when it was secured.

2 R INNISKS sent forward a strong fighting patrol, commanded by the Second-in-Command, Major R. C. Thomson, which found a bridge over the Simeto, to be known as Lemon Bridge, not yet blown up, although they were suspicious that there were enemy tracked vehicles in the vicinity. The leading company of the battalion sent a platoon across the river to the east of the bridge to come in on the rear of any enemy there. They found a small enemy post which they beat off, and by last light the whole battalion was over the bridge. Almost immediately tanks were heard, and enemy advanced on them shouting "Don't shoot, this is the Jocks." The suspicious Irishmen let fly a few well-aimed volleys at "where their sporrans should have been", which started off a series of battles that lasted the night long all around the little bridgehead. By dawn the situation was restored but any further attempts to enlarge it were fiercely resisted by the Herman Goering paratroopers. When the latter threw in their last desperate attacks, the Commanding Officer, Lieut.-Colonel O'Brien Twohig, decided to withdraw temporarily and bring down a resounding Divisional Artillery concentration. When this lifted there was no immediate sight of the enemy. A few minutes later six of them, very shaken, were led in by a solitary

Royal Inniskilling Fusilier. The enemy attacked "Lemon Bridge" no more, thanks to the fierce and skilful defence of it by the battalion, for which the Battalion Commander was awarded the Distinguished Service Order. Another D.S.O. was awarded to Lieutenant H. T. Christie for his particularly inspiring and courageous leading of the foremost platoon throughout the battle. Two M.C.s and a M.M. were also awarded to the battalion for the battle of Lemon Bridge.

Another bridgehead was secured by 2 WILTS farther downstream from which, on the 19th, they contacted some Canadian tanks working with 50 Div. Some German tanks were encountered trying to get round the back of the battalion but these were dealt with by the Cameronians who had moved up into a central position, ready to help either bridgehead in difficulty. Some casualties were caused to the enemy and a score of prisoners taken from them.

It was now apparent that the bulk of the Herman Goering Division was positioned along the Etna foothills, reinforced by about six battalions who had either been dropped by parachute a night or so back around the Prima Sole bridge, or who had been flown in. Many of the former, in fact, dropped well behind our forward troops, some of them in the gun areas where they caused some sniping casualties and became a menace to our own collecting parachutists, a menace that had in some cases to be winkled out by single tanks. A great number of them, however, managed to make their way back unnoticed at night. To this nucleus must be added those Germans falling back before the Allied advance in the centre and west of the island. The German commander was determined to hold Catania and the north-east corner of Sicily as long as he could, so that some further reinforcements, promised by Kesselring when he visited the front on the 17th, would have a deep enough assembly area: these in fact never materialized and the room was needed instead for his rearguard perimeter. To this end he was making the fullest possible use of the magnificent observation offered by the Etna slopes in conjunction with well-placed strong points on the northern edge of the plain.

Whilst 13 Inf Bde were gaining their initial foothold across the Simeto, supported at extreme range by the Div Arty, the latter's reconnaissance parties were somewhat prematurely looking for gun positions south of the river. Indeed, some of them found themselves involuntarily helping the Cameronians in their mopping up operations.

When it was obvious that another brigade attack would have to be mounted, the guns had to be put in rather open positions on the southern edge of the plain, near the railway embankment to gain the necessary range. This move was accomplished without much incident just before last light on the 19th, although the Germans must have seen the dust, and have been able to count every gun, on its way past the unsavoury smells of "Dead Horse Corner", past the ruined vinery south of the Prima Sole bridge, littered now with derelict and burned out vehicles; past a crashed glider with a wrecked jeep spewed out of its belly, and along a dust-raising track elevated above the canal. There new gun positions were on the dropping zones used by 1 Para Bde and by the Germans who might well return to use them again, unaware of the presence of the Gunners. Every man collected a piece of parachute silk which was put to all sorts of uses and the doctors collected some excellent German medical equipment neatly packed in containers.

On the 19th, during the night, almost as soon as the guns were in, 15 Inf Bde put in a very hasty and thus ill-reconnoitred attack, in an attempt to enlarge 13 Inf Bde bridgehead. They advanced, 1 Green Howards on the right, and 1 Y and L on the left with 1 KOYLI following up in reserve. Machine gun support for 15 Inf Bde was provided by "D" Company 7 Cheshire (Major J. R. Ellwood) who had passed through "B" Company. The start line was crossed at 0045 hrs. under a barrage fired by all available guns in XIII Corps. The advance was almost immediately slowed down by unforeseen deep ditches within a few yards of the railway line. The barrage naturally ran away from the leading troops and although Bofors tracer was fired to mark the axis of advance, the infantry lost their sense of direction; the Germans merely waited for the barrage to lift before pouring withering machine gun fire into the bridgehead area. "B" Company Green Howards somehow got ahead of "A" Company and had a most bitter hand-to-hand fight with a strong-point of Germans in which the Company Commander, Captain Verity, received wounds from which he later died in captivity. Captain Verity sent back Lieutenant Bell with the few survivors: this officer returned again to try and

Major-General G. C. Bucknall, C.B., M.C.

rescue his Company Commander and other wounded, but he was unable to get to them under heavy fire. For this gallant attempt he was awarded the M.C.

Meanwhile in this night of chaos, the leading Y and L on the left had overshot the mark and most of one company disappeared into enemy territory. 1 KOYLI and 15 Inf Bde H.Q. followed on almost blindly, and when dawn came on the 20th, the brigade found itself pinned down in a very exposed and uncomfortable position, mostly in shallow ditches over which the German gunners put some effective airburst shelling.

1 Green Howards in particular were in a bad position, enfiladed by a Spandau post to their right, and overlooked from most of the front. 1 KOYLI were on a forward slope so that only the barest movement was possible; 1 Y and L were little better placed, and Bde H.Q. suffered most of all from accurate enemy shelling on its transport, revealed skylined nose to tail at first light. Brigadier Rawstorne spent most of the morning on a hazardous pilgrimage to try and find his mislaid forward companies, accompanied alone by his Gunner, who was quite unarmed!

During the night 20th/21st under artillery cover, the luckless battalions were extricated and moved back about a mile to better positions. Here they planned another attack for that night but this was to be cancelled. It was by now evident that neither 5 nor 50 Divs could get much farther across the plain with circumstances as they were. Accordingly General Montgomery decided to wheel XXX Corps around the pivot of XIII Corps, who were to hold firmly to their shallow bridgehead over the Simeto, so hardly won. They were to keep probing so that the enemy was continually kept guessing as to future Allied intentions. This period was to be the first of several where 5 Div had to hold such uncomfortable positions. On this occasion enemy domination was limited to excellent observation, curbed by a limited amount of available ammunition. Quite apart from the nuisance imposed by the enemy, the Catania Plain was one of the most notorious malarial areas in the Mediterranean, and, despite elaborate precautions by the Div RAMC, often difficult to apply, the division was suffering grievous malaria casualties as a result of this enforced stay on the plain.

F.D.–K

On the night 21st/22nd, 15 Inf Bde, less 1 KOYLI, who remained in position under orders 17 Inf Bde, were relieved by 17 Inf Bde. For the following ten days or so the divisional frontage, about two miles in all, was held by a four-battalion brigade supported by the Div Arty and more guns if required. The battalions of 15 Inf Bde took turns to come under command of 17 Inf Bde as the fourth battalion. "C" Company 7 Cheshire (Major F. S. Scott) provided machine gun support the whole time, without relief.

5 Recce Regt was now fully deployed in the six-mile gap between XIII and XXX Corps roughly along the line of the Gornalunga River. One squadron had arrived on the plain on the 19th when it made an unsuccessful attempt to find a crossing place for 13 Inf Bde. On the following day one troop was detailed to reconnoitre roads on the left of the 15 Inf Bde attack; this troop lost most of its vehicles and nearly twenty men when it ran into a strong enemy post. Troop Sergeant Fisher was awarded the M.M. for particular gallantry in personally rallying the remainder of the troop. On the 21st July, 3 Squadron attacked some enemy positions but was pinned down by a heavy concentration of mortar and small arms fire. This squadron was forced, after many casualties, to withdraw by night. Now the whole of the regiment was committed, during the pivot movement, to active patrolling of the Gerbini gap. This was no mean task, particularly as the plain, at this point, was not tank-proof country, and it was a day or more before they could be reinforced by some anti-tank guns, two Canadian tank regiments and a machine gun company from 7 Cheshire. Later the patrolling had to be done on foot as the dusty ground showed up the movement of every vehicle. These were mostly static patrols, confined to watching by day from farmhouses and being moved about and relieved by night. Regular wireless patrols built up some useful information and provided many targets for the Gunners who had F.O.O.s with the reconnaissance patrols. The enemy was patrolling fairly actively as well, but nothing larger in the way of an enemy force ever walked into the trap so carefully laid for them by the waiting armour. Much useful information was picked up on the hastily evacuated Gerbini airfields and, on at least one occasion, a Messerschmitt fighter left one of the airfields flown by a pilot of the Royal Air Force who had been

carefully infiltrated on to the airfield by one of these patrols of the 5 Recce Regt.

The Div Arty made good use of this static period to practise itself in divisional concentrations and even to demonstrate to infantry officers assembled on the ridge the effect of various types of artillery fire, using known German posts as targets. The air O.P.s, flown by Gunners, did some excellent observed shooting and particularly on to Motta Santa Anastasia railway station, where a complete ammunition train was blown up with an effect that could have been seen almost all over the island. The enemy was always active in reply, but by the number of explosions of his dumps of materials, it was soon obvious that he would pull out when it suited him to do so.

After a few days' rest, on the 23rd July, 13 Inf Bde Gp embussed and moved round to the west coming under command of 51 Highland Div, to help their advance towards Adrano by forming a firm base in the Sferro area. By various reliefs they eventually held an area around the desolate corpse-strewn town of Sferro, in very close contact with the Germans opposite them. On the 31st, the 51 Highland Div attacked, but as the preliminary bombardment was put down opposite Sferro, almost all of the exceedingly concentrated enemy defensive fire came down on 13 Inf Bde; this, naturally, enabled the Highlanders to attack more successfully.

On 4th August 2 Cameronians passed through 2 R INNISKS over the Simeto and into close wooded country which was liberally mined. Although enemy tanks were heard and seen, no contact was made except with 2 WILTS who had come up on the right flank. On the next day a sharp battle was fought for the high ground overlooking Paterno on the south-east, with 2 WILTS on the left and 2 Cameronians on the right, supported by 91 Fd Regt, machine gunners of 7 Cheshire, and Canadian tanks. When this high ground was taken, 2 WILTS entered the town at 0900 hrs. on the 6th August. From here the brigade was ordered to move across to the west to join up with the remainder of 5 Div who by now had crossed the plain into the foothills.

Meanwhile on the divisional front the enemy's intentions became clearer still by the 25th July when they realized that the Americans were well round the north coast, that XXX Corps' offensive in the centre of the island was going well and that, much to the obvious delight of the Sicilians, Mussolini had resigned. On the 29th July gunfire to the west could be heard getting nearer: 78 Div were attacking Catenuova and 51 Div were attacking Sferro. On the 30th a further characteristic message arrived from General Montgomery first speaking well of the fighting so far, then of knocking Mussolini "off his perch" and finally, exhorting the Eighth Army to "get on with the job" and "drive the Germans out of Sicily".

The ominous explosions from the foothills opposite the divisional front became more frequent and then died out altogether; the tempo of artillery fire from both sides increased; patrols went forward making no contact with the enemy up to the foothills. Centuripe had fallen to 78 Div and Kesselring had appreciated that he could no longer hold Catania, that he must extricate as much of his forces and material as he could and that to achieve this he must hold off the Allies until the last possible moment.

3rd August, however, was a particularly sad one for the division. Major-General H. P. M. Berney-Ficklin, who had been allowed an extension of his tour to lead the division into Sicily, had now to take his farewell in a jeep-borne pilgrimage around the units already getting ready to advance for the last round. His familiar Highland Light Infantry bonnet fluttered its way round for the last time and there was not a man in the division unmoved at his going. He had commanded 15 Inf Bde from the outbreak of war until it went to Norway, and took over 5 Div from General Sir Harold Franklyn in the summer of 1940, after Dunkirk. He had built it up into a well-trained formation by sheer weight of personality and leadership, and by the most relentless and realistic training methods. He gathered around him a most efficient and understanding staff whose experience and thoroughness enabled him to move the division half-way across the world with hardly a hitch, and the minimum interference to morale and training. He must have felt proud of the division's first showings in Sicily and he must have been convinced that he was handing over to his successor, Major-General G. C. Bucknall, M.C. (later Lieut.-General G. C. Bucknall, C.B., M.C.), an extremely efficient fighting machine.

By now General Montgomery was already planning to seize the advantage of a quick follow-up across the Straits of Messina in pursuit of the retreating enemy. 5 Div and 1 Canadian Div had been earmarked for the assault, and the former was now to advance on Misterbianco and Belpasso before going into reserve to plan and refit for the invasion of the Italian mainland.

Fighting in the Foothills

On 4th and 5th August, 5 and 50 Divs were advancing northwards side by side. The advance of 5 Div actually started on the 3rd, and continued on the 4th, with 17 Inf Bde on the right and 15 Inf Bde on the left. The former, led by 2 Northamptons and 2 RSF, encountered a few minor enemy posts covering many mines and booby traps which slowed up their advance considerably. On the evening of the 6th, they eventually entered Misterbianco to be overwhelmed by its reception from the almost delirious population. The main Catania-Adrano road was now cut and the enemy forced towards the narrow eastern side of Mount Etna. To their right, 17 Inf Bde contacted 50 Div who, similarly delayed by mines and booby traps, had entered Catania on the 5th.

On the left, 15 Inf Bde had several small battles before they entered Motta Santa Anastasia in the evening of the 4th, having marched some fourteen miles in twenty-four hours, crossed three rivers, and mounted a night attack. On the 5th, 15 Inf Bde advanced on Belpasso, 1 KOYLI on the right and 1 Green Howards on the left. They soon ran into some Tiger tanks well placed at Fondaco, an important crossroads about a third of the way between Motta and Belpasso on the main lateral road. This was to be known to the brigade as "Hell Fire Corner" and it was to be responsible for quite a few casualties. Subsequently the brigade was delayed until 1600 hrs. before the opposition could be cleared by a heavy Div Arty concentration.

From Fondaco onwards the going became more and more difficult as the leading troops got farther into the lava rocks and cactus forests immediately south of Belpasso. They were forced to spend an uncomfortable night just short of the town in the rocks, widely scattered, machine gunned from the east and with their wireless communications distinctly upset by the lava.

Next morning, the 6th, 1 Green Howards attacked Belpasso at 0500 hrs. behind a Div Arty barrage and the machine gun fire of "D" Company 7 Cheshire. They got into the outskirts fairly easily, but the enemy, and particularly the same Tiger tanks, refused to be dislodged so easily. The infantry spent some time chasing them, and being chased in and out of back gardens and side streets to the accompaniment of exhortations and directions bawled in Italian from upper windows and from their characteristic wrought-iron balconies, by the excited citizens, some of whom were dropping the strangest of objects on to the Germans in particular. The final entry was one of triumph and mass hysteria as never seen before by most of the soldiers, who were quite overwhelmed by the unreality of the hand-clapping and throwing of flowers.

When 15 and 17 Inf Bdes advanced on the night 3rd/4th August, 5 Recce Regt, on the extreme left flank, was ordered to harbour at a map reference, well into enemy country. In attempting to get there they had several casualties from mines, and when the road was blocked on one occasion, had to back all their vehicles in pitch darkness to make a diversion. Next day, when it was discovered that the enemy's evacuation was not quite so complete as had been hoped, patrols were sent out to Paterno, Biancavilla, Belpasso, Nicolosi and Masaculucia to contact 51 Div on the left and 15 Inf Bde on the right. None of these patrols got through but all of them behaved most gallantly against heavy odds, gaining one M.C. and three M.M.s on that day alone.

On 7th August a bold partially successful attempt was made by the division to strike laterally at the enemy's right flank and threaten his whole position. Two mobile columns were formed mainly from 5 Recce Regt, which had now joined up, and the tanks of County of London Yeomanry still supporting the division. Colonel Blockley commanded the southern column, known as "Blockcol" which included two squadrons of 5 Recce, a squadron of Shermans, some Scorpions, a field battery and an anti-tank battery. The other similarly constituted was named "Camcol" also after its commander, Lieut.-Colonel Cameron, Commanding Officer of the C.L.Y. Despite the ground and roads being hardly suitable for open mobile warfare, both columns started off well. "Blockcol" clearing Mascalucia, quickly joined elements of 50 Div to the

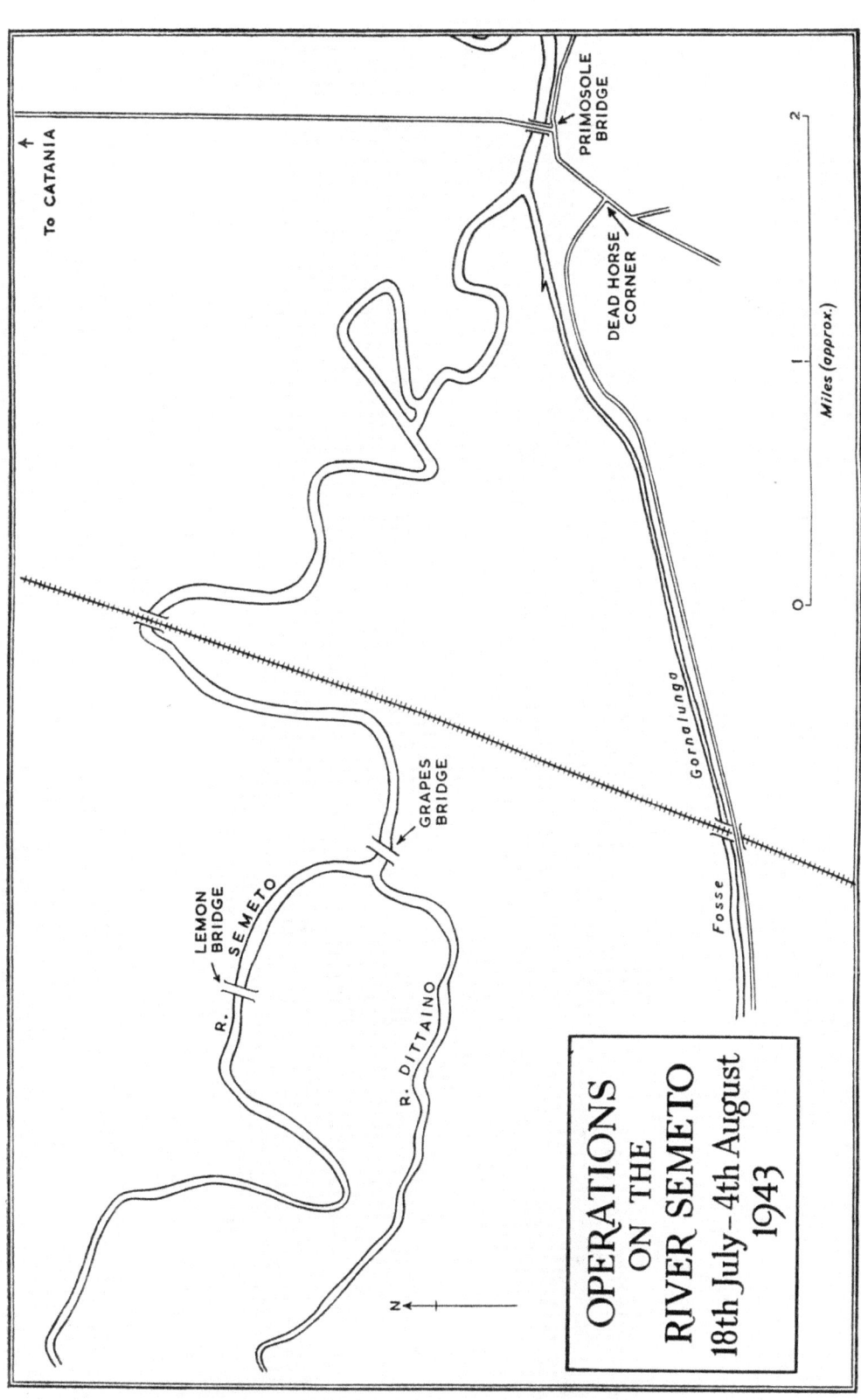

south of the town; as a result of this threat the Germans were cleared back for about five miles. "Camcol" in more hilly country found the going hard, and ran into some enemy tanks not far beyond Nicolosi whence it started operating. The rocky area was also becoming more and more difficult country for siting the supporting guns in large enough numbers.

On the same day 13 Inf Bde arrived from Paterno and debussed in the vineyards on the eastern outskirts of Belpasso now in the hands of 15 Inf Bde. From there they marched through Nicolosi which was heavily mined and booby trapped: in some cases actual German corpses were used for this. The town was being fairly severely shelled at the time. Despite all this 2 Cameronians were soon established to the north and north-east of it. 2 R INNISKS occupied the high ground to the south-east. For the next few days there followed some very hard and confused fighting in the lava foothills against a stubborn, relentless enemy fighting for every possible hour of delay. This enemy appeared to be on about three sides of the divisional area in the hills, and to add to the confusion, civilians continually arrived at the various headquarters with more and more lurid reports of odd parties of Germans committing all sorts of atrocities. To the north of Nicolosi 1 Y and L had a private expedition some way up Etna, and their accompanying Gunners had some good shooting observed by the air O.P.

On the 8th August 2 R INNISKS sent two companies to capture Tremonte, three prominent hills between Pedara and Etna. They soon reported that they were on Tremonte, but battalion H.Q. became a bit sceptical when they were later heavily shot at from Pedara and the area between Pedara and Tremonte. They advanced to Pedara where they spent a most eerie night; collaborators being reported everywhere and there were strong suspicions that Germans also were still lurking in the neighbourhood. It was then discovered that the first two companies were in fact in Tregastani, some way farther east, due to mistaken map reading, so easily achieved in such country. The other two companies then mounted a strongly supported attack on Tremonte from Pedara, but even with the help of 91 Fd Regt and Canadian tanks, they were unable to reach the hilltops.

While the battles for Tremonte were in progress, 2 Cameronians had successfully attacked two other prominent hills, Monte Arso and Monte Gervasi on the latter of which they surprised from the rear some enemy who were firing on to Tremonte. 13 Inf Bde then ordered 2 Cameronians to attack Tremonte from their advantageous position on the morning of the 9th. In the meantime, however, General Montgomery had visited 2 R INNISKS and threatened to put in another brigade if they were unable to take Tremonte. The Irishmen made no mistake about their second attack which saved 2 Cameronians a long walk and duly earned the applause of the Army Commander. 2 WILTS entered Tregastani on the right and this was to be the last enemy stand against 13 Inf Bde as the Highland Div passed through them a day or so later. They were then withdrawn to the Motta Santa Anastasia area to rest and plan for the coming invasion of Italy in which they were to be one of the assaulting brigades. 17 Inf Bde were already concentrated in the Mistabianca area with Div H.Q.

It had been the intention of the Army Commander to hold the enemy on the eastern slopes of Etna with a single division from XIII Corps, whilst XXX Corps advanced more widely round the northern slopes. As 5 Div was to be one of the assaulting divisions for the next operation it would thus now be freed for resting and planning. The northern advance of XXX Corps, however, had been slowed down at Randazzo and the enemy were actually being reinforced from the east. General Montgomery, when he learned this, ordered XIII Corps to bring back 5 Div and advance with a renewed effort on a two divisional front, even if this meant postponing D-day for the next operation. This entailed more lava fighting for the division in the foothills.

15 Inf Bde, being the reserve brigade for Operation Baytown, the landing on the mainland, were ordered forward from the Belpasso area. On the 10th the Green Howards, who had reached Mascalucia, were ordered to attack the mountain village of Milo on the left flank of 50 Div, advancing with some difficulty up the coastal road. The Gunner reconnaissance parties moved up so closely that they only just missed being blown up with a bridge that was being dealt with by a last minute German demolition party. Milo was entered at 0500 hrs. on the 11th without actual opposition but very closely on the heels of the withdrawing Germans. There they were

A detachment of the 2 WILTS Anti-tank Platoon wait for a possible counter-attack beyond Paterno.
Machine-gunners of 7 Cheshire cover the Infantry of 15 Brigade as they enter Belpasso.

Bren Carriers of 2 WILTS pass through Pedara in the Etna foothills.
Members of 141 Field Ambulance give blood transfusions at Misterbianco.

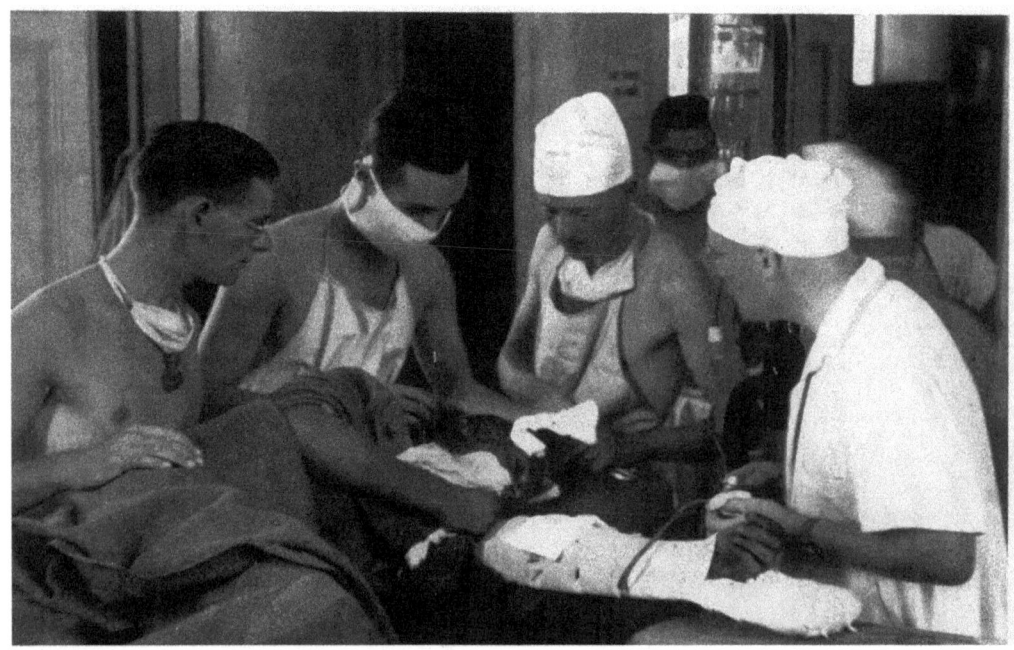

The Sappers with 17th Infantry Brigade are helped by civilians in
their search for mines in Misterbianco.

A troop position of 91 Field Regiment in action near Zafferana in
the last action in Sicily.

2 Northamptons (above), 2 R INNISKS (below)
embarking for the Italian mainland.

heavily shelled, particularly in the area of the church, with some casualties. This routine was now recognizable as the signature of retreating Germans about to pull back farther. 15 Panzer Grenadier Division actually started to cross the straits of Messina on the 12th leaving 29 Panzer Grenadier Division as rearguard.

That same day it was learned by division that D-day for Operation Baytown was being advanced to 1st September to get the fullest advantage of the German "Dunkirk" across the Straits of Messina. This withdrawal was now in full swing. It was very successful from the enemy's point of view, under an anti-aircraft umbrella, that was, in the opinion of R.A.F. pilots, as effective as the well-known Essen Corridor, and far too costly for them to get low enough to direct hits on the small craft and ferry rafts being used to transport the retreating German soldiers. The skilful use of demolition and cratering of the coastal road was preventing ground interference from getting too close.

To release the whole of 15 Inf Bde at once, 51 Div was brought into the line in the Milo area, north of which the Green Howards were being held by heroic German rearguard actions amongst a particularly heavy concentration of anti-personnel mines. 15 Inf Bde had decided to send 1 KOYLI mountaineering up Etna in an attempt to force the German right flank. It was an arduous and dusty climb calling for a good deal of portering although little opposition was met. The Gunner O.P. however, had some excellent shooting, being able to look into the rear of the German position. This operation was eventually called off on the 12th August and on the 13th, 15 Inf Bde, having handed over to a brigade of 51 Div, pulled back to the divisional rest area after having marched most of the way from Cassibile in just over a month.

Preparations for Crossing the Straits of Messina

The 5 Div was now concentrated around Misterbianco, Motta Santa Anastasia, and to the west: resting, bathing, eating, attending concerts in Catania from ENSA and from the division's own talent; and generally getting what relaxation that was possible before the second much longer round. On the 16th August, Messina fell and the Sicilian Campaign, which had cost the Germans some extremely heavy casualties, was at an end within thirty-nine days of continuous fighting in some very difficult country at the hottest season of the year. The division had every reason to be proud of its share in this campaign.

On 21st August, planning started in earnest at Div H.Q. in Misterbianco. The planning of the assault was a simpler affair this time, requiring only certain alterations to those landing tables used for "Husky". Brigadier Buffey, the C.R.A., and his Brigade Major, Major Zambra, in conjunction with H.Q.R.A. XIII Corps, were busily engaged on a monster fireplan in support of the landing that was to be fired by 630 Allied guns precariously perched wheel-to-wheel in mountain-side positions above Messina. On the next day the rear parties and "B" echelons of various units started to arrive in the concentration area. The troops having already at least partially restored their physical wellbeing now fell to the tasks of replenishing their equipment, arms and vehicles and to absorbing the many lessons of the fighting. By now they had mastered the heat and the dust of Sicily, but malaria, contracted whilst on the Catania Plain, was still taking its toll and continued to do so. And as the necessary work and refresher training was completed more relaxation was packed into the all too brief spare moments. The mobile cinema and the mobile bath appeared to be well patronized although the latter was mainly forsaken for the sea. Sightseeing in the once beautiful city of Catania and other excursions, were arranged. This welcome break, however, was soon at an end. On 31st August, now refreshed and ready once more for the road to Rome, the division moved up to concentration and embarkation areas north of Taormina, that lovely holiday resort on the Etna Riviera, in which the Germans had had their headquarters. From this area all units in the division could look down across the Straits of Messina on to their Italian objectives. The channel, now free of the fleeing German craft was majestically entered first by destroyers, then next day by a monitor and, as a final gesture, by the battleships of the Mediterranean Fleet who mercilessly pounded the areas around Reggio with well-aimed broadsides.

One minor adventure by small parties from the division at this stage, must not go unrecorded here. On 28th August, before D-day, some radio operators and their sets from 156 Fd Regt crossed the straits with the commandos to

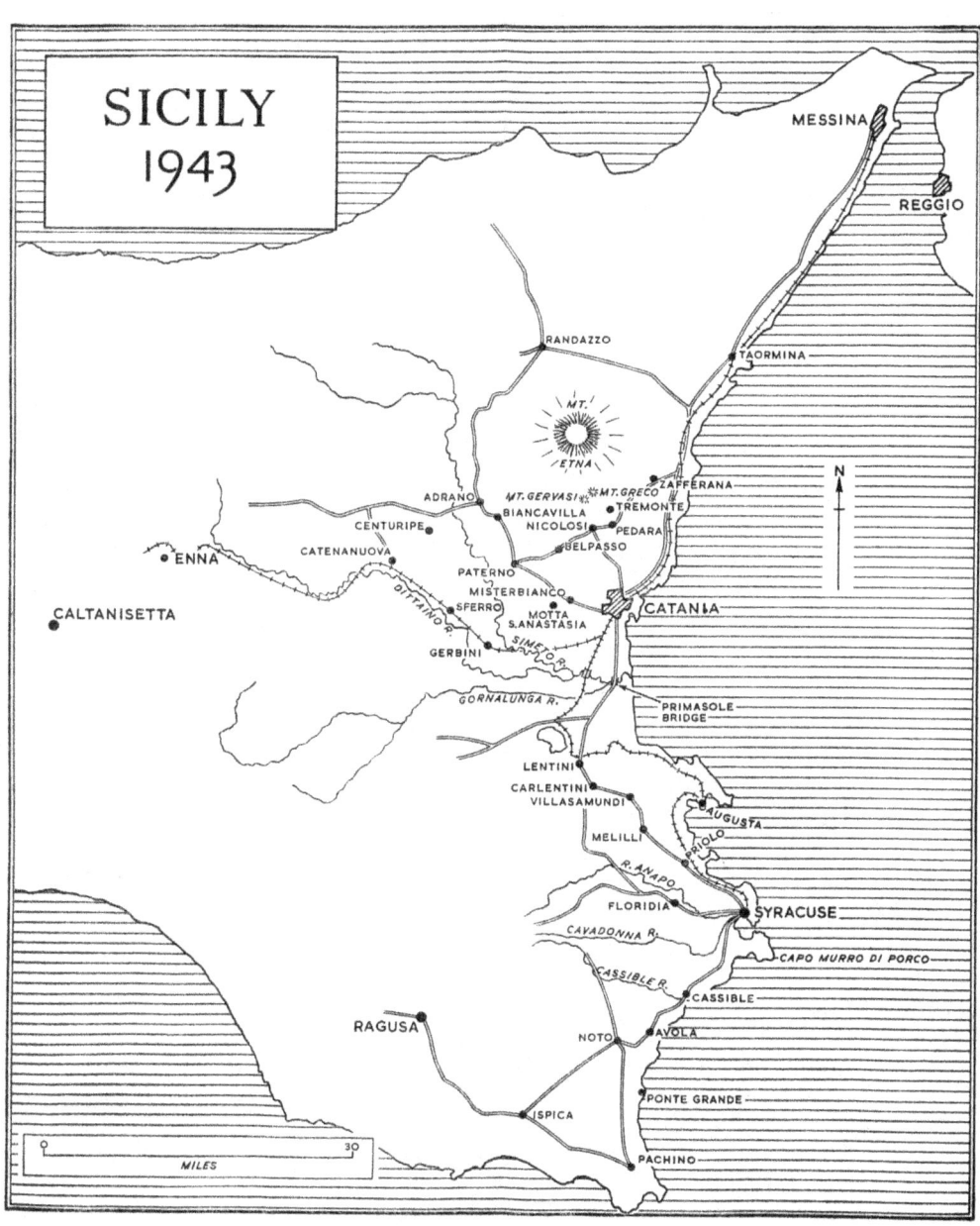

supplement the latter's communications. These commando parties were to lie up, watch and report enemy movement and disposition. They had many adventures, some pleasant and others not so pleasant; some managed to remain hidden, others were captured, temporarily at least; some were just missing, others died. A great deal of valuable information, however, did get through, and theirs was a worth-while last-minute contribution to the successful assault of Italy.

Last minute packing, stowing, driving the vehicles down to the hards for loading into the landing craft was the order of the last few days of the division in Sicily.

CHAPTER TEN

THROUGH SOUTHERN ITALY TO THE ADRIATIC

In which 5th Division still part of XIII Corps of Eighth Army, crosses the Straits of Messina on Operation 'Baytown' and starts a long trek through Southern Italy to join up with the United States Fifth Army, after the latter had landed south of Naples. In which, after campaigning in the Abruzzi and Molise Mountains, the Division moves across to the Adriatic sector near Lanciano, to spend Christmas in action alongside the New Zealanders, Canadians and Indians.

The Setting and the Plan

As early as May 1943, in Washington, the Allies had decided that the main attack against the northern coast of Hitler's European Fortress could not be made until the spring of 1944 at the earliest. To relieve the pressure on the protesting Russians, Sicily had been taken and any ensuing plan against the softer underbelly of Europe had to be designed to get the quickest results in the most economical way. It was clear that an advance up the narrow Italian mainland could not only be achieved with relatively few divisions, but could also be greatly helped by Allied superiority in the air, and by sea over the long coastline. From the enemy point of view this air and sea superiority enforced the keeping of a large garrison, not only on the Italian mainland, but also in the Balkans and Southern France. The latter two areas had been expecting invasion at any time and were being kept increasingly busy by active partisans and guerillas.

When it was obvious that the fall of Mussolini on 25th July had virtually put an end to any organized Italian resistance, General Eisenhower was instructed to hasten a complete Italian surrender and to secure a bridgehead on the mainland of Italy. This was to include Naples and an area large enough to draw as many German divisions as possible to the south. Various negotiations proceeded for the Armistice which was finally accepted by Marshal Badoglio, and was secretly signed in Cassibile on the afternoon of 3rd September, by which time 8 Army was across the Straits of Messina. This Armistice was not to be announced publicly until General Mark Clark's United States Fifth Army, in which was included British X Corps, had completed landings at Salerno, south of Naples, with the object of hastening the advance, and cutting off any German formations opposing 8 Army. Operation, "Avalanche" as this was to be known, was to take place some days after Operation "Baytown". It was hoped that the latter would have penetrated by then far enough to keep the maximum enemy reserves in the south.

General Montgomery's plan was for XIII Corps to assault with two divisions, 1 Canadian Div on the right, 5 Div on the left, to the north of Reggio, supported by artillery fire from XXX Corps and other artillery in position above Messina. 5 Div would then make the main advance along the western road axis, whilst 1 Canadian Div took the eastern route, to squeeze out the narrow part of the "Toe" of Italy, around Cantanzaro. Two commandos and 231 Independent Brigade Group from Malta, were in reserve ready to make seaborne landings when required.

The plan of 5 Div was almost a repetition of that for the landing in Sicily. This time 15 Inf Bde was to follow through beachheads secured by 13 and 17 Inf Bdes. This operation was to be supported by bombing and sea to shore bombardment from the warships *Rodney*, *Valiant*, *Nelson* and *Warspite*, as well as by the overwhelming fire support from XXX Corps artillery. The latter, in the form of a barrage, started at the water line, moved inland to cover coastal guns, and then returned to the beaches, just to make quite sure that any surviving defenders were in the right frame of mind to receive the assaulting battalions.

The lovely wild mountain country of Calabria, and its neighbouring provinces of Apulia and Lucania, have suffered the same stormy past as Sicily. The influence of the Greeks is still noticeable in that part of the heel known as Magna Graecia. To-day, as a result of successive earthquakes, this is, in places, an overpowering wilderness, malarial, and lacking all sanitation. The Normans dominated Apulia in the eleventh and twelfth centuries, to be followed by representatives of the houses of Hohenstaufen, Anjou, Aragon, Spanish Bourbon and Savoy. In the nineteenth and early twentieth century the land was acquired by landlords who remained in the more civilized parts of Italy, north of Naples. This absenteeism, after the misrule of the Bourbons, has left the people in a decadent and impoverished condition, crude, ignorant and dishonest by nature. They exist in squalid huddles amongst their pigs, fowls and vermin. To the latter they have become quite impervious like the beasts they keep on their large straggling farms. And if you ask the Calabrian farmer for his philosophy of life he will probably reply "Si Campa"—one exists—or else one goes to America and makes a big fortune as a waiter! This sense of fun, bequeathed him by his Neapolitan ancestors, is still one of his greatest charms, and somehow helps to console, when hearing him tell that he is starving, with no prospect of employment. His inherent love of money and gambling accounts for the popularity of all sorts of lotteries which are more often than not influenced by pure witchery and knavery. The Southern Italian is a musical fellow who loves his "tarantello" when, after the heat of the day, fortified by his flagon of vino, he can summon the energy to dance it. So idle is he that most of his conversation is confined to ample and exotic gestures of which he is a past master. He sleeps so much by day that one wonders how any of the farm-work ever gets done. He lives so much by night that Chateaubriant wrote of the Calabrian night: *Ce ne sont pas des ténèbres, mais seulement l'absence du jour.*

Opposite the Etna Riviera, where the division was now making its final preparations for the crossing of the straits, towered the huge granite mass of the Aspromonte Mountains, the southern end of the long chain of Apennine Mountains, that form the backbone of Italy. Almost everywhere these mountains fall away sharply into the sea, leaving here and there small sandy bays, surrounded by lush vegetation cultivated by small colonies of the more intelligent fruit farmers and fisherfolk who have traded for centuries, almost in a world of their own. Their terraced domains stretch upwards to the hinterland where the Calabrian peasant farmers take over the land, intersected only by poor mountain cart tracks. In and out of these little bays the main coastal road and railway run almost continuously. Here and there are bigger colonies in sizeable towns; three such towns, Reggio, Villa San Giovanni and Mariana Gallico, were now to receive the full weight of the grand barrage that was to herald the arrival of 8 Army, so soon after the weary ruthless Germans had abandoned them, in their headlong flight northwards. This withdrawal was confirmed by the commando parties, mentioned in the previous chapter, who had given clear indication that this area was no longer seriously defended. The retreating Germans had been covered by the 29th Panzer Grenadier Division backed up by 26th Panzer Division, small mobile rearguard parties of which were still in the area. Their task was to try and bolster up the almost non-existent Italian Coastal Garrison.

It seemed once more that the nature of the country was to prove a greater deterrent to 8 Army than its defenders, but General Montgomery was taking no chances of unnecessary casualties, and the fireplan across the straits was to go on as planned.

The Landing and Securing of the Beachhead

At 0430 hrs. on 3rd September, 1943, exactly four years after the outbreak of war, 13 and 17 Inf Bdes landed on the beaches at Gallico Marina to the north of Reggio. Opposition was confined to some sporadic shelling from the odd self-propelled gun in the hills, and mortaring, particularly on the southern end of the beaches. Later on in the day a few casualties were caused by bombing, but that was about the sum total of the effective resistance put up by the demoralized Italians. It was reported, however, that an Adjutant of one of the battalions was temporarily incapacitated by a brick hurled at him by an Italian artilleryman. The latter's commander was found weeping in his dugout, with the muzzle covers still in position on his coastal guns. It is assumed that the brick was the only alternative means of offence left to his outraged gunner.

The crossings of landing craft, on a ferry basis, were a bit erratic, partly due to the darkness and the tremendous smoke and dust thrown up by the intensive supporting barrage; at least one lost landing craft skipper was successfully beached by a Gunner from the Div Arty correctly reading his map! Some sub-units, particularly of 13 Inf Bde, landed on the wrong beaches. Others, in the same brigade, hit the shore with such a bump that they were thrown into a confused and undignified heap on the deck of the craft. It was as well that there was little opposition from men, mines or wiring. These men of 2 R INNISKS were greeted at first by silence; there was no sound of 2 WILTS or 2 Cameronians who should have secured the beaches ahead of them. The only sound came from a few peering Italians who meekly cried "Viva Inglesi". However, by 0700 hrs. most of the companies in 13 Inf Bde were reported on their initial objective, and "D" Company of 2 R INNISKS was ordered to go for Pt. 210, a very steep and difficult climb; their only consolation for this was a magnificent view backwards down on to the steady regatta-like streams of little ships, plying backwards and forwards across the straits. The final phase, the extension of the initial beachhead, was completed in the early afternoon without much further incident.

At 1600 hrs., after the cancellation of a proposed move forward to take over positions from 2 Northamptons of 17 Inf Bde, 2 Cameronians moved northwards towards Villa San Giovanni, covered by a small mobile column of the battalion's carriers. By 2030 hrs., without meeting any noticeable opposition, they were in position around Pezzo and a patrol from the carriers pushed on to drive away an enemy armoured car on the edge of Scylla, a little seaside town named after the Greek heroine who was turned into a monster by her rival Aphrodite; she developed the habit of devouring mariners thrown ashore there by the whirlpool of Charybdis off the Sicilian coast, opposite Scylla.

Meanwhile 17 Inf Bde had pushed forward to the high ground about four miles inland from the beaches. 2 Northamptons had led this advance to San Stefano, against very light opposition, until 1500 hrs. when they came to a quite impassable crater in a mountainside road, with a sheer drop into a deep ravine below. This was covered by Spandau and rifle fire. Up to this point they had been supported by the self-propelled guns—known as "Priests"—of 24 Field Regt., but even tracked vehicles could certainly go no farther than this. At this stage 2 Northamptons came under command of 13 Inf Bde and pushed out night patrols towards Scylla which met further slight opposition. The other two battalions were meanwhile consolidating the beachhead area.

Landing craft crossing the Straits of Messina.

THE BAGNARA TUNNEL.—Lieut.-Colonel C. B. Wood and members of his Tactical Headquarters emerge at Bagnara.

A Patrol of 2 WILTS in the Aspromonte Mountains behind Villa-San-Giovanni on the 3rd of September, 1943.

In a brickfield near Goia, the Army Commander, General Montgomery, congratulating Captain H. J. Christie of 2 R INNISKS on his award of the D.S.O. for continued first-class patrolling activities. Behind the General is Brigadier Campbell, Commander, 13th Infantry Brigade.

The Advance from the Bridgehead to Potenza

At midday 15 Inf Bde Gp embarked and after what many described as a "pleasant little cruise", landed to the south of Villa San Giovanni and assembled in the dried up ravine of a river-bed ready to break out towards Scylla and Bagnara. They set out along what was already signposted as "Monty's Highway". There was an additional and significant notice which directed "all traffic for London straight on. 1870 miles". 1 Y and L, leading along the coast road, reached Favazinna by 1600 hrs. on the 4th, followed by 1 Green Howards. 1 KOYLI had meantime been doing some expert mountaineering in the high ground, on the western flank of the advance, followed by 92 Field Regt, who, like the "Priests" with 17 Inf Bde, found it difficult to get practical gun positions, and the infantry were soon out of range.

During the previous night of the 3rd/4th, a commando had landed ahead of 15 Inf Bde at Bagnara where they met some troops from 29th Panzer Grenadier Division. After a fierce fight they took part of the town, driving the Germans into the northern outskirts. 1 Y and L, after having had to advance through a long tunnel, which was the sole route, the road being completely blocked by expert demolition, found themselves up against German rearguard forces in between them and the commandos in the town. Those who had to trundle through this tunnel, over the sleepers, in a jeep or carrier were certainly not likely to forget the liver-shaking ride. General Alexander had previously said that all roads certainly lead to Rome and were all of them mined into the bargain. This was to be the first of many such demolitions to slow down the long and tenuous line of communication of the division. The first real rain fell in those Calabrian Hills that night to add a further difficulty, the flooded river-bed, to the many obstacles to which the divisional Sappers were soon to become used.

The night 4th/5th was spent around Bagnara. 1 Green Howards had joined 1 KOYLI in a defensive position overlooking the town, from the high ground to the south of it. 1 Y and L were still held up on the coastal road. The Brigade Commander, Brigadier Martin, joined the two battalions on the high ground next morning and ordered them to advance and turn the enemy left flank; the order of march was the Brigadier, his gunner Lieut.-Colonel Wood, and the two

Battalion Commanders. The two latter and the Brigadier remarked how strange it was that they, all three of them "neutral" Irishmen, should find themselves together in such a position.

At noon on the 5th 1 Green Howards reached the road from Bagnara to Euphemia whence they were ordered to occupy the high ground to the east of Cerimido. A patrol from "D" Company contacted the enemy outside Cerimido. These were the last Italians to resist the division. They were grouped round machine guns with a great deal of ammunition and with good command of the roads: L/Sergeant Parkin of the company attacked them single-handed and forced them to give up the contest; for this he was awarded the M.M.

The remainder of 13 and 17 Inf Bdes spent a quiet day on the 5th, while the divisional vehicles and guns contrived to arrive over the beaches, with only the occasional bombing raid to harass them. Later in the day 2 Northamptons were relieved by the Canadians and reverted to their own brigade, moving to Villa San Giovanni. Of the casualties that had to be evacuated, most of them were malaria cases still arising from the stay on the Catania Plain. Hoards of deserters from the Italian Army were overwhelming the inadequate prisoner of war cages in the beachhead area.

Congestion around the Bagnara tunnel was so serious now, that it was decided to use landing craft to pass 13 Inf Bde to the seaward flank of 15 Inf Bde, landing them at a beach twelve miles ahead, and three miles south of Gioia. This was successfully done during darkness and the landings made early on the morning of the 6th, but not before the swell had caused many of the infantry to wade a considerable distance. 2 R INNISKS in particular suffered from a seriously swirling surf, which prevented their craft from reaching the beaches. Life-lines had to be used and some men were swept away, but were rescued by Lieutenant N. J. Crawford, a champion swimmer, and Padre Power both of whom showed great courage. A strenuous mountain march soon revived all concerned. 17 Inf Bde followed 13 Inf Bde on the 7th, using the same craft between Scylla and Gioia, whilst 15 Inf Bde proceeded by the coastal road, and reached Barretlera. The motor transport used the road and eventually met up with the battalions in a concentration area east of Gioia. On the 7th September opposition appeared to be slight, and 13 Inf Bde were ordered to advance, capture Rosarno, and occupy the high ground north of the River Mesima. 2 Cameronians moved off at 2045 hrs. towards Rosarno, but were fired on by the usual self-propelled gun and Spandaus within sight of the town, and lost their two leading carriers. Any further attempts to enter the town were strongly resisted although one company did get a foothold in the railway station. During the evening, enemy shelling became intense, and the enemy still held the river line. Early on the 8th the shelling ceased, and at 0800 hrs. the forward Cameronian companies were in the town without further opposition. Three hours later, 2 WILTS and 2 R INNISKS passed through to continue the advance. 15 Inf Bde reached Gioia on the 8th, marching from the lovely little cliffside orange groves of Palmi, once destroyed by earthquakes. The supporting arms got a little mixed during these land/sea manœuvres and 7 Cheshire were no exception. "C" Company, who had been in action with 15 Inf Bde on the high ground east of Cannitella and Scylla, reverted to command of 17 Inf Bde on the 5th whilst "D" Company went back to its normal affiliation with 15 Inf Bde. This may sound trivial but, so long had the infantry, gunners and machine gunners worked together, that they took some time to get used to strange faces. This close affiliation was to be a salient feature of the division's fighting in Italy.

One bridge laid by the Sappers was marked "Achtung! Go slow. Musso's Bridge. Almost Finito!" In a minefield on its verge lay several Italian dead, killed by the mines. A few minutes after their demise the comedian George Formby and his wife passed by on their way to give an impromptu concert at Div H.Q. The latter was seen to put her head out of the staff car and remark, in an unmistakably Lancastrian dialect, that it was a good thing she was not the fainting type!

On the night 7th/8th September 231 Inf Bde, and some commandos, made a successful but extremely difficult landing in Porto San Venere, near Pizzo in the Gulf of San Eufemia, ahead of 5 Div. This was a little town famous for the exploits and burial there of the French Marshal Murat, former King of Naples. Unfortunately some German troops, also at the point of landing, put up strong opposition against the Malta Brigade, whose foothold was only gained at great cost. 13 and 17 Inf

Bdes, at that time, some fifty miles south of Pizzo, were immediately ordered to advance in relief, which they accomplished in twelve hours by means of mobile columns.

These columns left in the afternoon of the 8th, and joined up with 231 Inf Bde. The 13 Inf Bde column was commanded personally by Brigadier L. M. Campbell, and the other by Lieut.-Colonel Ballard of the Northamptons. The latter met little opposition, and by 1400 hrs. on the next day, had reached the River Angitola north of Pizzo. The column was disbanded at 1600 hrs. and 231 Inf Bde came under command of 5 Div for further movement to the north.

In the evening of the 8th, Rome Radio and the B.B.C. broke the news of Italy's Unconditional Surrender on the 3rd of September. Immediately, at every available window and balcony, appeared white sheets, and the Italians gathered and madly clapped their hands at every street corner, as the division marched on northwards. The peasants were loudmouthed in their disrespect for Mussolini and the "tedesci", all the while demanding "biscotti" and "cigaretti" from their "Inglesi amigo". The Germans, on the other hand, only fought more bitterly, enraged, probably, by the many home-made Union Jacks and Stars and Stripes that had now suddenly appeared in the hands of the Italian peasants.

On the 9th September, Operation "Avalanche", the landing by General Mark Clark's United States Fifth Army at Salerno, south of Naples, crashed into German troops who were rehearsing their defensive rôle. Farther south, at Taranto, elements of 1 Airborne Div had been landed by V Corps of 8 Army. 15 Inf Bde moved to a hide area south of Mileto with a view of its lovely Norman castle. 13 Inf Bde were marching to a concentration area north of Vibo Valentia where 8 Army had gained an important airfield.

On the next day, the 10th, patrols from 231 Inf Bde, now under command of 5 Div, started to move across the diversions over the Angitola River, whose bridges had been previously destroyed by the R.A.F. A mobile column formed from 2 RSF and 2 Northamptons commanded by the C.O. of the former, advanced in the afternoon and, meeting no opposition, reached the Nicastro area by 1830 hrs. On the 10th also, elements of 5 Recce Regt. arrived in the Nicastro area, to take their proper place at the head of the divisional advance.

The regiment had been delayed in Sicily to allow the very highest priority to the Sappers, who by now, were fully stretched in making bridges and diversions, filling in craters and clearing the many demolitions and ubiquitous mines of all descriptions, so cleverly laid by the retreating German motorized troops. On the inland route Cantanzaro fell to the Canadians, and by now, the "Toe" and "Instep" of Italy were firmly gripped by 8 Army. Since landing around Reggio, XIII Corps had covered a hundred miles in seven days with insufficient transport and over very difficult roads. This achievement was considerably helped by the short sea trips undertaken by landing craft.

5 Recce Regt. established its R.H.Q. at Sambiase on the 11th and sent scout patrols with attached Sappers farther north. Other of their patrols were trying to contact the Canadians farther inland. 17 Inf Bde, concentrated in the Nicastro area, had similar patrols out. The same day, in the afternoon, 1 Green Howards landed from the sea near Pizzo and marched to establish themselves some six miles or so west of Nicastro, at Gizzeria, by 2100 hrs. that evening. The Gunners meanwhile had been moving from position to position, by road, to keep up with the advance and there had been no shooting since Rosarno.

On the 12th, 5 Recce Regt. moved farther up the coast to Amantea, probing northwards all the time. Patrols were sent inland to the Cosenza area; one of them held up by the blocked roads discovered a train with steam up and driver standing by. In the confusion, nobody had stopped this railway running, and the patrol in question boarded the train, not without some argument with the ticket collector, and lay on the floors of the carriages out of sight of German patrols. They reached Cosenza and captured the airfield without further difficulty. Apart from this, all seemed very peaceful on the divisional "front" and there appeared to be no contact with the enemy as far as Paolo, where St. Francesco lived in a cave on the shore. The effect of the Salerno landings must have caused the Germans to look back over their shoulders a bit at this stage.

5 Div H.Q. were now fully established in the Nicastro area and 13 Inf Bde were ready to make another sea trip as far as Scalea, followed by 17 Inf Bde. 15 Inf Bde were

marching up the coastal road to Belvedere and Santa Agate. The road along the Tyrrhenian coast was thick with white dust and wound in and out of the little bays over many diversions. In Santa Agate, Brigadier Martin, commanding 15 Inf Bde, found a luxurious caravan inhabited by an Italian Admiral who preferred to command his fleet, based on Taranto, from this retreat in the mountains. The Admiral obligingly rang up some of his friends, by means of the railway telephone, to find out whether the retreating Germans had passed by their way. The road back to Belvedere was afterwards found to be filled with bombs timed to go off under the bridges used by 15 Inf Bde. Those of the division who spent the night at Belvedere will remember its particularly vicious mosquitoes, the luscious lemons and raisins and the excellent anchovies.

In the meantime all was not going well at Salerno, where 5 Army were being heavily counter-attacked, and although its communications were stretched to the fullest, 8 Army was racing north to relieve the pressure. 5 Div. was ordered to step up its advance and pin down the enemy on the southern side of the Salerno bridgehead. 5 Recce Regt., well ahead, were experiencing some difficulty in maintaining their wireless communications owing to the long distance between sets and the difficult mountainous country between.

At times during this period R.H.Q. of 5 Recce Regt. was a hundred miles ahead of Div H.Q. and leading patrols often as far ahead again of R.H.Q. Vehicles throughout the division began to feel the strain of their tremendous mileages, and, on top of all this, the division began to outrun its map supplies. For a few days the only maps that covered the area of operations in the possession of the 5 Recce Regt., were two very aged and small-scale motoring maps that had been borrowed from a friendly retired Italian general. Some of the division's Gunners recalled the days of the last stand at Dunkirk when they tried to fire predicted fire from Michelin motoring maps!

On went the patrols as far as Sapri, with reconnaissance and harbour parties trying to keep up. Those of the latter who were jeep-borne, had to mask their faces with silk handkerchiefs, desertwise, in order to keep out the persistent thick white dust which was churned over the roadside fruit trees and verges almost resembling snow.

The first contact with the enemy was made at Vallo, northwest of Sapri by a reconnaissance patrol, on the night of the 15th, but the enemy immediately pulled back; the same procedure was repeated the following night. These were only rearguards of the German 1st Parachute Division keeping contact as they fell back towards the Salerno battles. It was then decided to advance from Sapri, with a column from 5 Recce Regt. which included a squadron of Canadian tanks, 365 Battery from 92 Fd Regt and some machine gunners from 7 Cheshire in the lead. Meanwhile 13 Inf Bde formed a firm base at Sapri, 2 WILTS being in position on the left to cover the main coastal road. On 17th September, 1 Squadron of 5 Recce Regt. was under command of 13 Inf Bde at Sapri, and it was a troop of this squadron that, at 1120 hrs., met a patrol of the reconnaissance troop of the American 36 Div., working south from the Salerno bridgehead. The Americans then contacted 1 Squadron H.Q. at Vallo and 5 Recce Patrol went on to deliver a personal message from Brigadier Campbell to H.Q. 36 Div. On the same day the Canadians contacted V Corps on their right, so that virtually all Allied forces were in touch across the breadth of Italy. General Montgomery immediately ordered XIII Corps to push on, to let the enemy know that 8 Army had arrived on the scene, with the object of taking the important communications centre of Potenza.

The 3 Squadron of 5 Recce Regt. heading inland towards Sala Consilina on the 17th had the first serious clash with the rearguards of 26th Panzer Division at Lagonegro. The leading troop was quickly pinned down at a blown bridge which was covered by mortar and machine gun fire; two armoured cars were set on fire and two troopers killed. The Gunner Troop Commander of 365 Battery had some good shooting despite the use of his O.P. as a grandstand by all the C.O.s of the Bde Gp but the reconnaissance troops could get no farther. All manner of fire was poured down into the village; one of the 17-pounder anti-tank guns, then known as "Pheasants" for security reasons, was fired by a detachment of 52 A Tk Regt., whose first shot with the weapon it was. Some German machine gunners were operating from a tunnel down which one could see, from the high ground to the west of the Gunner O.P. The "Pheasant" was trundled up to this position and one or two armour piercing shots were sent whistling down the tunnel. This must have had a terrifying effect on the machine gunners and certainly silenced them. After a lot of difficult ranging, the field Gunners delivered a few high explosive rounds down the mouth of the tunnel which undoubtedly finished off anybody still sheltering there. At 1950 hrs. 15 Inf Bde arrived at Lagonegro and ordered 1 Green Howards to advance across country to the west of the town, to secure the high ground and approaches from the north-west by first light on the 18th. During this advance the German Panzer troops devised a new kind of defensive horror when they petrol-soaked the scrubs on the hillside, and, at the appropriate moment, set it off with well-placed incendiary bombs. This did not deter the infantry who merely avoided the affected areas. The Divisional Artillery was backed up by 66 Med Regt. then under command, and a fireplan was arranged. Once more the German rearguard withdrew during the night and 1 Y and L were able to occupy the town early in the morning, without the help of supporting artillery fire.

On the 18th, 13 Inf Bde led by 2 Cameronians entered Sanza, and occupied positions on the far side; the same evening 2 R INNISKS passed through the town.

15 Inf Bde, 1 Green Howards leading, pushed on to cross the River Noce and, after a long march, arrived at Casalbuono in the afternoon. There they received orders to move forward in the troop carrying vehicles at 0400 hrs. in the morning of the 19th to seize and hold Montesano. 1 KOYLI led the advance this time, and reached Montesano without contacting the enemy. On the next day the Canadians entered Potenza against 1st German Parachute Division and their western patrols contacted 5 Div.

Bringing up the rear, 17 Inf Bde were south of Lagonegro on the 19th, and continued their march on the 20th; on the 21st they concentrated in the Atena area, where they came into divisional reserve again, until the end of the month. There was now only one road open to the divisional advance and 15 Inf Bde were using it.

On the afternoon of the 21st, 1 Green Howards left Montesano, arriving at Brienza in the early hours of the 22nd. Within three hours they were marching to Picerno, to the west of Potenza, and here they arrived at noon on the same day. On the 22nd, 5 Recce Regt. reached Vietri in touch with the

2 Cameronians enter Rosarno on the 7th of September.

Resting in a hide on the way up the toe of Italy.

Detachment of 18 Light Anti-Aircraft Regiment at Rosarno.

Musso's Bridge.

158 and 164 Field Ambulances at work in Nicastro.

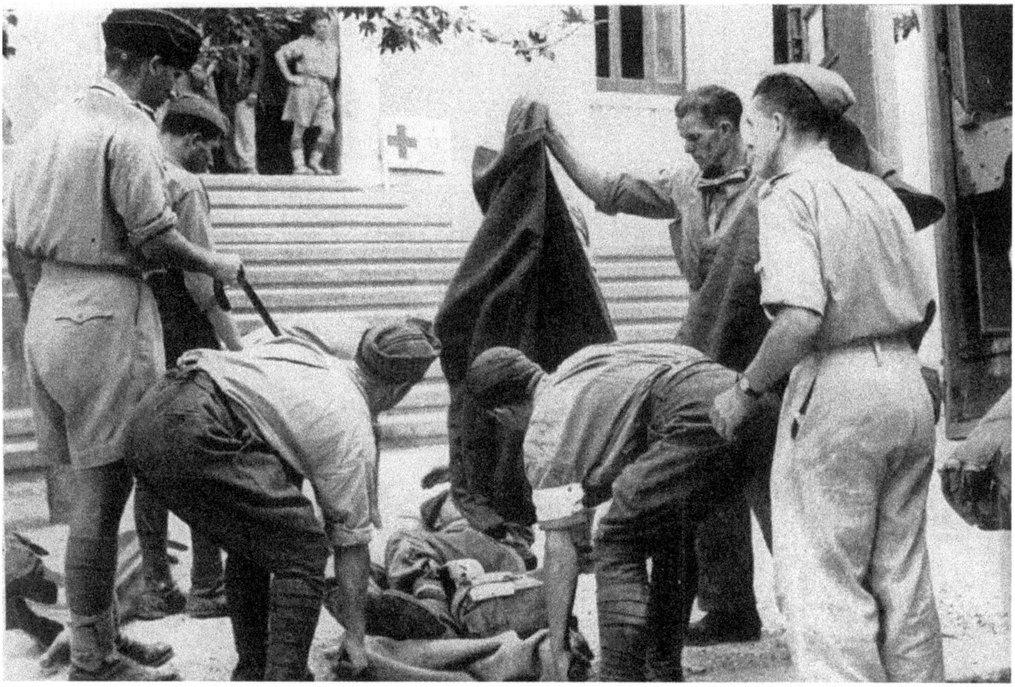

The L.A.D. with 91st Field Regiment make friends over a cup of tea.

Lieut.-General Dempsey, 13th Corps Commander, learns of the position from Major Colville, Brigade Major of 13th Infantry Brigade.

Canadians on their right, and the Americans on their left, forming a light screen in front of the advancing division. On the 22nd also, 13 Inf Bde moved to a concentration area farther west still, around Auletta, partly by foot and partly by truck. Here their patrols were in contact with those of 36 American Div.

5 Div., now up on the Potenza line, to the west of the Canadians, had travelled over 250 miles in less than twenty days. The capture of Potenza had forced the enemy to release his pressure against 5 Army at Salerno. With Potenza captured in the centre, the weight now shifted to 8 Army's next objective, the port of Termoli across the Foggia Plain, with its valuable airfields, on the Adriatic coast, and in the path of V Corps. Above all, the long line of communications was now stretched farther than was practicable, punctuated with many diversions, Bailey bridges and other defiles. At this stage General Montgomery decided to move the Army's lines of communication across to the Adriatic sector, using the much larger and more efficient port of Taranto.

It would take at least ten days before an advance of any size to the Foggia Plain, could be supported by the new base. 5 Div were ordered to halt around Auletta and Picerno, to protect the right flank of 5 Army, and the left flank of a slower Canadian advance north of Potenza. This advance was made against more frequent and determined rearguard action, using to its fullest advantage by demolition and mining the even more difficult and mountainous country ahead. On the right V Corps, which now included 78 Div and 4 Armoured Bde, was pursuing the retreating enemy up the Adriatic coast. During this time, 5 Recce Regt patrols were active, and one from 1 Squadron had a fierce battle in which it lost two vehicles at Castel Grande. This squadron formed a base in front of the divisional positions at Muro.

This pause enabled 5 Div to get in some more training for the mountains ahead and some relaxation and athletic recreation in the modern university town of Potenza which towered above the pine-clad surrounding slopes. It had been severely bombed by the Allied air forces only a few days previously.

On the 24th 1 Green Howards were ordered to stage a diversion; they advanced through the 1 KOYLI, down the railway line, much of it through tunnel, to Bella Muro Station, the base of German patrols that included self-propelled guns. After an eerie march, they arrived at the station to find a platoon of the 1 KOYLI in possession of it. Moving on, they met a patrol of 45 U.S. Reconnaissance Unit who reported that 5 Recce patrols were being mortared south of Castel Grande. Just as they were going to do something about this, 1 Green Howards were ordered back to Picerno, to prevent the lines of communication being any further stretched. Here they remained with the rest of the brigade until 8th October, although a small party was sent to deal with some civil disorder in Maschito on 5th October.

By now the rain storms were more frequent and so were the caustic allusions to "Sunny Italy" made by the troops. A notable occasion was when one of the divisional military policemen in Potenza unknowingly rebuked the King of Italy for proceeding against the one-way traffic; His Majesty withdrew and completed the circuit correctly.

Across the Foggia Plain into the Central Apennines

On the 2nd October, 5 Div, now grouped under V Corps, started to move to the Foggia Plain where it was to form a firm base, whilst the Canadians moved up into the Central Apennines, and V Corps advanced across the big rivers that flowed across their front into the Adriatic. 5 Recce Regt led the advance as far as Bovino, on the main Foggia-Naples road, and then concentrated, less 2 Squadron, who were to continue with 17 Inf Bde. The country north of Potenza consisted of winding roads going up and down through little valleys and over small mountains. It had been well sprinkled with demolitions and mines; abandoned and wrecked Canadian vehicles testified to the efficiency of the latter. The Foggia Plain was very similar to the Catania Plain but much vaster. It had been considerably bombed and had not really been defended against V Corps. 5 Div was concentrated near Troia on the eastern end of the plain, not far away from the historic battlefield of Cannae. On the 4th October, 13 Inf Bde concentrated in the Foggia area. 17 Inf Bde, who had moved up to Potenza on the 1st, arrived in the Troia area on the 3rd, where they were to remain in reserve for a few days. Here a great deal of refresher training was done to get ready for the vigorous winter warfare in the mountains that lay ahead.

There was yet time for some relaxation, and the football matches that had always been such a feature in the Middle East were started for a few days. The 2 RSF ran an excellent donkey race meeting! 15 Inf Bde followed the other brigades on the 8th, but did not stay in the Foggia area. The next night, partly by transport, and partly by marching, they moved through Lucera, on Highway 17, up to a line overlooking the Biferno River, with the Canadians on the left and an Indian division on the right. 1 Y and L led this advance, which was made along roads that had had extra special destructive treatment from the Germans, there being several demolitions to every mile; the railways were also smashed up every few yards. Now these obstructions were covered by increasingly intensive shelling, against which the Sappers, in three days, cleared twelve miles of road, built five Bailey bridges and constructed ten diversions. 1 Y and L had their first fierce battle against the enemy on Pt. 88 beyond Bonefro, on the 12th, supported by 92 Fd Regt and "D" Company 7 Cheshire. Several casualties were caused to both sides and the pressure was only relieved when 1 KOYLI put in a flanking attack on the right which took them to Casacalenda. The enemy had withdrawn behind his usual artillery fire. Meanwhile, on the 11th, in a heavy rain and mist, 1 Green Howards attempted to get to Montelongo. Just as it was getting dark the main body arrived at the river, to find the crossing washed away, with the first part of the battalion already on the other side; the cook's lorry was firmly bogged down in midstream. After much strenuous effort, they finally reached Montelongo by midnight. The next day the battalion took over 1 Y and L positions, making a further advance on the 13th to high ground overlooking Providenti. From Providenti, a track with a sheer drop on one side wound round a conical hill up to the little town of Morrone, perched on the top, like a fairy-tale castle. Here on the same night a strong fighting patrol from "D" Company met an enemy post on the edge of Morrone; against four well-placed machine guns, Sergeant Lambert stormed right into the enemy position in a farm and won the M.M. The enemy withdrew from this natural defensive position, and "D" Company, supported by machine guns of 7 Cheshire, took it over next afternoon and remained there until relieved by 1 KOYLI on the 18th. On 13th October the enemy had been driven back to the line Guardialflera-Petrella-Montagano-Busso-Baranello-Campochiaro.

The advance was now delayed some days by the increasingly difficult roads, by the atrocious weather, and by a build up of the enemy's strength. At the time, the strategic air force was moving into the Foggia airfields, so it was decided to wait for their support before pushing forward in strength.

On the Adriatic sector V Corps had taken Termoli by the 7th October, and were getting ready now for the battle for the crossings of the River Trigno. On the left of XIII Corps, 5 Army were just crossing the Volturno River, and by the end of the month, their patrols were on the banks of the River Garigliano.

The Canadians continued the advance on the 17th. The Green Howards had by then joined up with them in the neighbourhood of Petrella, where several casualties were caused by booby-trapped mines attached to trip wires and, from the 18th onwards, took up a wide front in that area, actively patrolling to give the impression that the whole of 5 Div was up there. During this time another M.M. was won for the battalion by Corporal Pears who returned, after a local attack by "B" Company across the Biferno, dragging to safety a wounded member of his patrol. The enemy were particularly persistent in firing into the area between the river and the high ground on either side of Lucito. On the 23rd, "C" Company (Major D. St. J. Radcliffe) managed to get through Lucito as far as Castelbottaclo, where they were later relieved by the Canadians and returned to Petrella.

By now a small trickle of Allied prisoners, who had escaped from the north when Italy surrendered, were drifting back to the divisional area, having walked many miles in the mountains from one friendly farm to another. One of these was Major Lewis of 5 Recce Regt., who had been captured in Sicily.

13 Inf Bde was now brought up into the forward area. 2 Cameronians took over a sector around Bojano from the Canadians who had opened up the road from Vinchiatura, in order to dominate the road to Isernia, after some stiff fighting for San Stefano, Barranello, Campochiaro, Colle d'Anchise, Spinete and Castropignano. For this fighting, the

Canadian Divisional Artillery borrowed 92 Fd Regt, although they actually never fired a round from their positions north of Campobasso. 5 Div now took over the lead of XIII Corps. The Canadians had come eighty miles in three weeks by 28th October, to form a firm base for a successful attack, two days later, by 2 R. INNISKS and 2 WILTS against objectives about five miles beyond Bojano. On 1st November the Cameronians moved up to some high ground just in rear of the other two battalions in reserve for 13 Inf Bde. A base was now secure for the capture of the important communications centre of Isernia, once an old walled Samnite city commanding a pass into the basin of the Apennines. This was designed to create the general impression that the main effort was going to be inland on the left of V Corps. In a steady downpour of rain on the night 29th/30th October, the leading battalions of 13 Inf. Bde. set off on the left flank, across the steep wooded slopes of the Matese Mountains, to occupy San Massimo and Cantalupo on the 30th; on the next day, a patrol entered the mountain-top village of Roccamondolfi, after a great deal of skirmishing. They were accompanied by their Gunner O.P. from 91 Fd Regt and machine gunners from "B" Company, 7 Cheshire, both of which were now getting valuable experience of carrying their heavy equipment on mules. These mules were made a special target by the enemy and heavy losses sustained, particularly by those with 17 Inf Bde. On one occasion at least, the Americans bombed the gun areas near Bojano in error. A German prisoner after one of these unfriendly acts, was heard to remark: "When British bombers fly over we duck, when German bombers fly over you duck, and when American bombers fly over we both duck." By now nearly a hundred guns of XIII Corps Artillery had come up into the central valley north of Bojano, and were helping both brigades on to their mountain objectives, now between three and four thousand feet high, and resolutely held by the enemy from 26th Panzer Division. The latter were based on Isernia, until the 3rd November, when, after they had lost San Angelo and Castelpetroso to 13 Inf Bde, they withdrew northwards. On 1st November, near Cantalupo, 2 WILTS found a German motor cyclist dispatch rider hiding in a ditch—his bike well camouflaged. Apparently he had broken down, had mended his machine, and was waiting for darkness to get him back to his own troops. One of his captors was referring to him in no uncertain terms as one of the adjectival persons of unknown descent who had knocked hell out of Coventry, when to his surprise, came the quick retort in very good English: "I happen to live in Hamburg."

Down in the valley, to stop the large gap between the two brigades, and in defence of the gun area, Battalion Tactical H.Q. and "D" Company of 7 Cheshire, together with one battery from 52 Anti-Tank Regt., formed a small force which, however, did not actually gain contact with the enemy. Ahead of 17 Inf Bde, 2 Squadron of 5 Recce Regt. patrolled to Carpinone and Sassano, to secure the division's right flank, but had to do this on foot owing to extensive cratering. 17 Inf Bde to the right of the valley, with their Gunners and machine gunners also, after some battling at Pesco della Messa, followed up with energetic mountaineering. The Northamptons took the village of Macchiagodena, forcing the enemy to withdraw westwards.

On 17 Inf Bde front there followed some particularly dogged fighting for several rocky pinnacles, against which enemy shelling, now becoming quite prolific, was very effective. The hard ground made it quite impossible to dig in, and the sole means of protection was to build up Sangar-like shelters, as in the fighting on the north-west frontier of India in pre-war days. When, on the 31st October, 2 Northamptons had secured Macchiagodena, 6 Seaforth opened up further high ground to the north. Their vigorous night patrols found the enemy still on the next bit of high ground, and next day, they fought their way into Castelpetroso, via San Angelo which was free of enemy, but under accurate shellfire. 6 Seaforth had a stiff battle for Pt. 1146 around St. Elena and after heavy losses, mainly from mortar fire were driven back; amongst those cut off was their Gunner F.O.O. Captain Bridie, of 156 Fd. Regt., who was awarded the M.C. for his gallant behaviour on that occasion. Next day a concentration was fired on the enemy by the Div Arty, and the 2 RSF took Pt. 1146 whilst the Northamptons took Pt. 1385 near by, with little loss, as the enemy had discreetly withdrawn once more. Patrols then pushed on rapidly to the road junctions around Isernia.

During this hilltop fighting the magnificently energetic and enterprising patrolling of all battalions brought back some very valuable information; this was handsomely acknowledged by Div H.Q. The going could not have been worse, nor indeed the weather. Maintenance of companies on these rocky outposts had to be almost entirely by mules, which suffered heavy casualties from shellfire and mortaring. Wireless was the only possible form of communication and it worked well despite the difficulties of battery maintenance. This mule maintenance had to continue until 13 Inf Bde had cleared a passable road at a lower level.

There were several parties interested in getting first into Isernia; the Americans and the two forward battalions of 13 Inf Bde were three of them. This town was to the enemy the last important stronghold that could be denied to Allied troops in Southern Italy; but once its southern mountain approaches were gone, the town itself would be quite untenable. During the night of 4th November 2 R INNISKS, having infiltrated among the enemy outposts rather successfully, decided they could save 2 WILTS having to mount the attack they were due to make. Lieut.-Colonel O'Brien Twohig devised a night patrol which included one of his pioneers armed with a brush and a pot of paint. By 0400 hrs. they had not only discovered that the enemy had withdrawn, but had also left a very artistic representation of their regimental badge—the Castle of Enniskillen—on one of the town's most prominent walls. Two hours or so later 2 WILTS arrived to find much of the sting taken out of their triumphal entry by this unmistakable signature. Two hours later still, an American patrol from 5 Army, thinking themselves to be ahead of all others, as was their wont, were even more mortified at the reception they got from 13 Inf Bde, by then most forcefully represented.

Whilst in the Isernia area, 2 R INNISKS and 2 WILTS did much patrolling, liaising with American patrols on their left. One of the Irish patrols snatched the village of Vincenzo from the enemy, and drove the Germans straight into the arms of an American patrol who happened to be coming in the other way. The latter with some reason insisted on sharing the bag! 2 R INNISKS also upheld the traditions of the division, much to the admiration of the Americans, by installing outside their R.H.Q., in the town, a life-size mirror inscribed "Do you look like a victorious British soldier *now*?"

The demolitions and other damage in and around Isernia

were so severe that the divisional Sappers had to employ all their resources, before the advance could be continued. Theirs had been a superhuman task so far and they were not then to know that this was to be their last big effort on the central axis—the bridging of the River Vandra under the able leadership of Lieut.-Colonel K. H. Osborne, the Commander of the Divisional Royal Engineers well to the fore as usual. Since landing in Italy the Sappers had undertaken a full and successful programme which included the development of beaches, many road diversions, two dozen odd Bailey bridges erected, repair of railway bridges, lifted thousands of mines, most of this in appalling weather conditions, and some of it under fire.

The Rionero Sector

13 Inf Bde were now on the high ground three or so miles to the west of Isernia, covering the River Vandra beneath them, with 2 Cameronians on the right and 2 R INNISKS on the left. 17 Inf Bde were continuing their epic mountain-top advance on the right flank and now it was the time, once more, for 15 Inf Bde to take the lead after a week's rest in the San Giuliano area. They moved up by transport on the 7th November, via Pesche, until they came to the great bridging activities, whence they proceeded on foot towards Rionero, a typical Apennine village, overlooking the upper valley of the Sangro River. 15 Inf Bde entered Forli two days later, scattering the enemy backwards, where his outposts were based on the wooded lower slopes of the hills. These were from the newly arrived 305th German Infantry Division, who had come in on the right of 26th Panzer Division. Their main positions were on the dominating high ground of Monte Greco, towering over the northern side of the valley, on either side of the main road from Barrea to Castel-di-Sangro. They had two regiments farther south facing 13 Inf Bde in the Pizzone-Colli-Atina area.

While this bridging operation was going on, using their own mine detectors and initiative, the Gunners of 1 Airlanding Regt. R.A., who had come under command of 5 Div when the latter passed through the Canadians, managed to get themselves into action on the north side of the river to support the advance of 15 Inf Bde. They also helped 92 Fd

Regt to get over the same way, and the two C.O.s, Lieut.-Colonel Thompson of the former and Lieut.-Colonel R. C. H. Kirwan, who had been G.S.O.I of the division until he took over 92 Fd Regt a few weeks previously, were the first to stroll into Rionero, to find it abandoned. After a pause, the Green Howards arrived in Rionero on the 4th November; they found it strangely quiet for the first few days, but it was not to remain so for long.

It was the intention of General Montgomery that XIII Corps should draw as much attention to themselves as possible in the Rionero sector for a few weeks, while V Corps completed its formidable task of crossing the Sangro River near the sea. The Corps artillery was to be brought forward as strongly as possible, and constant widespread patrolling by the infantry of 5 Div, combined with much artillery registration, was intended to portend a coming large-scale offensive, and thus draw enemy reserves from the Adriatic sector. Accordingly, 1 Green Howards, on arrival in Rionero, spread themselves on a wide front of some 5,000 yards, picketing all the heights in the approved manner. The rain poured down in torrents, making the main street of Rionero almost a swirling river; and wherever the infantry were able to scrape trenches, the rain poured into them while they were being dug. On the high ground by now, the infantry were resorting to sangars, in very exposed conditions, so exposed that no cooking there was possible. Really hot meals were never available to the forward troops, and all maintenance to them was by mule or porters, which took about seven hours to complete each journey; by which time the tea and stew in containers was lukewarm. The mules often returned with exposure cases from these forward companies. The best that could be done was a hot drying room in one of the less wrecked houses in Rionero.

After six days in these miserable conditions, and when Rionero was now getting fairly heavily shelled, its main street being very exposed to well-sited enemy O.P.s, 1 Green Howards went to billets in Forli. They were relieved by 1 KOYLI who existed in much the same sort of conditions. They in turn were relieved by 1 Y and L, and finally 1 Green Howards came back again to the same positions on the 19th November. By this time conditions were immeasurably worse; the weather was colder still, the enemy shelling increased in reply to the build up of XIII Corps artillery. Patrols became longer and more arduous; the mules began to break down under the strain, and the only replacements were horses and donkeys that could be found locally. When these were not to be found, the men themselves carried everything.

The Gunners south of Rionero were unable to go far from the road owing to the rocky nature of the countryside, and command posts were almost washed away in the roadside gullies. Almost everywhere mines were still being found; sometimes causing grievous casualties. The Gunners, to the north of Rionero—there was not enough room for more of them south of the town—had to go into boggy open ground where they were almost entirely overlooked by the German O.P.s and regularly shelled. Later on moves were made to alternative positions on the high ground east of Rionero but not before acute discomfort had been suffered in "Death Valley"—as the gun area came to be known. The road down to Castel-di-Sangro was particularly naked, being only used when it was entirely necessary and then by night.

With the Corps artillery almost entirely deployed around Rionero and Aquaviva it was decided to step up the simulated pressure on this front with an attack by elements of 17 and 13 Inf Bdes on Alfedena, an important centre of communications on the left front. This was to be known as Operation "Hook". On the 20th November, 2 Cameronians, starting from Cerro, attacked positions some six miles or so short of Alfedena from which 17 Inf Bde could advance to the objective. Although patrols had reported enemy positions in the area to be attacked, there were actually none to greet 2 Cameronians after a terrific Corps artillery bombardment, in extremely heavy rain. The area was lightly shelled an hour or so later in reply.

Early next day, at 0150 hrs., 2 RSF with two companies of 1 Green Howards under command, also started from Cerro and climbed up almost 800 feet of steep rocky cliff to a start line taped for them on the plateau above. This was typical of the many tests of physical fitness these attacks constituted, as all loads, including twenty-four hours' rations, had to be carried by hand. The usual bad dawn visibility delayed further movement, but later on "A" Company Green Howards (Major J. A. Purton), attacked Pt. 1086 supported by regimental concentrations of artillery fire. Again the slopes were steep and rocky, only broken up by small stunted trees sticking out at the most awkward angles. At the bottom of this hill they had to pass through a heavy concentration of enemy defensive fire and then scramble up to Pt. 1630, a similar rocky eminence. Consolidation in Sangar form was immediately begun, but a patrol later in the evening, to the snow line ahead, made no contact with the enemy. The next day 2 RSF passed through, after a very rainy night march, to cut the main road through Montenero. This was only reached after a very wet approach which resulted in the capture of the high ground beyond Montenero, complete with an enemy O.P. The battalion, with "Q" Battery of 156 Fd. Regt., held Montenero for several days and from it dominated Alfedena. Using this as a base, patrolling became active and the C.O. of the R.S.F., Lieut.-Colonel MacInnes, with his Gunner, Major Batey, made a spectacular private excursion into the hinterland claiming to have been the nearest Allied troops to Rome, at that time!

To the right of 5 Div, the Canadians had been having similar experiences, although opposition to them was mainly confined to extensive demolitions and the destruction of roads and the burning of villages. On 2nd December 15 Inf Bde took over from them in the area of Borella, San Angelo and Castel del Giudice, and the Canadians then passed over to V Corps on the Adriatic, where they were to have some bitter fighting for Ortona. This left the division with almost thirty miles of XIII Corps front to be held, and very strenuous and persistent efforts were made to keep the enemy guessing where the next blow was to fall. These efforts were stout enough to cause the German 1st Parachute Division to maintain strong rearguard positions just north of the tragically ruined town of Castel-di-Sangro, and to take full advantage of this lull by making widespread demolitions in the mountains; particularly around the Rome-Pescara main lateral road.

Patrols grew more and more energetic as conditions got more and more unpleasant; sometimes these patrols would come down off the icy mountain tops and be out for some days probing the German positions. Often a patrol would go out wading thigh-deep across the Sangro, to find, on the way back, that the swollen river would be neck-high for some of the men. Occasionally the torrent would sweep away a man to certain death; the others would only be saved by clinging together in a human chain. The first men of the division to cross the Sangro, the first also in 8 Army to do so—they actually swam—were the Northamptons. Even "S" mines fairly liberally scattered in a variety of inconvenient places failed to deter these patrols which continued to produce well-worth-while information. They certainly achieved the object of keeping the enemy guessing.

Communications, as already mentioned, were now proving extremely difficult. Div H.Q. was over twenty miles away from brigades as the cable layer goes. Battalions were nearly as far away from brigades in the most inaccessible places, as were companies from battalion H.Q.s and Gunner O.P.s from gun areas. The linesmen of the Royal Corps of Signals, and of the other arms, performed heroic unsung feats of line maintenance, and only the highest standard of training kept the battery-starved wireless sets working efficiently. Miles of roadways and diversions were patrolled, in all weathers, by the division's Provost personnel. Such was the reputation of these military policemen, that they were universally known as the smartest in the Eighth Army—even in the forward areas their immaculate turn-out was taken for granted, and was always a tremendous morale booster to the hard-pressed and often unavoidably filthy men of the battalions. Many will remember their efficient signing; many were comforted, when in doubt, to see the familiar "Y" route up signs. They even provided a divisional lighting-up time indicator clock which was displayed on telegraph poles en route.

By the end of November there was very firm liaison with the Americans on the left of the division. A small force from 5 Recce Regt., commanded by Major Prince, and known as "Princeforce", held this extreme left flank of the 8 Army in the Abruzzi north of Isernia. Their neighbours were first the American-Japanese Nisei Regiment, which was later relieved by the 2 Moroccan Div. of the Free French Force, better known as the Goums. For a time 92 Fd Regt provided an O.P. with the Americans and the French. This small reconnaissance force remained behind when the division moved east, and finally went back to the regiment's concentration area around Bovino, where earlier on Lieut.-Colonel M. F. Douglas-Pennant, of KRRC, had taken over from Colonel N. Blockley. Colonel Blockley,

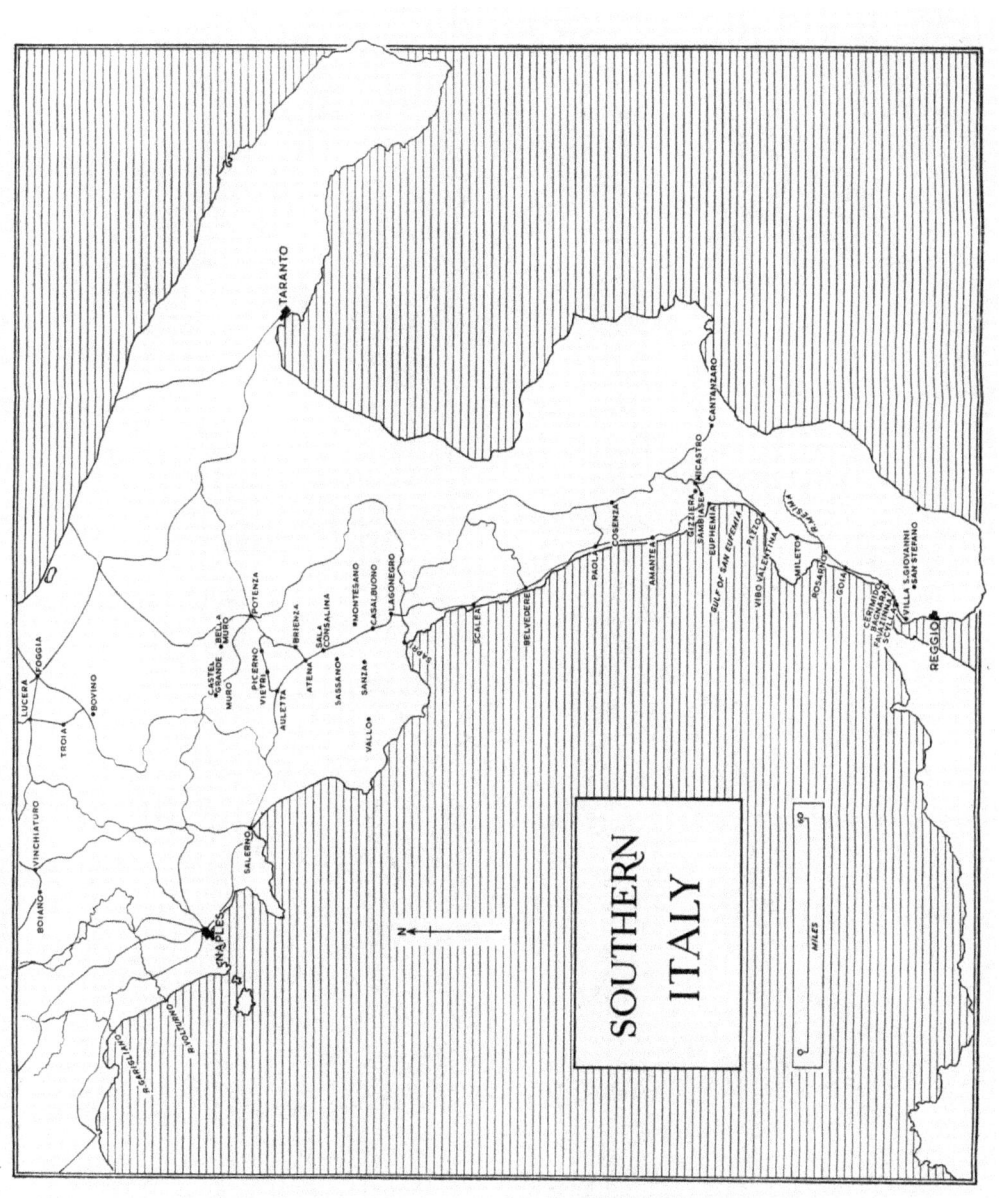

had great reason to be proud of the regiment he had virtually formed and trained so successfully; he was a personality to be missed throughout the division.

The war diaries of nearly all units for this period show a succession of reliefs within battalions and brigades, or O.P.s, and of patrol reports in profusion. They reveal valuable civilian confirmation of German movements, of the number of Poles and Czechs serving in 3rd Panzer Grenadier Division on the division's left front and of countless other useful scraps of information. From the listed map references, can be traced the almost chess-like moves of both sides, and the fully marked map of the divisional area at this time was heavily covered with markings of all colours and shapes indicating the great local activities that are so ably cloaked in the curt official communiques of such a period of "inactivity".

The artillery of both sides remained active. On one occasion the little village of Roccaraso was completely set on fire after a divisional artillery concentration. On another occasion a daylight patrol of the Northamptons saw an unusual concentration of an enemy platoon; the quick response from "Q" Battery of 156 Fd Regt kept German stretcher parties busy for the next two hours.

The Adriatic Sector

Over on the Adriatic sector, both the Canadians and the New Zealanders were having very heavy fighting in their slow advance. The Sangro had been successfully crossed and its northern ridge, which included the sizeable town of Lanciano, was now firmly in the hands of V Corps. The New Zealanders were particularly hard-pressed in their attempts to reduce the natural fortress of Orsogna. To give them further strength, it was now decided to hold the mountain sector even more lightly with elements of 78 Div., which had been in Army reserve, and to release XIII Corps to join V Corps in the Adriatic sector. 17 Inf Bde were to lead the division in this, and on the 11th December, after a very uncomfortable move that included a night in a muddy field by the Sangro, they crossed that river over the remarkably long Bailey bridge. The results here of the German scorched earth policy were very impressive. Parts of the Lanciano ridge looked remarkably like

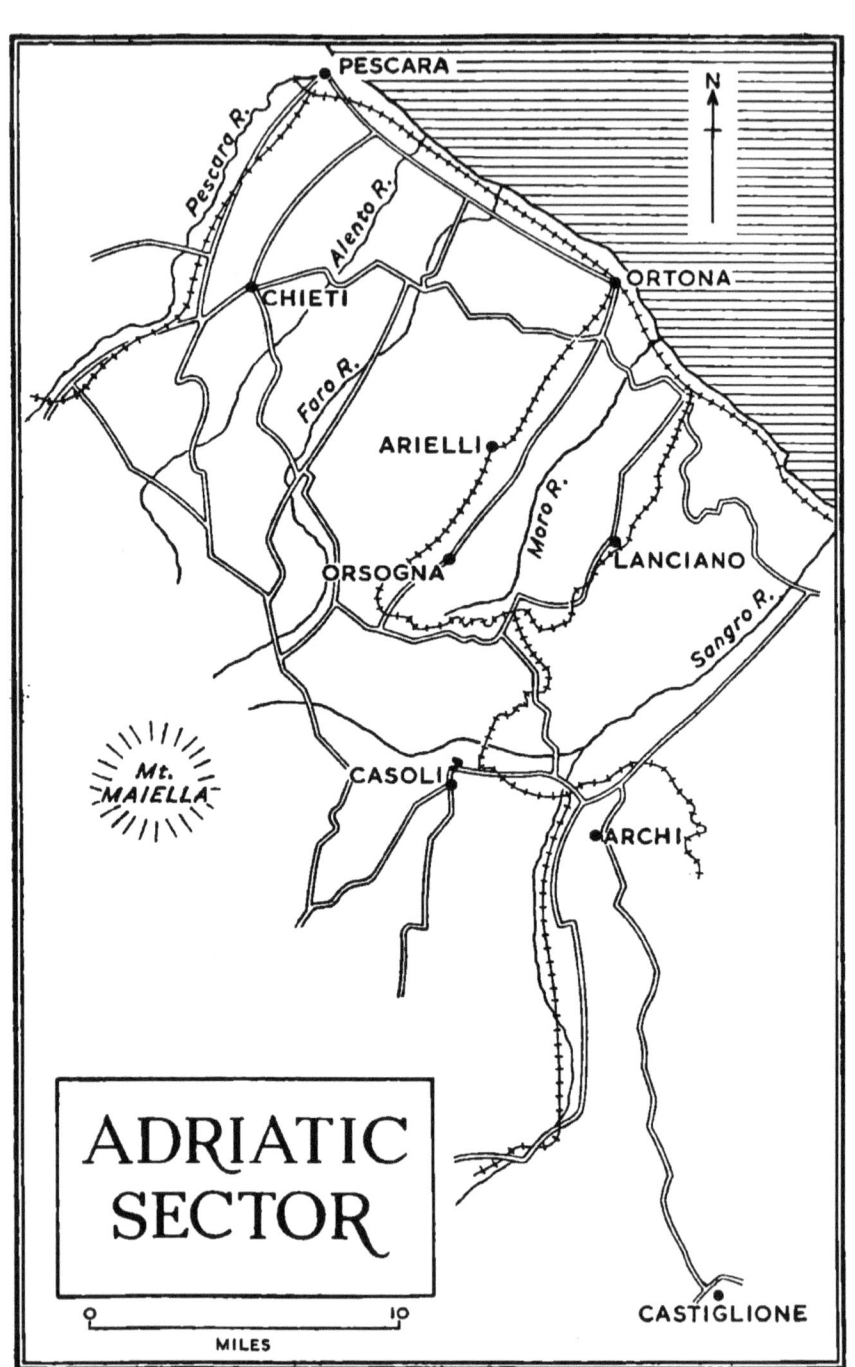

one of the lurid photographs of the mud of Flanders in the first Great War. Huge craters and the twisted wreckage of guns, tanks and trucks with gnarled tree stumps alone pierced this eerie wilderness; a veritable abomination of desolation. 17 Inf Bde came under command of 2 New Zealand Div, and the next day relieved part of 8 Indian Div on the New Zealanders' right flank. Their task was only to patrol, or to make small nibbles at the enemy, to protect the New Zealand flank while they were testing the Orsogna defences. They were not to take on any large scale offensive.

The brigade positions were overlooking the Moro River on the Colli Feature. This was very muddy cultivated ground, vastly different from the heights of Rionero, with olive groves and the odd farmhouse to give a little cover. From north to south, right through the brigade area, ran a Roman road which was to be much used by the division. The enemy of 65th Infantry and 26th Panzer Divisions were active with mortars and some tanks dug in hull down on the far crest. Movement during daylight was not encouraged and only permitted if absolutely necessary operationally.

On the 14th December, before dawn, part of 2 Northamptons moved across the River Moro to improve the positions. Here they dug well in and remained hidden by day. Late that night the remainder of the battalion moved across in a silence that was only shattered by the sudden barrage fired for another attack on Orsogna by the New Zealanders. "C" Company, and a platoon of "A" Company 7 Cheshire, got on farther, to a position just short of Poggiofiorito, when the Germans sensed them, and shelled the Roman road pretty heavily. By sheer hard work four anti-tank guns were brought forward during the night, partly by carrier and partly by mules; they were in position by first light.

For the whole of the 15th, into the early hours of the 16th, the battalion withstood heavy concentrations of artillery, Spandau, and mortar fire. At about 0400 hrs. three companies of Panzer Grenadiers supported by tanks formed up to counterattack. They had so many casualties on their start line that they finally abandoned the idea. Early on the 17th the enemy withdrew from Poggiofiorito, and "A" Company 2 Northamptons went into the town, while "B" Company moved to the high ground just west of it, where they joined up with the right hand New Zealand company. The battalion mule maintenance problem was not enhanced, at this stage, by the obvious unwillingness of the Italian muleteers to submit themselves to the effective German mortaring. On this day too, Lieutenant Hamer took out the Northampton Fighting Patrol and cleverly brought back some prisoners from 67th Panzer Grenadier Regiment. This was his hundredth patrol since Sicily, and it was suitably recognized with an award of the M.C. Other patrols had confirmed that both Arielli and Canosa were held in strength. At the same time the enemy was doggedly holding on to Ortona, and it appeared that he was acutely conscious of the fact that once Orsogna, Arielli and Ortona went, he would be unable to prevent 8 Army from reaching Pescara, and then wheeling down the road to Rome.

Meantime the 2 RSF were moving up, under shellfire, to relieve the 2 Northamptons and advance through them. So close were they now to the enemy posts that every time they dug the very sound of clinking shovels brought down assorted fire. "D" Company of 2 RSF captured an enemy mortar O.P. intact, who warned them that there were over forty Spandaus only 600 yards ahead down the road. The relief was completed by the 21st, when 2 Northamptons moved back to Lanciano, where they spent a snowy Christmas and actually received some reinforcements from the United Kingdom the day after Boxing Day!

156 Fd Regt had done some considerable firing in support of these battles from positions in the orchards northwest of Lanciano. They had fired over 9,000 rounds between 14th and 20th December at the cost of only a few casualties from enemy counter-bombardment.

It was now decided to relieve 17 Inf Bde with 15 Inf Bde, who had got themselves quietly organized to the rear, expecting a peaceful Christmas. At 0700 hrs. on the 19th, 1 Green Howards arrived in Lanciano, which was under shellfire, and marched straight through to relieve 2 RSF on the Moro. Battalion H.Q. was moved into the village of Colli and the companies forward of the river bed. By now the torrential rain had turned the whole area into a quagmire, and to get forward the soldier had first to slither down a steep bank to the river, wade through, and climb up the other steep bank. The mud was so thick and sticky that it almost sucked

Captain Culverhouse, Intelligence Officer of 2 WILTS, gets some valuable news of the Germans from Guiseppe Patullo of Bojano, through the Brigade Interpreter, L/Corporal Hardusty.

Sergeant Lay marks this information on the map.

A CREDIT TO THE ARMY.—Fusilier Whittle of The Royal Inniskilling Fusiliers whilst on guard consults the mirror installed outside Battalion H.Q. in Isernia. This mirror confronted the men as they came down from fighting in the hills.

ISERNIA.—Sappers supporting 13th Infantry Brigade clearing mines.
Entering Isernia.

2 Cameronians march up to Pt. 1260 near Rionero.

Cameronian Bren Gunners watch a flank on Pt. 1260.

A patrol goes out northwards from Rionero.
Cameronians hold an "O" up near Rionero.

The Divisional Military Police lighting-up clock.

Cypriot mules bring up ammunition and supplies to 15 Infantry Brigade in the mountains around Rionero.

An O.P. of 92nd Field Regiment on Pt. 1260.

The exposed gun positions to the north of Rionero.

After one of the few rainstorms south of Rionero Sergeant Hamilton and Gunner Tennant wring some of the water out of a blanket.

his boots off as he plodded through. The whole area was still pretty regularly shelled and mortared, enough to make the infantry dig their first dugouts in the banks. There were many cases of sheer exhaustion from the continual exposure.

For a fortnight 15 Inf Bde held these positions, 1 Y and L on the right, 1 Green Howards in the centre, and 1 KOYLI on the left, and supply was so difficult that their Christmas fare was confined to cold bully, biscuits and tea. Two or three feet of snow fell immediately after Christmas, and drifts formed up to ten feet high which broke down most of the timber cover to the dugouts. The only alternative to braving the elements now was to make use of sacking and gas capes. The signallers had a particularly bad time; exchange operators had to sit up to their knees in water, whilst lines were continually being cut by shell and mortar fire. The very gallant linesmen, in the most appalling weather conditions and under accurate fire in mined areas, went out time and time again at all hours of the day and night to repair these damaged lines. One such was L/Corporal Hill of 1 Green Howards, who was awarded the M.M. on 30th December when he continued to mend breaks in the line, although wounded, until he was ordered to withdraw. The Gunner O.P. linesmen worked in similar conditions and suffered many casualties in their devotion to duty.

Of one the most notable achievements was the bringing up of more anti-tank guns to deal with the increasing trouble given by enemy tanks, on to the very extended and lightly held sector. This involved taking the guns to pieces, an operation which required ten men to lift the barrel alone. These porters eventually got there staggering a few yards at a time. It was quite out of the question to bring tanks far enough forward, owing to the mud and mines.

All through this period patrolling went on in the most efficient way, and information, as expected by now, was regularly arriving at Div H.Q. On the left the New Zealanders were pounding away at Orsogna. On the night of 23rd/24th December, behind a terrific barrage from all the guns of XIII Corps, and from those of V Corps who could reach, the New Zealanders made a tremendous attack, which only just failed to get them into Orsogna. On their right flank, however, 15 Inf Bde managed to reduce the small town of

Arielli. Farther to the right, the fierce street battles of Ortona were in progress; the Canadians eventually capturing the entire town on 27th December.

Some extracts from Sitreps of the time give an apt picture of the front in a nutshell:

"*23rd December*. 1800 hrs. Sitrep. Seaforth of Canada and Edmonton Regiments gain 300 yards in Ortona. H. & P.E. Regt. estd. at 312150. Tps. 8 Ind. Div. still engaged with enemy in streets of V. Grande. 1 Green Howards attack gains part of objective—held up 400 yards on left—to cross Moro and drive 4 German Para. Div. off road Ortona-Orsogna.

"*24th December*. Div. Arty. fire barrage in sp. N.Z. attack towards Orsogna at 0400 hrs. N.Z. tps. 200 yards short of Orsogna and cas. light. Many enemy dead and wounded found in FOL's Y and L patrol returned from area 265095 and report enemy pl. localities at 265094, 265089 and 265092, with M.G. at 264092.

"*25th December*. Quiet. Little shelling from all sides.

"*26th–27th December*. Quiet. Intermittent shelling.

"*28th December* Y and L at 283086. Green Howards 270070. KOYLI 273054, after relief of 17 Inf Bde.

"*29th December*. 1800 hrs. Sitrep. PPCLI at 324180. Seaforth & Edmonton. Ortona. etc. etc."

This is how Christmas 1943 was spent by most of the division, the only Christmas of the war to be spent in action.

On Boxing Day, however, one of the divisional unit concert parties, "Low Gang" of the 92 Fd Regt, gave two shows during the afternoon, to packed houses of Canadians, Indians and New Zealanders, as well as British troops, in the opera house at Lanciano. Unfortunately the magnificence of this opera house had been somewhat marred by an enemy 17-cm. shell that had removed part of the back of the stage, thus subjecting both performers and audience to such a powerful draught that the show had to be finished in overcoats. Some of the performers left the guns for the performances and went back to them afterwards. It was snowing outside, and German planes attacked the town during one of the performances in spite of the growing ascendancy of the Desert Air Force, amongst which were Australian pilots flying Kittihawks. Those not actually on the Moro front, made the best of their Christmas, and on the whole the enemy respected this feast of

Peace and Goodwill and could be heard singing carols lustily.

13 Inf Bde were scattered partly in reserve and partly holding quieter parts of the line. 2 R INNISKS, on 23rd December, took over part of the Casoli sector in the mountains to the west and came under command of 2 New Zealand Div for a short time, with the 2 Parachute Bde. They had some interesting patrolling in co-operation with Italian guerillas, who produced some valuable information on the whereabouts of the German outposts to the north. 2 Cameronians moved across to Castiglione, some twenty-five miles south of Lanciano, where they patrolled in protection of the left flank of main Div H.Q. On 31st December they lost their Commanding Officer, Lieut.-Colonel E. Brickman, who left to take up another appointment. He had been with the 2 Bn since the outbreak of war, and had been responsible personally for much of their success. Lieut.-Colonel A. M. Finlaison, his previous second-in-command, who was then commanding 2 WILTS, took over 2 Cameronians. 17 Inf Bde were "resting" around Archi, about ten miles behind the New Zealanders, busily scraping mud from their bodies, trucks and equipment.

Snow was now falling fairly frequently and heavily, and those units of the division scattered in the high ground to the left flank were seriously hindered in their movement. Supply routes were closed and some transport was buried under the drifts. On 3rd January these troops had to be put on half rations, and some of these rations were successfully dropped from aircraft the next day. The dominating high ground of Mount Maiella looked more magnificent than ever, particularly with the red winter sun on its snowbound slopes. It had now become as familiar a backcloth as Etna became when the division was on the Catania Plain.

Although there was to be no major movement on the Moro, the drive of the forward positions was fairly fluid, in more senses than one, and there was much artillery fire again, after Christmas. The Gunner O.P.s reported continuously with valuable information, although some of them were in almost too exhausted a condition to hold the microphones of their wireless sets. One typical report was received at 1545 hrs. on the evening of the 31st by the headquarters of one of the regiments: "Infantry patrol has just located a machine gun position in a haystack. Mediums engaged, whereupon haystack moved hurriedly!" The Germans were certainly showing diabolical ingenuity, as well as stubbornness, to hold this vital winter line.

This German resistance and the appalling weather now brought the 8 Army to a standstill, just short of their objective, at the end of the year. Their main superiority over the enemy, in available armour, could not be fully exploited owing to the treacherous state of the ground. There was also some doubt, particularly after a disastrous bombing raid on Bari harbour, that sufficient ammunition to maintain the momentum of the advance could be brought up as and when required. Accordingly it was decided to abandon the right hook manœuvre on to Rome, and 8 Army was now to hold the enemy in a tight grip around Ortona and Orsogna, while the big effort on Rome was to consist of a left hook attack by the United States Fifth Army. To throw in a little extra weight for this, the practically intact 5 Div was to be transferred from the 8 Army to the 5 Army in the conditions of the utmost secrecy.

When it was known that the division was to move, and that small advance parties had already departed for a destination on the west coast of Italy, generally believed to be Naples, rumour became rife once more. Quite genuinely many of the troops believed that the *Queen Mary*, with a suitably inscribed "Y" on her, was even then at anchor in Naples Bay, waiting to rush the division back to the United Kingdom. This surmisal was accentuated by the farewell letter to the Divisional Commander from General Montgomery, himself on the way home to take over 21st Army Group for the attack against Northern Europe. This letter was published and contained the following appreciation of the division:

"I would like to tell you how very sorry I am that the 5th Division is leaving the Eighth Army. During the campaigns in Sicily and Italy the division has fought magnificently, and has played a notable part in the successes that have been achieved. I have always known that any job given to 5th Division would be well and truly done. It is a first-class division in every respect, and I hope we may all meet again soon. Good luck to you all."

To this letter Major-General Bucknall replied suitably, expressing appreciation of General Montgomery's inspiring leadership and expressing an ardent desire to serve under him again.

A further appreciation came from an ex-commander of 13th Brigade, Lieut.-General Dempsey, XIII Corps Commander, who wrote: "We took part in the capture of Sicily together, and together we have successfully invaded the mainland of Europe. During these six months you have shown the world what a fine division you are. Now we part. You take with you my sincere thanks and admiration for all your achievements, and the best wishes of the whole Corps for your continued success."

A further quite unintended and backhanded compliment was later paid to the division by Brigadier Kippenburger in his book *Infantry Brigadier*. Opposite Orsogna at that time he was commanding the 5 New Zealand Bde and was worried about 5 Div's failure to keep up with his battalions. He attributed this to the division's lack of fighting experience, and remarked that when he went to visit Lanciano he was quite defeated by the fact that everyone in sight saluted correctly or marched at attention! It was perfectly true that the division's fighting against the enemy had been limited to short sharp battles since landing in Sicily; but the battle against the elements had been as prolonged and as severe as had been experienced by any division outside Russia. That such impeccable demeanour on the part of its soldiers should be possible after these strenuous efforts, showed that there was little wrong with discipline or morale. That it should distinguish itself as completely in close quarter fighting, was to be only too evident during the next few months with 5 Army. Maybe the New Zealanders were upset that the XIII Corps code name for Orsogna was "Bunfight"!

On 3rd January, 15 Inf Bde were relieved by the 2 Parachute Bde and moved back to the Lanciano area. For the next few days a succession of convoys took the division across from the east to the west coast of Italy via Furci, Termoli, San Severo, Lucera, Cancello, on bad roads much cut up by constant traffic. The tail of the division did not arrive in the Mondragone concentration area until the 11th January.

Before leaving 1943 and the long trek of some 380 miles of 5 Div up Italy, and whilst still thinking of bad road conditions, it is timely to mention the quiet methodical work of the Divisional R.A.S.C., whose unfailing delivery of the goods had always been taken for granted by all ranks. They mastered the many different forms of transport: mules, jeeps and trailers, Dukws, landing-craft and porters, taking them all in their stride. They even organized civilian evacuation where that was necessary, and arranged for delivery of rations from the air, as already mentioned. They themselves would be the first to admit that the indomitable divisional spirit and the mutual confidence between all arms of the service, had made this smooth running possible; but neither of those happy qualities would have been of use without their particularly excellent and flexible organization, backed by sound training. This enabled them to maintain the momentum of the advance by means of a series of Divisional Maintenance Areas: miniature reproductions of the Corps Maintenance Areas. In these D.M.A. were seldom held more than four days' stocks, except for specially dumped ammunition. Fortunately there was adequate transport to keep up with the infantry, who were partly marching and partly riding, sometimes in boats as well as in vehicles. These vehicles were efficiently maintained, and only very rarely did the correct number fail to arrive as ordered. The two troops of mules who supported 15 Inf Bde's initial mountain excursion around Bagnara in the first days of September were not needed until the division passed through the Canadians north of Campobasso. They kept up with the division the whole way, however, at their own speed, although, at times, they were actually many miles behind the leading troops.

The division certainly had reason to be thankful for its R.A.S.C. and Sappers during this long advance. Any critic of the speed of movement of 5 Div in the autumn and winter of 1943 should have been there to see the almost superhuman efforts made by every member of a truly magnificent team.

Having chased the elusive enemy half-way up Italy, in the most appalling conditions, the soldiers of 5 Div were now about to come to close quarters with the magnificent defensive fighting of Kesselring's German divisions, on the west coast, with General Mark Clark's 5 Army.

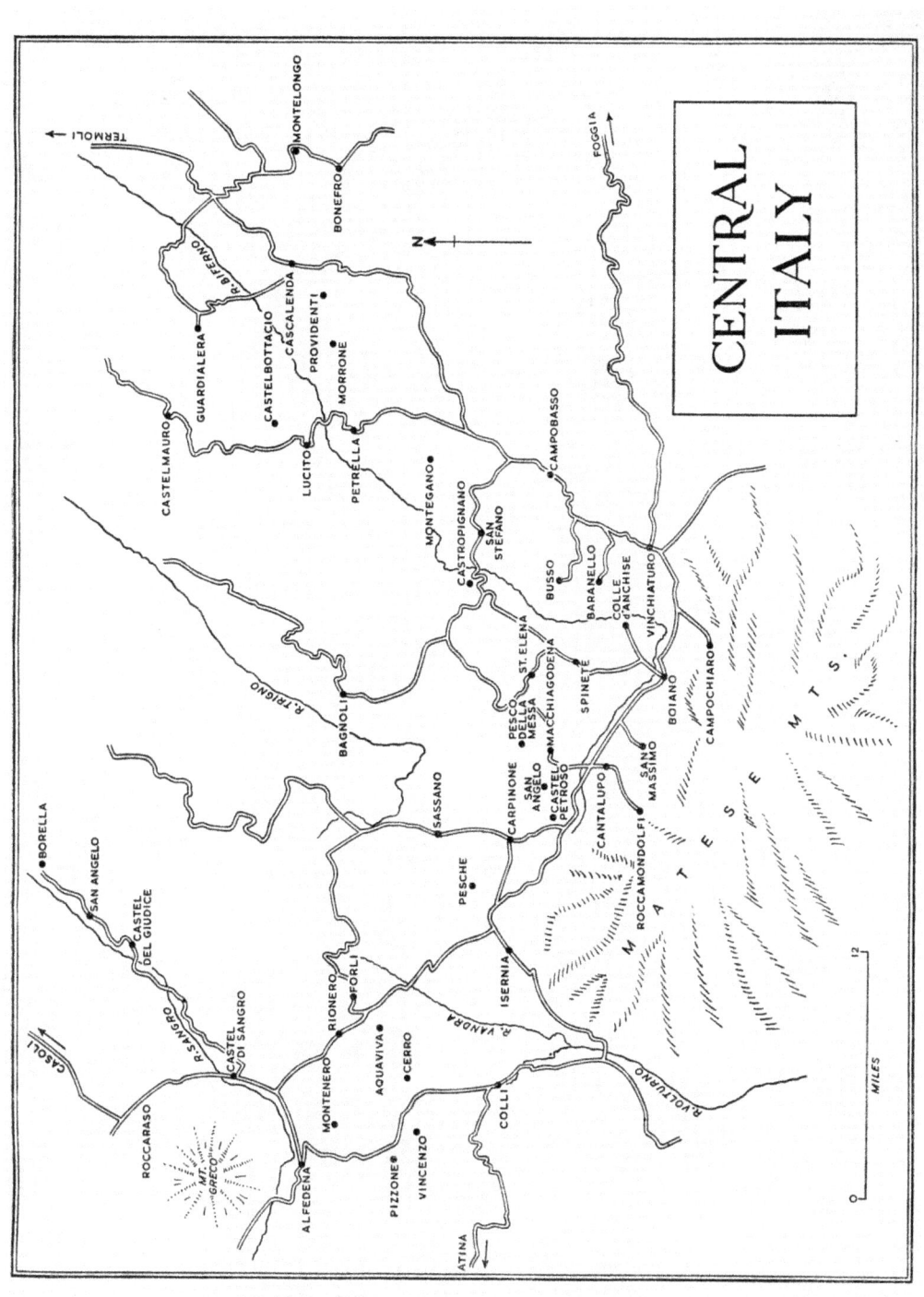

CHAPTER ELEVEN

CROSSING THE GARIGLIANO RIVER

In which 5th Division now transferred from the Adriatic Front of Eighth Army to the Fifth Army north of Naples, attacks the Hitler Winter Line across the Garigliano River. In which a small, uncomfortable bridgehead is held successfully against vicious counter attacks.

The Setting and the Plan
Several attempts had been made by 5 Army to dislodge the enemy from the Hitler Winter Line. Many fierce battles had been fought between the Volturno and Garigliano Rivers; the latter river, well covered by superb German positions in the mountains, had proved too strong for the battle tired Divisions of General Mark Clark's Army. By mid-December it had become obvious that the projected 8 Army advance from the Adriatic, which had been directed on Rome from the Pescara-Chieti flank, had become bogged down in the difficult terrain to the north of Ortona and Lanciano.

At this stage, robbed of any possible reserves, all of which were now wanted for "Overlord" in N.W. Europe, A.F.H.Q. at Caserta decided to switch to a left hook whilst 8 Army held tightly on the Adriatic front. Among the most important contributions to 21 Army Group was General Montgomery, who left after Christmas; soon afterwards, several divisions moved from 8 Army to 5 Army. 5 Div was among those that transferred their allegiance, to be allotted the difficult task of forcing the crossing of the Garigliano at its wide mouth and under the very eyes of the enemy. This was to be part of the assault by General McCreery's X Corps whilst the II (United States) Corps attacked in the mountains to its north. On the immediate right of X Corps was 46 Div with the French Expeditionary Force farther to the right again.

When both these Corps had advanced far enough thoroughly to commit Kesselring's reserves, the United States VI Corps was to land in the Anzio-Nettuno area to exert rear and flank pressure on the German Southern Army and thus open up the famous Appian Way to Rome.

The scene of this river crossing was to be where Highway 7 and the main Rome-Naples railway line cross the river around Minturno. Now a small town in the foothills, this was once Minturnae and near it there are ruins of an ancient amphitheatre and aqueduct. Here was the place of exile of Gaius Marius who hid himself among the rushes of the river and thus escaped from the barbarians sent to kill him.

Caesar founded a fashionable colony here and, much later in 1504, Gonsalvo di Cordova finally defeated the French in these same marshes.

The River Garigliano was to be crossed between Monte Casteluccia and the sea. It was a difficult obstacle offering poor lines of communication and was completely dominated by the German positions to the north of it, not only by observation, but by the excellent fields of fire offered by the flat plain. Two brigades of the 94 German Infantry Division were holding the high ground around Minturno and Castelforte, with active outposts patrolling down to the river line and, in certain cases, to the south of it. Any permanent positions to the south of the river had been cleared some time before the attack.

The plan of X Corps was to cross on a four-brigade front with 56 Div on the right, directed on Castleforte and Monte Damiano, whilst 5 Div on the left assaulted Minturno and Tufo. All four brigades were to establish a Corps bridgehead some seven miles deep.

5 Div were to make use of landing craft round the river mouth and to exploit up the valley of the River Ausente, a tributary running due north from the Garigliano and serving as an inter-divisional boundary, to secure the San Giorgio defile. The river was wide and fast flowing around the blown bridges of Highway 7 and the railway, making the bridging problem, particularly under fire, a difficult one; boats of all sizes and shapes were to be fully utilized. 210 Guards Bde were put under command of 5 Div and 40 Royal Tanks were split between 5 and 56 Divs. The latter had 40 Royal Marine Commando under command to tackle the slopes of Monte Damiano. In the actual assault all available Artillery was to fire a programme in support of 56 Div whilst 5 Div were to cross the river in silence. Naval and Air support were to

A Green Howards Patrol in the Casoli sector.

Men of 5 Recce hang out their washing in the ruined amphitheatre outside Minturno.

THE LINK WITH HOME.—The home letter and home news supplied an unshakable link wherever the Division went.

be used mainly to isolate the battlefield. Further help in this direction was to be contributed by 46 Div, farther to the right, in the form of a "Chinese" attack.

56 Div had fought with X Corps since the Salerno Landing but the arrival of the 5 Div, on this front, was to be treated with great security; and once more the "Y" temporarily disappeared to be replaced by a cryptic "7". The Division's sector was lightly patrolled by an 'ad hoc' force made up from 56 Recce Regt. and known as Hicks Force. When the road signs showing a white "7" on a black ground were planted by the Provost, a member of that force solemnly declared to an officer of the 2 Northants that he didn't know of this 7 Div., but he was pretty well certain that no one would get over that river until 5 Div arrived! That sentiment was later to be endorsed by the hard pressed Americans at Anzio who are alleged to have uttered the plea, "Praise the Lord and send the Fifth Division!"

To ensure that this security was maintained, any pre-battle preparations in the assembly area had to be worked guardedly, by night by troops moved up from their bases between Naples and the Massico feature. This particularly applied to the preparation of the gun positions which had to be sited in full view of the enemy. Gun pits had to be dug and much ammunition to be dumped.

The operation was to be carried out in two or three phases. The first, the assault of the river by 13 and 17 Inf Bdes and the securing of a Divisional bridgehead in the foothills on the northern end of the plain. The second phase was the exploitation and expanding of this bridgehead by the 15 and 201 Guards Bdes passing through the other two brigades respectively. 17 Inf Bde on the left were to make use of beach landing around the mouth of the river and from their positions in Tremonsuoli and Minturno, 201 Guards Bde were to exploit to the Scauri feature, whilst to the right of them 15 Inf Bde were to advance up the Ausente Valley, from 13 Inf Bde positions in the hills around Tufo, securing St. Maria Infanta and the Bracchi feature.

Behind this apparently simple plan, an exceedingly difficult series of brigade and battalion operations presented themselves; one for which the odds had been openly allowed of five to one against the crossing being achieved. It is worth noting that a senior officer who lost his money on this transaction declared that had he been aware that it was 5 Div who were to tackle it, he would have allowed far less generous odds!

Within each brigade the operation was further subdivided into two main phases, the first was a two battalion assault of the river and the second a follow through by the third battalion to the foothills as already indicated. On the left, 17 Inf Bde planned for RSF, on the extreme left, to make a sea landing north of the river in D.U.K.W.s whilst the Seaforth arrived in assault boats near the blown Ponte Fiume on the Appian Way. Northants were then to pass through to the high ground. On the right both the WILTS and the R INNISKS were to cross in assault boats and the Cameronians were to pass through. The first phase of each was timed for 2100 hrs. before the moon rose, with no Artillery support. The second phase was timed to start at 0330 hrs. supported by a barrage.

The enemy although not formidable in numbers held an almost ideal defensive position. The German 94 Inf Div was holding the Gustav Line from Scauri to Damiano —well dug in, 12 ft. deep, with all available comforts; even hot breakfast was captured intact by one of the battalions during the battle.

Barely ten days separated the move of the Division into 5 Army, and the attack. A great deal of preparation was achieved in that time from concentration areas out of view of the enemy, behind the Massico feature, famed for its vineyards. The assaulting battalions practised boating on the Volturno, the scene of a previous X Corps crossing assault. Special sleds were knocked together for getting forward anti-tank guns and scaling ladders, and other unorthodox paraphernalia were improvised out of local materials.

The engineer bridging problem on the Divisional Front was a major one. It was planned to use:—

> Two assault boat rafts, Class 2.
> Two pneumatic float rafts, Class 2.
> Five tracked rafts, Class 2.
> Nine shore loading rafts, Class 2.
> Forty Bailey pontoon rafts, Class 1.
> Nine folding boat bridges, Class 2.

Intensive study was made of air photos and patrol reports, to gain the best possible advance information. Sapper reconnaissance was made from planes at heights between 300–500 ft. and Sappers accompanied specially arranged patrols.

Yet time was found for relaxation in Naples and, for the first time, most members of the Division saw the famous Bay backed by that "peak of hell, rising out of paradise" as Goethe described Vesuvius. Quite a few were disappointed to find that the liner *Queen Mary* with a large "Y" painted on her funnels was not, as rumour had had it, waiting with steam up to take them home to England. They were comforted by the fact that it would undoubtedly be waiting at the mouth of the Tiber near Ostia when they got that far!

The Night of 17th/18th January

On the extreme left of 5 Army Front, 2 RSF set off from the seashore just north of Mondragrone to land on the north bank of the river between the estuary and the Argento feature: the latter being a prominent mound that dominated the whole of the front of 17 Inf Bde. The Fusiliers were to land in two waves; the first, consisting of "A" and "B" companies, was to seize and hold the Argento feature, the second, consisting of "C" and "D" Companies, sailing half an hour later, was to go through them and secure the features known as Pt. 141 and Pt. 156 to the north-east of Minturno.

It was a very dark night and the currents of the fast moving river made navigation round the mouth exceedingly difficult. The D.U.K.W.s were manned by American crews who were relying on landing lights that materialized too late to be of much use; the phosphorescence of the sea stirred up by the boats must have been obvious to the Germans, who brought down accurate defensive artillery fire on the D.U.K.W.s when they were some 200 yards from the water line. For all these reasons the ultimate landing was somewhat confused and the first to land was a detachment of 141 Field Ambulance with Major Houchin of the Northamptons, and a small stores party. Later a 6-pounder detachment of 2 RSF complained that these store dumps obscured their fields of fire. Of the main body, a party of RSF and A Coy 7 Cheshire (Major E. G. S. Mather) were landed south of the estuary and almost attacked their own Bde HQ. One D.U.K.W. went so far out to sea that it came into contact with a cruiser then busily shelling the German positions across the Gulf of Gaeta. Quite lost, they were just about to hail the Navy for instructions when a submarine surfaced alongside the D.U.K.W.s. Uncertain of its nationality the Fusiliers manned their Piat and were about to sink it when a head popped out of the conning tower and shouted:

"Who the hell are you?"

"Royal Scots Fusiliers," was the prompt and somewhat relieved reply.

"Never heard of you," was an even prompter rejoinder as the hatch closed and the submarine submerged.

Thus the start of operations on the left was inauspicious and nothing appeared to go to plan. When "C" and "D" Companies landed, unaware that Argento was still in enemy hands, they managed to get a footing on a small sandy ridge some twenty yards from the sea, but as the two companies moved forward they suffered many casualties in the minefield the explosions from which brought down a hail of spurting fire from the Argento feature, where, according to the battalion plan, there should have been a platoon of "B" company. This was quickly and efficiently silenced by a concentration from the Div Arty. "D" company then moved along the beach to secure the feature only to run into "A" company who had at last found the beach after their cruise out to sea. Despite accurate artillery support, "D" company failed to make much progress. The Sappers could not be found to help clear the mines and the battalion had only two mine detectors; there was no sign of 6 Seaforth who should have been on the right, but the three companies that had landed, and Bn H.Q., managed to clear a narrow lane through the main minefield through which they advanced with caution. By first light they had only penetrated to a depth of 1,000 yds. and were somewhat bunched around cross tracks. Argento, however, was still in enemy hands after three vain but glorious attacks from "D" company. Then the missing "B" company arrived, having landed on quite the wrong beach. Very soon afterwards "D" company managed to get on to Argento and a much depleted battalion sat down in an extremely uncomfortable position, to hold on to the precarious bridgehead it had so hardly won.

In fact the whole of 17 Inf Bde (Brigadier Dudley Ward, later General Sir Dudley Ward, G.C.B., K.B.E., D.S.O.)

were in an extremely difficult position; they had lost so many men that they were now hard put to it to hold the triangle between the Appian Way, the River Garigliano and the sea.

To the right of 2 RSF, 6 Seaforth had planned to cross the river at Pontefiume by the blown bridge, ferried across by "B" company of 2 Northamptons. This was eventually achieved, at great loss, as a result of heavy defensive shellfire, and by 0200 hrs., with but eight serviceable boats left, each of which was limited to an Infantry section, the Northamptons were only just about to take over "D" company 6 Seaforth (Major R. C. R. Roche).

The north bank was riddled with anti-personel mines, so concentrated that the battalion's taping was quite inadequate. The Germans were undoubtedly expecting the main attack around Pontefiume. They had the minefields well covered by Spandaus firing on fixed lines, and mortar defensive fire, and were able to mount a strong counterattack against 6 Seaforth. The latter, without any information of the whereabouts of 2 RSF, found themselves so pinned down that they were unable to secure the start lines for 2 Northamptons' Phase II attack, by the planned time of 0400 hrs.

The counterattacks against 2 RSF and 6 Seaforth continued until first light when the whole of 2 Northamptons, less "B" company, who dug in on the south bank, had been ferried across the river into the shallow bridgehead. At first light further discomforts were added by observed enemy shellfire restricted in intensity only by the shortage of ammunition available to the German gunners. Targets were nevertheless easily presented by the movement of the long rushes around the northern bank, and the still frequent explosions of mines. Pockets of enemy remained on the plain and tanks were used by them with comparative impunity; the only anti-tank defence available to the brigade was provided by their own Piats, the guns of 52 ATk Regt, R.A., having been landed on the wrong side of the river.

There were many incidents and stories of the crossings made of that wide and swirling river; one of the best was told of Major Bates, Commander of 593 Bty supporting 2 RSF and their Commanding Officer, Lieut.-Colonel McInnes. When the forward company had arrived, these two distinguished officers stepped into a rubber assault boat and seizing the paddles lost no time in striking out furiously. Remembering his Cambridge days, Major Bates exhorted the Battalion Commander to "Take the time from me. Right. In—Out. In—Out!" To their consternation, however, black as the night undoubtedly was, it was apparent that they were not making much headway. Undismayed and remarking that the current was obviously strong in that stretch of water, the gallant Major continued to shout "In—Out. In—Out." Yet still they remained in the same position until at last he turned round to see that their boat was still securely tied to the bank!

Assault boating also provided excitement farther to the right, on 13 Inf Bde's crossings. 2 WILTS crossing, to the east of the railway bridge, was the most successful. A few casualties were caused by mortar defensive fire. By a few minutes past midnight they had got all save one of their companies over the river and were forging ahead towards the foothills. Their advance was only halted by 13 Inf Bde when it was seen that 2 R INNISKS were seriously delayed by sunk boats. They eventually reported on their objective for Phase I at 0455 hrs., and the second phase was postponed until 0530 hrs.

Supported by the Div Arty, 2 WILTS reached the lateral road from Castleforte to Minturno, by first light, and crossed it into the foothills soon afterwards. "B" company on the right reached point 201 by 0800 hrs. They were counterattacked very sharply, however, and had to withdraw to the high ground to the east of Tufo.

2 R INNISKS had a check to their assault at the outset. When "D" company (Major Bradley) arrived on the river bank some time before zero, they found no boats there for them. The porters who were to have brought them forward from their hiding places took the wrong turning. These were being brought up by the reserve battalion, 2 Cameronians. After a frantic rush two boats were brought across the fields just as the barrage in support of 56 Div started, at 2100 hrs. Captain Long with a small party immediately used them to secure Epitaffio Farm, as an initial bridgehead. This party had a sharp fight to gain the farm, but, an hour later, Major Grant's "A" company were able to start ferrying across its leading platoons. By now all surprise had gone and they were heavily shelled both in their assembly area, and on the banks of the river itself. Mortar fire was particularly effective and many

dead and wounded were lying in both areas; furthermore, most of their boats had been holed and were in a sinking condition.

Soon after midnight the Commanding Officer, Lieut-Colonel O'Brien Twohig, with Major Bradley, went to see if the crossing of 2 WILTS was more feasible. There they found things quieter and the crossing going smoothly with several boats still water-worthy. They ordered "B" company of the 2 R INNISKS to move up, use 2 WILTS boats and then to move sharply right to join the planned forming up place. It soon became obvious that it would be impossible to be ready for the second phase by the original time of 0330 hrs. By 0100 hrs., with practically all 2 WILTS across (their support company, the last, being in process of crossing) only one company of 2 R INNISKS across, and that having had a very sharp battle, 13 Inf Bde Headquarters ordered Phase II and its barrage to be postponed for ninety minutes. It is interesting to note that this message was actually transmitted through artillery communications. From 91 Fd Regt whose Commanding Officer was with the Bde Comd (Brigadier Campbell) it went to 92 Fd Regt who, for the crossings, were supporting 2 WILTS and who had set up a forward telephone exchange near the river bank. This method was to be almost the only sure way of controlling progress across the river for some time.

By 0200 hrs. 2 R INNISKS had Bn HQ and two companies over by using 2 WILTS boats, and completed their crossing by 0300 hrs. Major Grant, with a very depleted "A" company, attacked with the bayonet on the right flank against the strongly held group of buildings at Massa Rossi. Murderous mortar fire killed Major Grant and four German prisoners he had acquired. Company Headquarters now consisted of two signallers. The only remaining officer, Lieutenant Fleming, was seriously wounded a few minutes later. L/Sergeant Banton now found himself in command; he collected the remnants, reorganized them, and by outstanding personal and courageous leadership, carried the farm buildings and formed a defensive position which was never retaken. There were twenty survivors from the whole company. Zero hour for Phase II was then fixed for 0530 hours and the fire plan started at that hour, with "B" and "C" leading. "B" company (Major Nixon) almost immediately ran into a minefield and suffered a score of casualties. "C" company (Major Blake) were more lucky. Bn HQ, however, caught the full attack of the enemy counter-shelling. One shell killed the adjutant, the R.M.O., some artillery and battalion signallers and a runner. The Commanding Officer and many others were wounded. Dawn was now breaking and the barrage was behaving exactly as required. 2 R INNISKS struggled on against powerful small arms and artillery fire, and eventually by noon, had got a foothold some 800 yards in depth.

The 18th

The B.B.C. news of the 18th contained the following extract:—

"In a new attack by British Troops in Italy, the crossing of the Garigliano River has been made, an entry in the main defences of the Gustav Line."

Dawn certainly revealed the Division to be in a very uncomfortable and delicate position, recalling to memory a similar river crossing over the Simeto river in Sicily which took place six months past, almost to the day. Fortunately a ground mist limited visibility in the early hours of the 18th, an advantage denied in Sicily.

17 Inf Bde were in the most exposed position, being pinned down by mines and small-arms fire to the flat plain around the river mouth. They would have suffered much more had pressure not been relieved by the advance of 13 Inf. Bde. soon to be followed up by 15 Inf Bde. Brigadier Dudley-Ward and the Commanding Officer found it hard to contact the battalions, and on their way to 6 Seaforth were fired on from a strong outpost position which had to receive a special attack from No. 9 Platoon of "A" company, 2 Northamptons, led by Sergeant Bell, who received the D.C.M. as a reward. This was a model platoon operation. The outpost which had been left behind as an island during the night, gave up no less than five M.G. 34s, seven prisoners of war, several dead, two wounded British soldiers, after a fierce battle, whose end was signalled at 1000 hrs. by the simple message "Strong point ours".

The minefield meanwhile proved a very extensive obstacle and many wounded Seaforth were retrieved and evacuated. "A" company 2 Northamptons had to be supplied by using two Wellington Bomber rescue boats which were found booby trapped in the amphitheatre ruins on the Appian Way near by. They must have been found by German patrols moving south of the river before the crossing.

The Divisional Commander realizing that 17 Inf Bde could go no farther in the circumstances and that Minturno would have to be attacked from the right, ordered 2 Cameronians who had got two companies in reserve, to close up more to the left towards Minturno in support of the hard pressed 2 WILTS fighting for Tufo. In haste "A" and "B" companies of the Cameronians under the direction of Major R. O. Mitchell ("B" company) attacked Tufo unsuccessfully and Major Wishart of "A" company died next day of wounds received in the attack. These two companies remained under Command of 2 WILTS on their left.

It was now clear that although the river had been successfully crossed, the bridgehead was dangerously shallow. Only on the extreme right of the Division were the planned objectives secure; 2 R INNISKS were on the heights to the east of Tufo. In fact, nowhere on the whole Corps front were the forward elements far enough forward.

The 2 R INNISKS had made a rapid recovery after their delay at the river bank. With "A" company initially a loss at Massa Rossi, "D" company somewhere to the rear; "B" company somewhere well ahead but out of touch; "C" company were left to take the battalion objective, although they were joined by "B" company for the final assault. They ran into a further minefield soon after—a minefield that by a miracle caused no ill to "C" company. Their ultimate success was due almost certainly to very skilled use of a first-class artillery barrage. In the First World War, troops had learned to "lean on the barrage"—it was not a practice much resorted to in the Second World War. It was well this was done as the Germans were deeply dug in and had little time to come out to meet the bloodthirsty bayonets of the Irishmen. The two companies cleared about half a mile on the ridge east of Tufo, a salient which was to relieve much pressure on the rest of the Division during those difficult hours that were to follow.

Much had now to be done to retrieve the position. On the left in 17 Inf Bde area, a smoke screen was quickly generated. 2 WILTS in the centre made special watch of their open left flank and everything possible was done on both sides of the river to meet the inevitable counterattack. The first marked one appeared at about 1100 hrs., after it had been observed to be coming up to the west of Tufo about an hour previously. It was not a well co-ordinated attack and was easily broken up by the battalion and the Divisional Artillery.

"A" class Navy ferries were now being operated across the river but the building of the larger bridge near the demolition was proving a difficult task, being under direct observation of the enemy until an artificial smoke screen was generated around it.

The Divisional Commander now decided that he could do no more until the original objectives of 17 Inf Bde, around Minturno and Tremonsuoli had been secured. This he could only achieve by using the reserve brigade. Accordingly he planned that 15 Inf Bde should cross the river on the following night, at 2200 hrs., pass through 2 WILTS' positions and advance westwards in the early hours of the 19th.

Meanwhile, sporadic incidents occurred all over the front. The gunners soon claimed direct hits on some tanks that tried to infiltrate around 2 WILTS who went on to finish them off with Piats. 2 WILTS during that attack, received two enemy ambulances which reported to their Regimental Aid Post in error and were detained.

In the late afternoon the Cameronians made an unsuccessful bid to take over point 201 but received very heavy mortaring which spread along the whole front and heralded a further and probably more organized counterattack. This series of counter-attacks lasted for almost an hour and a half, from 1800 hrs. to 1930 hrs., and was only finally beaten off when the enemy had nearly overrun O.P.s and forward positions. Most credit must go, as it had already done, and will continue to, to the solid steel wall of defensive Artillery fire that was invariably put round our positions when they were being counterattacked. No infantrymen in the Division need feel ashamed or would be unprepared to acknowledge that the gunners probably held the small Garigliano bridgehead when called to do so at frequent intervals. So frequent were these demands for this that the Divisional Artillery fired practically unceasingly for many days, a feat it was later to repeat at Anzio.

It was obvious that the enemy realized the instability of the bridgehead and would make further persistent attempts to dislodge the hard pressed battalions of 13 Inf Bde. An enemy wireless message was intercepted at that time from 274 Inf Regt of the 94 Inf Div who reported to their division "Enemy in Tufo and we are being shelled intensively. Request objective counterattack." This message was timed for 1700 hrs. and throws interesting light on the highly centralized control exercised by the Germans.

Again the Gunner communication was used by Brigadier Campbell to instruct 2 WILTS to hold on at all costs and if pushed off the ridge, to get back again.

2 WILTS spent most of the afternoon of the 18th in hand-to-hand fighting in the village of Tufo. Two reserve companies of 2 Cameronians went through them to try and hold point 201 but were driven back by heavy and accurate mortar fire.

Later on in the early evening three German tanks attacked the 2 WILTS positions just below Tufo shelling them on the 102 feature but the Piats of the Cameronians compelled them to withdraw.

Meanwhile Brigadier Martin was preparing to get his 15th Brigade over the river that night for the attack planned by the Divisional Commander, and a warning went out at 0130 hrs. that the barrage in support of that attack was to be fired at 1000 hrs.; the necessary replenishment of field-gun ammunition was already under way.

The night was a quieter one for the exhausted troops of 13 and 17 Inf Bdes but was not without its alarms and excursions. At 0440 hrs. it was reported that the enemy were again coming up for a counterattack in the Tufo area, but this never materialized.

19th January

The plan of 15 Inf Bde was to advance through 2 WILTS positions with 1 KOYLI on the right and 1 Green Howards on the left, the latter directed on to Minturno itself. 1 Y and L were in reserve and there was a very strong artillery barrage, moving from east to west, arranged in support from 0956 hrs. to 1130 hrs. This was to include all the guns of the Corps artillery that could be brought to bear. The crossing and advance through 2 WILTS' positions went without incident and 1 Green Howards reported at 1030 hrs. that the forward elements of "C" company (Major Radcliffe) were entering Minturno against only moderate opposition and that their casualties had been slight; "A" company (Major Gosden) followed close behind and took over the north-east corner of the town, "B" company (Major Tanner) bringing up the rear. At the same time 1 KOYLI had reached point 141, their objective and were in the process of completing a "job of mopping up".

The advance continued slowly with 1 Green Howards moving up towards point 141 and 1 KOYLI reporting "Tufo clear after fighting; small counterattack now beaten off. Few casualties. Damage to enemy not yet known. Time of origin 1223." Both battalions were helped or hindered by a heavy mist over the whole front, caused partly by the warmth of the sun on the river, and partly by the haze of cordite from the intensive shell fire of the past few hours. That the latter was effective was confirmed by both battalions who reported "quite a number of enemy dead after barrage".

It was apparent that the enemy, until the arrival of reinforcements, could only mount small local counterattacks and that full advantage must now be taken of the situation. Unfortunately throughout the Divisional Front casualties were being caused by mines and booby trapped obstacles and these had to be cleared as they were slowing down the advance. 15 Inf Bde had received several casualties from mines on the verges of the road as they moved up during the night.

The Seconds in Command of 91 and 156 Fd Regts (Major L. M. Buffey, M.C., later Lieut.-Colonel L. M. Buffey, M.C., T.D. and Major E. J. H. Bates, M.C., later Colonel E. J. H. Bates, O.B.E., M.C.) went down to reconnoitre positions for their guns near the main Minturno-Castelforte road. Both gun areas were very vulnerable and exposed to enemy observation so they tossed a coin on the level crossing at Tab Cinquanta. 91st won and took first choice, just out of sight of the Castelforte area and Damiano O.P.s. These new positions produced technical probems of gunnery, as the forward troops were less than 2,000 yards away with a fairly high ridge of hills in between. This meant that the infantry might expect the odd shell to land amongst them, a risk they were always prepared to take.

By the end of the 19th, the Minturno-Tufo ridge was secure against anything but the most formidable counterattack from a reinforced enemy. The casualties sustained by the Division in getting so far were, however, by no means light and, even with the assistance of 201 Guards Bde, as yet uncommitted there appeared to be little possibility of achieving the planned exploitation up the Ausente Valley.

The night of the 19th was spent in planning and preparing for a further attack by 15 Inf Bde on the following day—and in active patrolling to gain information for that attack. It was at this stage that the C.R.A. made the momentous decision that some of the guns at least must move across the river to be able to work more deeply into the enemy country. Their present positions although well concealed were in an open plain and to move forward they had to cross open ground for most of the way.

It was decided that 91 Fd Regt (Lieut.-Colonel Hendley) should move down first, and that 92 Fd Regt (Lieut.-Colonel Kirwan) should fire a smoke haze to screen them, as they moved, from O.P.s on Damiano. The move was to be followed by a similar one for 156 Fd Regt (Lieut.-Colonel Osmond) and eventually 92nd were to join the other two regiments in the new areas south of the lateral road that ran along the bottom of the Minturno-Tufo ridge. This last move was cancelled when it became impracticable to make the bridgehead deeper.

Patrols in the early part of the night reported little signs of the enemy but it was decided to proceed with the full fire plan for the attack next morning.

Just before midnight the carriers of 2 R INNISKS, together with extra ammunition and spare wireless batteries, were rafted across the river.

The 20th

The weather held and it was still possible to take advantage of the early morning mists and the fact that any sun shone directly into the eyes of the German O.P.s.

The 15 Inf Bde plan to exploit westwards was carried out in two parts. First 1 Y and L attacked on the right towards the Natale feature. Here all went smoothly and fifty prisoners were taken; this was increased to 150 for the loss of only two wounded. The battalions were held up continuously, however, in the final stages of the attack.

The second part of the plan followed at 1100 hrs., when 1

Green Howards attacked Tremonsuoli on the left and point 110 on the right with "B" and "C" companies respectively behind a barrage. This entailed moving down a very steep valley in front of Minturno and up again to the near ridge upon which were the objectives. In view of the exposure of the Battalion, 98 Self Propelled Regt (Surrey and Sussex Yeomanry) who were under command of 5 Div, laid smoke to indicate the target of Santa Maria to air bombers. During this advance they were mortared. They were also bombed by their own planes. They achieved their objective by noon, after some heavy fighting in Tremonsuoli, for which Major Tanner was awarded the M.C.

This now left 1 Green Howards in an uncomfortable salient in which they were allowed little rest from shell and bomb until relieved the following day. 1 KOYLI, who had collected ten prisoners during this battle, were ordered to straighten out their posts to conform with the gains of the Green Howards, with their own local fire plan.

The enemy now reacted strongly and shelled the whole brigade area. At 1530 hrs. they counterattacked in about a company strength but they were soon repelled by the usual means and with many casualties. Their retreat was harassed effectively by Divisional Artillery concentrations.

That night, 201 Guards Bde were moved up to relieve 15 Inf Bde's extended front. Most of the night was spent in exchanges of artillery and mortar fire and very active patrolling all along the front.

It had been a day of fluctuating fortunes with nobody quite getting the ground they wanted for stability. The field ambulances were kept busy doing some fine work; particularly a light section of 164 Fd Amb which was established right up close to point 102. During the day 13 Inf Bde H.Q. established themselves in the quarry, a pronounced landmark on the river side of the Tufo ridge, a rendezvous later to house many more headquarters.

21st January

Soon after first light four enemy aircraft, the first seen for some time flew in from the sea and lightly bombed Minturno. At this time 5 COLDM GDS were relieving 1 Green Howards. There was still a confused situation on all battalion fronts and 1 KOYLI reported that the enemy appeared to hold the Natale feature with many machine guns. Enemy patrols were still active and it looked as though another counterattack could be expected on the left flank. A small counterattack was later repulsed; 1 KOYLI got up on to Natale, killed a sniper and captured another. The 91 Fd Regt made a dash for their new area and were able to get in quite a lot of digging before the enemy reacted with counter battery fire.

In the afternoon, enemy artillery activity heralded a further counterattack from the direction of Natale; this was once more very effectively broken up by the Div Arty. To what extent was laconically described by Major Price, Commander 368 Battery with 1 KOYLI, who reported "The Boche caught no mean packet." Farther to the left of Minturno, however, the depleted 1 Y and L were having a difficult time and the Green Howards only just relieved by 5 COLDM GDS, sent their "A" and "C" companies across to help. The latter company put in a quick counterattack under command of 1 Y and L, but were forced to abandon it under heavy pressure.

By now it was certain that the depleted 94 Div had been augmented by the arrival of 90 Light Div and was trying hard to drive a wedge into the Divisional Front by pressing through Minturno to the river. All the afternoon repeated attempts were made to hammer in 1 Y and L positions, and by 0200 hrs. the positions were still very insecure. In the temporary absence of the Brigade Commander who was involved somewhere or other in the thick of the fighting, the Brigade Major, Major F. W. de Butts, alerted and moved 1 Green Howards into a longstop position and contrived to get a battalion of 201 Guards Bde. facing the same way. This was to be the peak of the enemy's efforts and he was within an ace of achieving his aim.

Mention must be made here of 17 Inf Bde which faded out of the picture after their landing round the river mouth. Surrounded by mines they were firmly pinned down. The Sappers were devoting all their effort to completing the Class 9 bridge under great difficulty and with many casualties. This bridge was started on the 19th under the great handicap of coverless exposure to enemy fire. On the 20th, construction was partly covered by smoke and little interference as a result. It was finally completed by 1830 hrs. on the same day and work began immediately on clearance and reconstruction of the railway bridge to the north of Highway 7, which it was intended to develop as a road. 17 Inf Bde reported they could follow the fortunes and misfortunes of 15 Inf Bde from their enfilade position by observing where the various barrages and other fire plans landed on the ground. Plans were now made to relieve them and use them to help enlarge the front around 15 Inf Bde's sector. 11 KRRC came under Command of Division for this purpose and took over the Argento sector from 17 Inf Bde.

22nd January

The alarums and excursions died down as night fell, but both sides patrolled actively throughout the night. Patrols from 13 Inf Bde reported that the enemy was preparing a large scale attack against the Tufo area and sure enough, at first light, preceded by a heavy artillery and mortar bombardment, he launched a sharp attack that overran "A" company of 2 WILTS, forcing them to give up about 200 yards of valuable ground. The Company Commander (Captain Clarke) together with his F.O.O. (Captain Plant of the 91 Fd Regt), and a platoon, went forward immediately to restore the position but they were likewise overrun. Captain Plant called for D.F. fire on to their positions and most of the party were extricated, but the two captains themselves were shot up and taken prisoner. Whilst they were receiving attention from a German medical orderly, a heavy concentration from the Divisional Artillery came down on to point 201. This forced the enemy to withdraw and abandon their two prisoners who managed to struggle back to the main positions. A successful counterattack was made by 2 Cameronians who secured point 201 for good.

To the right of 2 WILTS, 2 R INNISKS had been having a comparatively quiet time, for once. They had planned in great detail the original second phase attack on the Bracchi feature and had, as always, shown their mastery of the preliminary patrol work involved. They explored into the vacant Ausente Valley and were able to confirm that 56 Div, on the right of 5 Div, and across the other side of the valley, were not in fact firmly on Damiano, as they had originally claimed to be. This accounted for the accurate shelling of Divisional gun positions and of the traffic moving along and up to the main

Major-General P. G. S. Gregson-Ellis, C.B., O.B.E.

Minturno-Castelforte road, which they could plainly see from their O.P.s on the top.

On the extreme left of the sector 2 Northamptons, then under command of 13 Inf Bde, came into Divisional reserve and moved up into the foothills of the Minturno-Tufo Ridge to reconnoitre a counter attack on to point 156. This counter-attack plan was later cancelled. They remained dug in, and suffered only a few casualties from heavy shell fire. In the evening a few lonely enemy bombers added to their temporary discomfort.

On 15 Inf Bde Front, where 1 Green Howards were planning an attack to restore the position, the enemy forestalled them and launched a counterattack into 1 KOYLI at 0700 hrs. Shortly afterwards an enemy S.P. gun supporting this attack got in to the northern outskirts of Minturno near the cemetery and made a nuisance of itself until chased out by our own tanks. The attack was driven back with losses to both sides.

Shortly after 0900 hrs. it was announced that one British and one American division had landed some forty miles south of Rome—to form the Anzio beachhead. These landings were to be timed in conjunction with the Garigliano battle which had been fought to drain away all possible enemy reserves. It was now confidently expected that the enemy in front of the Division would withdraw to meet this new threat to Rome or at least would be looking uneasily over their right shoulder. But it appeared to make no difference to them.

1 Green Howards attack on to point 172 started at 1700 hrs. "C" company, now only thirty-three all ranks strong, led the way to the cemetery north-west of point 172. "B" on the left and "D" on the right followed them. Two German tanks held them up but, after some confused fighting, "D" company then secured their objective and several prisoners. "B" company had to withdraw backed by part of the carrier platoons. The battalion held on where it was, under heavy shelling, for the whole night and all next day.

For their fine work in this battle the Battalion Commander, Lieut.-Colonel P. G. Bulfin, was awarded the D.S.O. and six D.C.M.s were also gained. Sergeant Roche gained a bar to the M.M. he won at Otta in Norway some four years previously.

23rd January

Major-General P. G. S. Gregson-Ellis, O.B.E. (later Major-General P. G. S. Gregson-Ellis, C.B., O.B.E.), who had arrived two days previously now took over command of the Division from Major-General G. C. Bucknall.

The following farewell message to the Division was given in this Special Order of the Day:—

SPECIAL ORDER OF THE DAY

By

Major-General G. C. Bucknall, C.B., M.C.

I must now tell you that I am commanded to take over a new post in the Army of Invasion and the time has come for me to leave my 5th Division.

It is my firm contention that our Division is the best fighting Division in the Army. Every task committed to us during the campaign in Sicily and Italy has been well and truly achieved, and by its discipline, smartness, and soldierly bearing in all circumstances, you have earned a fine reputation which I am confident you will keep bright.

I know that these tasks have been achieved by the magnificent fighting and cheerful endurance of officers and men often in the most trying conditions and against severe opposition. To them I give my unstinted praise and thanks. And although all arms and units have combined to wipe out the German formations on our front, I purposely single out the Infantry of the Division for special mention, for in them always fall the first sweat and discomfort, strife and hard fighting—and with the grand help and close co-operation of the supporting arms and services, they have carried all their objectives victoriously.

I have been proud indeed to lead you, and from the bottom of my heart I thank you, one and all, for your splendid efforts and for your whole-hearted support and co-operation in our job.

The importance of the Garigliano Battle to the operations in Italy generally is such that it should have special remark. In having the river crossings and securing firmly the Minturno Ridge in the face of strong opposition, the 5th Division has smashed up the 94th German Division and has not only contained the 90th Division and parts of the Hermann Goering Division but has given them crippling casualties. This action has materially assisted the Anzio operations and has enabled the landings to be established virtually unopposed. The fighting has been grim, but the results victorious, and the Corps Commander asks me personally to express to you his heartfelt congratulations and admiration.

Closely associated with us in this operation are 201st Guards Brigade, 23rd Armoured Brigade, 98th Field Regiment, 102nd Field Regiment, 213rd Engineer Field Company, 2nd Troop No. 10 Commandos and other units of the Services. To them I would say how pleased and proud we are to have them fighting with us, and express our gratitude for their invaluable help.

I have no doubt that much will soon have to be done and strenuous training completed to repair the ravages of the continual moving and hard fighting of recent months, but I am confident that the opportunities will be given to you and that you will be ready to seize them.

I know you will give the same loyal support to my successor as you have invariably given to me, and I can assure you that there is no leader in the Army to whom I would more readily confide your future and fortune.

I hope we shall meet and fight together again, and I shall always look out for you and for the "Y".

Good luck to you all and every happiness to you and to your homes and families.

Signed:—G. C. BUCKNALL,
Major-General

22nd January, 1944　　　　　Commander 5th Division.

It was arranged that 17 Inf Bde, now relieved and reassembled, should attack the Natale feature and the spur to the west of it. The object was to open up the way for an attack on Santa Maria.

The Brigade plan was for 6 Seaforth to go for point 156 and 2 RSF for point 141. 2 Northamptons were to push on to point 156 via Santa Maria on the following day.

The attack went in at 1600 hrs. On the left 2 RSF suffered

casualties on their way to the start line. "A" and "B" companies led, with a troop of three tanks that moved forward as the barrage came down and disappeared. Thinking that "A" and "B" were lost, as indeed they were, "C" followed, led by an exuberant young officer. Some of the men went in singing, but enemy machine guns took their toll. Lieut.-Colonel MacInnes, the Commanding Officer, was mortally wounded by a heavy concentration of mortars and Major MacMichael ("C" company Commander) took over. He too became wounded and his place was temporarily taken by Major Batey—the Commander of 593 Battery of 156 Fd Regt. The Germans on the objective had an English speaker among them who shouted, "Come on you yellow B . . . and fight." This demand was answered by a lone fusilier who, slinging away his Tommy Gun, was last seen disappearing into a German slit trench armed solely with a jack-knife.

Small arms ammunition began to run low and Major Batey organized a D.F. plan which enabled "C" company to withdraw towards Minturno with the minimum of casualties.

"A" and "B" companies had in fact completed almost a semi-circle and finished up amongst 201 Guards Bde, too late to take any effective part in the attack. Major Batey was awarded the M.C. for his leadership on this occasion. It was not the only time that he showed a fine personal example.

The Seaforth likewise were unable to reach their objectives in much the same circumstances, so the Northamptons remained uncommitted.

About the same time an enemy counterattack was launched against 201 Guards Bde. in the Tremonsuoli area, but it was repelled without much loss or difficulty. 13 Inf Bde Front remained remarkably quiet all day.

The Battles for the Natale Feature

The 24th of January was a quiet day with the enemy making a big effort against 56 Div on the Division's right. On the Divisional Front activity was confined to reorganization and patrolling. There was much activity in the quarry that now housed Tactical Divisional Headquarters, 13 Bde Headquarters, 201 Guards Bde Headquarters and the Tactical Headquarters of at least one Field Regiment. 15 Inf Bde, who were now commanded by Brigadier J. Y. Whitfield (later

Major-General J. Y. Whitfield, C.B., D.S.O., O.B.E.), less 1 KOYLI, who were to remain under command of 17 Inf Bde, were to be withdrawn that night. 17 Inf Bde were warned to be prepared to attack the next day, and the guns of the 92nd were moved to more open positions near the river mouth, so as to be able to reach farther out towards the left part of the Divisional front.

25th January was an even quieter day. Corps warned Division that they must secure Natale. 2 R INNISKS stalked and killed a tank with a Piat. On the following day, Lieut.-Colonel O'Brien Twihig of 2 R INNISKS was ordered to hospital as a result of a mortar wound he received on the original crossing.

The main bridge was at last opened—a triumph of dogged and courageous determination on the part of the Sappers. It was shrouded in an artificial smoke screen during all hours of daylight and as the approach to it was open for some time, a fact which attracted enemy fire, only those bearers of special pink permits were allowed to use it by daylight and in jeeps. By night there was much transport bringing up ammunition and supplies. Until this was possible a jeep and trailer train operated by the RASC unfailingly produced field gun and other ammunition by night at the rate of 700 rounds per gun per day of 25-pounder alone. The build up was now started for the Natale attack which was planned for the 28th/29th.

Patrolling was active, 2 RSF established a listening post at point 141, and a fighting patrol to point 172; 2 Northamptons found that Natale was occupied by about 150 enemy in reverse slope positions by day; they also patrolled to the cemetery and to cover a gap in the minefields. 11 KRRC had standing patrols on the left flank. Both the 91 and the 156 Fd Rgts had casualties from shelling during the day. The enemy had now amassed a great many guns, their ammunition supply, however, was considerably rationed. The Divisional gunners captured a naval balloon, but nobody appeared to know what to do with it.

The bridge was temporarily cut by shelling, almost as soon as it had been opened. The Sapper task of repairing damaged bridges was as arduous on the Garigliano crossing as anywhere during the whole of the Divisional travels. During the nine days between the 22nd and 31st of January, the following damage was done to the Highway 7, Bailey pontoon alone:—

22nd	one bow pontoon holed.
23rd	slight damage to approaches.
24th	three bow pontoons holed.
25th	no damage.
26th	one bow pontoon sunk, two bow pontoons holed, two centre pontoons holed, and two pumps damaged.
27th:	very little superficial damage.
28th:	one bow pontoon holed.
29th:	two Bailey panels damaged.
30th:	no damage to bridge but one pier of spare end floating bay sunk.
31st:	one bow pontoon holed and motor boat sunk.

27th January

The over-all Corps plan now became known. The 3rd United States Division was reinforcing the American II Corps front. 46 Div was to attack between Ausente-Castelforte, whilst 5 Div were to take Natale. This was to be attacked by 2 Northamptons from the direction of Tremonsuoli, probably on the night of 29th/30th or during the day of 30th January. As barrages were becoming rather commonplace this attack was to be preceded by a "Chinese" barrage followed by a comprehensive counter bombardment programme. The real attack to follow it was to be supported by concentrations of Artillery fire. 15 Inf Bde were brought back to the line and 1 Y and L were to take over point 141 and the cemetery area.

A very full patrolling programme was laid down by Division for the night 27th/28th. 56 Div were reported to have made some gains during the day.

There was little to report on the 28th January except for further restless patrolling activity.

The next day, the 29th, started quietly. The Corps Camouflage Officer reported the completion of dummy guns contrived to decoy enemy counter bombardment fire. He requested that his dummies should be used to cover up harassing fire planned for that night. Columns of smoke denoted heavy demolitions and explosives in the enemy positions. A special smoke screen was fired by a battery in 92 Fd Regt to screen the move of the Guards from enemy O.P.s known to be on Scauri.

At 1900 hrs. the Guards attacked and secured their objective; Grenadiers on the left and Coldstream on the right to the west of Tremonsuoli. This was planned to give room for 2 Northamptons and 6 Seaforth to attack Natale and the cemetery respectively. The whole of X Corps Artillery and two cruisers were to fire in support.

30th January onwards

The Chinese barrage opened at half an hour after midnight. The Germans immediately reacted by shelling all possible forming-up places exploiting fully the fragmentation of shells on rocky ground. As a result, the attack itself started an hour late. On the left the Guards took all their objectives, with one minor exception. Some excellent and prompt wiring, in conjunction with defensive fire, helped to stave off determined counter-attacks.

2 Northamptons had much assistance for their advance over difficult ground in the shape of porters and carriers for their ammunition and extra stretcher bearers provided by 41 Fd. Amb. The lower terraced slopes of Natale with their 12 ft. banks particularly caused the rate of advance to be considerably slowed down. Despite this, by 0230 hrs., the attack was proceeding smoothly with "C" and "D" companies on the lower slopes.

An hour later these two companies ran into the enemy defensive fire while "A" company to their right was forming up for the final assault on to the north-west end of the feature. No. 8 Platoon of this company led by Lieutenant Garner, moving down a river to take a smaller hill, met an enemy party advancing to counterattack the battalion. Resolute action, in the form of an old fashioned charge, gave the enemy no chance. They fled, leaving 8 Platoon with twelve prisoners and two machine guns, and "B" company in possession of the western ridge of the feature.

By 0545 hrs. "C" company (Captain F. W. Kitchin) had cleared the highest point and, shortly afterwards, "D" company (Major R. R. Greaves) had cleared the eastern ridge of the feature. The whole position was consolidated for the inevitable counterattacks at dawn. It had been a most successful and well conducted attack.

Equally successful and without much incident was the

attack of 6 Seaforth on to the cemetery itself. By first light they were in complete control of the area with some prisoners from 301 Inf Regt of 90 Light Div. It was then possible to send some tanks to strengthen the position and the battalion was able shortly afterwards to patrol to Santa Maria.

This was an undisputedly successful day for the Division. All its objectives had been taken for less than 100 casualties and in return for at least 120 prisoners. The field guns fired over 500 rounds per gun in the attack and a further 200 rounds per gun against the counterattack.

The counterattack came in on "C" company of 2 Northamptons at 1330 hrs. For half an hour previously the enemy had been seen coming up in strength and the forward platoon, No. 14 of "C" company, was heavily shelled. The Divisional and Corps Artillery rose to the occasion but the German gunners put down a very neat box barrage round the attack to isolate it from a well sited section of 7 Cheshire machine guns and the left half of 14 Platoon. By sheer weight of numbers the platoon was overwhelmed, but the enemy's success was short-lived. 12 Platoon of "B" company (Lieutenant Hammer) counterattacked and restored the position by 1430 hrs. There was no more trouble that day.

On the next day 31st January however, from first light onwards, 12 Platoon was heavily shelled on its spur position. A desperate counterattack in the afternoon was promptly dispatched by well controlled small arms fire and the familiar artillery "wall of steel". A patrol, sent out in the evening, counted over sixty bodies caught in the first D.F. Captain Kitchin and Lieutenant Garner were awarded M.C.s and Lieutenant Hammer a bar to his M.C.

Back on the river, traffic was now moving normally and the Sappers had started a ferry service for motor cycles and jeeps across the mouth of the Garigliano, thus saving some fifteen miles on the route from the gun areas. The enemy no longer shelled the crossing with much vigour, his valuable ammunition being needed in the Natale area where he kept up both mortaring and shelling consistently. Patrolling again became the order of the day. Back south of the river the guns of the 92nd were moved up well forward and in full view of the enemy O.P.s on Scauri. Here they were shelled only spasmodically and suffered less casualties than their sister regiments over the river.

There had been scares of hostile landings in this unprotected area, and accordingly 52 Anti-Tank took over the sea flank to provide all round defence. Some spartan enthusiasts took to bathing until an 88 mm. from the Scauri area used them for target practice. Another popular form of sport was duck shooting. Every morning at dawn thousands of wild duck would wheel in from the sea and settle on the lake which was a few hundred yards inland.

The Corps Commander was well pleased with the ultimate securing of Natale. The Division was now holding a long and uncomfortably small bridgehead with no reserves to commit further. Almost all the battalions had lost about 150 men apiece since they crossed the river and had now been in almost continuous action for more than six months. Far from retreating, the Germans had reinforced their defensive line which had achieved one of the greater objectives of the plan. Thought of further advances, in these circumstances, was far removed. The task of the Division was now to hold on to what it had so grimly won, to recuperate as quickly as possible, and to give the enemy no peace. It was anticipated that the VI Corps bridgehead at Anzio would now force the pace and loosen the German hold on the Gustav Line.

Thus days now consisted of routine exchanges of artillery and mortar fire, patrolling, resting, cleaning, receiving reinforcements, eating and sleeping. The bases behind the Massico feature had been maintained by rear parties, and battalions rather than brigades, were relieved in turns, and thus enabled to refurbish themselves out of range of the enemy. After but a few hours there of respite they went back to the routine as resolutely as ever.

Occasionally the enemy would sally forth against the Division. In the early hours of the 2nd February a patrol which got among 2 RSF needed some methodical mopping up. Some hours later a Guards patrol was ambushed and severely handled. That morning "C" company of 1 Green Howards, under command of 17 Inf Bde, supported by the whole Divisional Artillery, attacked a spur at point 165 to keep everyone there busy. They left booby traps and came out before dawn, unscathed.

On 3rd February General Mark Clark, the Army Commander, visited the Division.

On the night of the 7th/8th February, L/Sergeant M. Robinson, of 1 Green Howards, and two men from "D" company went out on patrol towards point 165. A German grenade burst in front of the sergeant wounding him in the face and eyes, cut him deeply in the shoulder, and in the legs, but he carried on and sent one of his men back with information. A German Spandau then opened up. He remained there to find the exact whereabouts of the Spandau, in intensive pain until the effect of the blast on his face completely closed his eyes. He staggered back to the battalion area, some fifteen hours later, with some valuable information and for this he was awarded the Distinguished Conduct Medal.

On the 5th, Major Houchin, second in Command of 2 Northamptons took over temporary command of 2 RSF who had lost both Commander and Second in Command.

On 6th February, explosions in the Spigno and Castelonorato areas made it look as if the enemy might pull out. An attack was planned on to the Bracchi feature by 2 Northamptons who had taken over 2 R INNISKS area. It was postponed 24 hrs. and then cancelled.

On 10th February it was decided to send 56 Div to help at Anzio and 5 Div was to extend its front eastwards to include the whole of the Ausente Valley and Monte Damiano, less the summit which was still held by the Germans. This made the shallow bridgehead even wider and entailed thinning out the present positions. The rain was now coming down persistently and everywhere was mud. 13 Inf Bde took over Monte Damiano on the 12th February when the weather improved. The 52 A Tk Regt sent an improvised Infantry company to help out 2 WILTS on Salvatitio; the latter now had a mobile bath unit also in support. Their life centred again on the mules and Indian porters of the Central Appenines—living in sangars on bare slopes and rocky paths. The only sure way to find the various positions was to follow the signals cables. Prefabricated cereal again appeared in the rations, consisting of partly cooked porridge in containers to which hot water was added at the last minute. Jam tarts and cakes made at "B" Echelons were packed into 2-in. mortar ammunition boxes and carried up to the sangar positions. It took 6 hrs. to get a casualty down to the Regimental Aid Post and another $1\frac{1}{2}$ hrs. to ambulances at the foot of the hill. A pontoon broken loose from a neighbouring Divisional area farther up the swollen river nearly broke the Divisional bridge—and a 6-pounder anti-tank gun was promptly positioned to sink any further intruders.

On 13th February, 15 Inf Bde relieved 201 Guards Bde, who now left command of 5 Div. They had done some magnificent work in the last three weeks; although this is not the place for a full description of this, they deserve every praise for their splendid example.

During 15th/16th some enemy had the audacity to cross the river and some of them remained behind for mining, but they soon vanished into thin air when sought out.

Amongst the diversions provided by an imaginative staff was a pigeon race on 21st February. The following report was taken from a current Army newspaper:—

"A Grand Pigeon Race."

"Pigeons will carry two days' reserve rations. A.A. Gunners will take notice that all Pigeons will be regarded as friendly. Spectators are warmly welcomed at the Starting Point but all are advised to wear hats." These briefly were the competition instructions.

All bird choosing was done by drawing lots—a certain C.Q.M.S. drew "Sarum Sally" who rose straight into the air and flew down to Corps Headquarters a distance of approximately twelve miles in 16 min. 15 sec. to win 1st prize of N.A.A.F.I. supplies. "Bit O' Brass" belonging to 1 KOYLI flew 2 hrs. 50 min. to come in last—having dallied with local birds on the way!

On the 22nd February 2 R INNISKS went across to Tremonsuoli, where they had casualties to their patrols from mines, which were very prolific in that area.

Enemy shelling remained active but the 25 pounders of X Corps were limited to 40 rounds per gun per day. Demonstration was given also on that day of the "snow shoes" that were invented within the Division for moving about unscathed in minefields. They appeared to be effective.

On 22nd February 17 Inf Bde took over on Damiano and Salvatitio with 11 KRRC under command as a fourth battalion. It was now raining very hard for hours on end and occasional thunder cracked around the mountains like a gigantic artillery concentration.

On Saturday, 28th February, 13 Inf Bde came back from their rest area, and relieved 15 Inf Bde on the left hand sector. Two days later, the Division was warned it was to go to Anzio and relieve 56 Div just about as quickly as was possible; the next day, advance parties from the United States 88th ("Florida Wildcats") Division came to start taking over. A day or so later Major-General Gregson-Ellis made a quick trip to visit General Templer and 56 Div and to see for himself the reported horrors of the bridgehead. On 2nd March, the first Regimental Combat Team of 88 Div relieved 17 Inf Bde on Damiano. Also on that day the Corps Commander, General McCreery, visited units of the Division and the Class 9 bridge was broken by shelling which was most inconvenient at the time of the approaching relief. On the 4th, a further Regimental Combat Team relieved 13 Inf Bde and on the following day, General Sloane took over the whole sector from General Gregson-Ellis and the scene moved to Anzio.

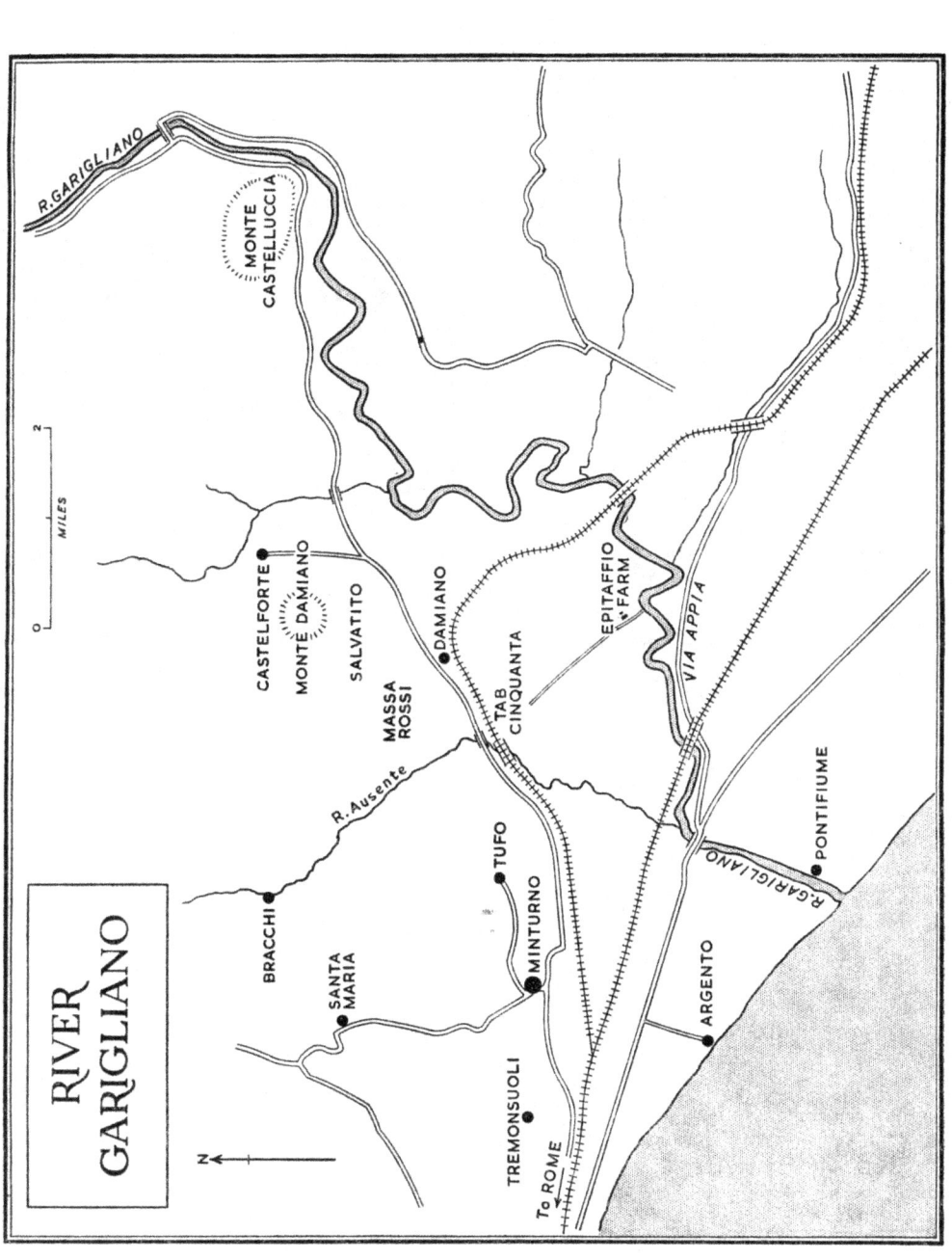

CHAPTER TWELVE

THE ANZIO BEACHHEAD

In which 5th Division moves from the Garigliano front, to relieve 56th Division in the United States VI Corps Beachhead at Anzio. Where after minor attempts to improve the position the Division becomes locked in bitter and intimate conflict with the enemy and maintains its operational integrity by experience and high morale in face of rapidly dwindling numbers. In which the Division finally breaks out of the beachhead in the battle for Rome and eventually reaches the banks of the Tiber near Ostia Antica.

The Setting

The United States VI Corps, then commanded by Major-General Lucas, landed on the beaches around Anzio and Nettuno on 22nd January, some five days after X Corps had crossed the River Garigliano. 1 British Div was among the assaulting troops who initially met very little resistance; this was greatly due to the success of X Corps operations across the Garigliano in which 5 Div played a major part. The plan was for VI Corps to seize a bridgehead and then advance across the flat Latium marshland and secure a footing in the Alban Hills overlooking Rome. It was a fortunate landing for not only were the enemy conspicuous by their absence but weather conditions were almost ideal and by nightfall on the 22nd a comfortable bridgehead had been secured with the port swept clear of mines and in normal use. The following day saw an expansion of the beachhead to a semi-circle of some fifteen miles to a depth of half that distance, and some real strength in the way of ammunition and other supplies was being built up in the harbour, almost entirely unmolested. This was just as well, as by the 29th, not only had the weather broken into gale force but also the enemy had reacted very violently using 88 mm. and 170 mm. shells, mines in the sea-lanes and bombs, torpedo and even glider-bomb attacks from the air, to some good effect.

On the 30th the expected attack towards the Alban Hills materialized. Eight previous days had been allowed to pass by in overcautious preparation and this had given Kesselring just enough time to gather together all the possible reserves he could find to meet it. He wisely resisted the temptation to attack the Allied Corps by taking away troops just holding on to the Gustav Line and waited for his scratch force to relieve them properly before counterattacking. He was in a good position of observation from which he could follow the entire build-up of the beachhead. Having collected all his reserve he disengaged 26th Panzer Division from 8 Army's front and 3rd Panzer Division together with the old enemies of 5 Div, the Hermann Goering Division, from the main Gustav positions. Some further weaker divisions came from Northern Italy and France to augment this force which was now to make VI Corps pay dearly for their hesitation in the first few days.

The battles, bitter and ferocious, that waged around the factory area of Aprilia and along the Mussolini Canal during the next three or four weeks do not belong here. Suffice it to say that the attack on the Alban Hills did not get very far against a determined enemy who had all the advantages of observation. The German Southern Commander, General von Mackensen, brought the 1 Parachute Corps against the British element alone and the main attack was aimed down the road that ran straight into Anzio and which, if held, would split the British from the Americans of VI Corps. It was now no longer a question of how to get to the Alban Hills but rather of how to keep a footing at all on the beachhead, which Hitler had personally ordered to be eradicated. The first of the German attacks was on 3rd February and the next day an Inf Bde of 56 Div, which had just arrived from having been alongside 5 Div on the Garigliano, made a successful local counterattack.

The battle raged for the month following and before 5 Div were to arrive to replace 56 Div, by now reduced to a very weak condition. The Germans had paid dearly for their containing of the bridgehead and could no longer be expected to be able to stage anything larger than local attacks. It was to a stalemate of mutual exhaustion in atrociously wet weather that 5 Div were now moved. Although the weather was to improve, the relentless grip held by von Mackensen on the Allied Force was not to be released for three months longer.

The Corps Perimeter

The American Divisions of VI Corps held the more open country from the sea to the east of Nettuno following roughly the line of the Mussolini Canal to the area of Padiglione. From here the 1 British Div held a line across to the main Campoleone–Anzio road at a point where a fly-over bridge of some prominence crossed it seven miles north of Anzio. The road that once took this fly-over bridge cut at right angles to the main Anzio road and swept on westwards almost to the sea. This was known as the Lateral Road and its length was the length of the 5 Div front. It ran from the bridge upwards gently to the hamlet of La Cogna from which area it dominated the enemy positions but was also equally exposed to their fire; it continued its pot-holed track through some cuttings down to a junction with the coastal road on a steady downward slope. To the north of it were small valleys known to the Division, after their spell in the Middle East, as Wadis, to the Italians as Fossa; these were interspersed near the sea with a few prominent woods. To the south of the lateral road lay open rolling farmland with here and there a young wood and valley. The junction of the Lateral and Coastal Roads took place at the hamlet of S. Lorenzo, an extremely exposed place known appropriately as "Stonk" Corner and only used by those with charmed lives, at least by day. From the woods near by the front line ran across country in a north-westerly direction to where the Moletta River ran into the sea. The Divisional Sector ended there.

The Divisional Sector

To make the following account understandable the Divisional Sector will be divided into certain areas which although they were not necessarily Brigade or Battalion areas as such, will suffice to keep the reader sufficiently informed of what was a very complex system of forward positions. At no time can it be said that any brigade or battalion was in a cut and dried position without reeling off a string of map references, quite undesirable in this context. Indeed, in some cases there were German localities interspersed between the companies of a battalion in the Division. From west to east the major areas were known as "The Coastal Sector", "La Cogna", "The Fortress", and "The Lobster's Claw".

(a) *The Coastal Sector*

The extreme left of the Divisional Front was a tongue of dune where the Moletta River swung into the sea. From the dunes the country was dead flat and with no cover right across to the lines of poplars indicating the coastal road that ran back from S. Lorenzo to Anzio. Here were long fields of fire and little close contact with the enemy, except by patrols. On the right, however, there was close contact in the woods to the north of the road. It was good country for snipers and nowhere was more popular for this than the dune near where the gunners had an intriguing O.P. that could look right back into the enemy and across to the triangle of roads south of Ardea. It took some time before the enemy in the area of La Fossa, another hamlet beyond Lorenzo, realized that they were being watched, when they got accurately shelled almost every time they went to relieve nature; they never discovered the whereabouts of that O.P. There were three minefields between the Germans and the battalion in this sector, one laid by each and one that had been laid by the 36 United States Combat Engineers, who were in the sector when 5 Div first took it over and stayed on under command for some time. Patrolling was made difficult by the lack of accurate knowledge of the whereabouts of those mines laid by the Americans. On the extreme left of the sector it was possible to dig right in, which was just as well, as German mortars were always active in that area. Being more open, the Coastal Sector was a relatively quiet one, and the one from which the final break-out was launched.

(b) *La Cogna*

This was the only major position south of the Lateral Road and the Divisional Reserve position. La Cogna itself was the remains of a hamlet situated between the Coastal Sector and the Fortress but much nearer to the latter. It was on the highest ground and much sought after as an Artillery O.P. although, being equally easily observed by the enemy it was never free from shelling and other unwelcome attention. The positions were dug in to the south of the ruins, on reverse slopes from which there was a certain amount of covered approach to positions which might have to be counterattacked from it.

(c) *The Fortress*

This was the most famous of all the areas to be held and one that epitomized the performance of the Division. To the right of the right hand position in the Coastal Sector and across the Lateral Road from La Cogna lay this the grimmest sector of them all. It consisted of a winding wadi full of shell holes, mines, splintered tree trunks and wired bushes, surrounded by banks. On one side the German positions were dug in close by, and deep into, the bank. Just south of the wadi system and overlooking part of it was a little bump of ground with one or two prominent bushes on it—this was the Fortress of the position, in that if one stood on it erect one could command the enemy lines of approach and indeed right across to the fly-over bridge to the right rear. Needless to say nobody ever could stand erect there and remain alive. Here was the ever pungent smell of the dead, most of them unburied because they could not be got at, and those that were marked by a wooden cross were but lightly covered with earth. The whole area was littered with the abandoned paraphernalia of fighting belonging to both sides, odd bits of equipment, clothing and paper, of rotting fragments of food, or twisted brightly coloured telephone cable. All of this was continually being churned up by shell and mortar fire into some gigantic stew of which the individual elements could be recognized less and less easily as the days went by.

Nothing stirred here by day unless it was ordered to attack. All essential work such as bringing food, mending broken cable, sorting ammunition, had to be done under cover of darkness.

Both sides here lived shoulder to shoulder. They could hear each other talking in their holes, calling the roll in particular. They did not see much of each other because they did not venture to put their heads out of their holes by day, to encourage many eager snipers who patiently waited on both sides for just such an opportunity.

The Gunner O.P could see little from this area and efforts were made to find higher places elsewhere. Mines were so thick that it was impossible to chart them accurately; this was a deterrent to movement even by following taped routes at night. Patrolling was made difficult for even the determined experts. The enemy were not very keen on patrolling in such circumstances, preferring to probe with the mortar bomb.

As can readily be imagined, the take over between one battalion and another in the Fortress, to which normal access was almost impossible, was a very nerve-racking experience. Many took the wrong track and disappeared without trace; many were the casualties caused by enemy mortars alerted by the slightest false movement.

As battalion relieved battalion, so the position became more difficult, although every effort was made, the whole time and by each of them, to improve the actual dug-outs and fire-trenches. The Fortress remains a grim memorial to those who died refusing to yield a foot of it to the redoubtable enemy positioned to dominate every inch of it.

(d) *The Lobster's Claw*

This was a form of wadi immediately to the S.E. of the Fortress and so named because on the map it looked exactly like a lobster's claw. It tapered off to the Lateral Road just before that went into the front of the neighbouring 1 Div near the fly-over bridge. This was a more elaborate trench system than the Fortress and really resembled one of the 1914–18 War. Conditions were much the same, with even more evidence of death, buried and unburied. There was a gap of about 200 yards between the two areas covering a convex slope that was swept by spandau fire of deadly accuracy. This area had to be covered nightly by the porters who brought up ammunition, food and water to those in the "Lobster's Claw".

These were the principal forward areas that were to be occupied by the Division for the next three or four months. There were other spots that will be remembered eternally by those who had to live in them, pass them regularly, or even to come within their influence, such as Chokah Wadi, Commando Wadi, The Yellow Bungalow, Sheep Pen Farm, Recce House, Lorenzo Tower, to mention but a few of them. When the Division arrived in the area nicknames had been given to all the recognizable tracks, roads and features because the Italian names, picturesque as they undoubtedly were, did not come easily to the lips of the English fighting man. For instance, the Lateral Road had been known as Watling Street, the Coastal Road as Piccadilly.

On the map, some 3,000 yards behind the Lateral Road ran another track at right angles to the Coastal Road, called Stradane Di Macchiane, which was known more colloquially by the Division's predecessors as Regent Street and familiarly to the Gunners of 5 Div as "Gun Alley". To the north and south of this road lay the Divisional Artillery Areas. They were mostly pretty exposed and ranged from the right hand troop, being less than 2,000 yards from the enemy positions, to the left hand troop that was almost twice as far back. Many of the positions suffered from enemy artillery, mud at the outset, and thick undergrowth. The guns were cramped in this area and it was not easy to expand or find alternative positions without having guns immediately behind others with consequent disastrous effect. Later on when early summer came the area became liable to fire and to be given away by dust raised by ammunition and other vehicles.

Where Gun Alley met the Coastal Road was an exposed stretch of track and a solitary farm building which was used as a Police Station by the Divisional Provost. This was under observation from the enemy and used, frequently and punctually to a time-table, to be subjected to bursts of gun fire. To the west of the Coastal Road was a peaceful world of green grass, sandy dunes and glades of pine and cypress trees wherein innocently lurked Divisional H.Q. and other elements of Divisional Troops. This area got shelled and bombed but a fraction of the times that such things happened across the way in the gun areas.

Behind the line of the guns was a prominent wooded hill feature, the Colle Rifondo, upon which was a Tower, Le Torre St. Anastasio. This had been a favourite target for enemy gunners but was still, nevertheless, used as an O.P., particularly for the counter bombardment folk; another was the famous Tower of Lorenzo on the coast line about a mile nearer the enemy. Behind the Tower of St. Anastasio lay the rear area of the Divisional Sector. Here in fields and vineyards with only the occasional building, stood the "B" Echelon, close to the forward areas and very much a part of them. Behind this was the ever expanding Corps Administrative area along the Coast.

Great strides had been made before the war to make this

area of the Pontine Marshes a self-supporting agricultural one free from the malarial curse that had been with it for centuries but which was now but a fraction of that experienced by the Division in Madagascar, or on the Catania Plain. For 2,000 years Roman Emperors, Popes and even Napoleon himself had tried and failed to reclaim this land. It must be credited to Mussolini, so aptly called the "Bullfrog of the Pontine Marshes" by Mr. Churchill, that this was well on the way when the landings in Anzio caused considerable damage to the whole area. Anzio and Nettuno had been fishing places and summer resorts for the Romans for hundreds of years, indeed the former was once the famous Antium, birthplace of Caligula and Nero, who has left the remains of an elaborate villa there. It has been established at least from 348 B.C. when it was named in a Protection Treaty with Carthage. Here was the famous Temple of Fortune of which mention is made by Horace; here was fought a famous sea battle and near by was the Volscian City which was defended by high walls and a deep ditch which can still be traced.

This, then, was the setting into which the Division was sent early in March of 1944 to help hold an uncomfortable bridgehead in preparation for the final advance to the Eternal City. Rome was only 33 miles to the north, or less than an hour in an electric train, in more favourable circumstances.

The Take-over

Much advance publicity of the horrors of Anzio had reached 5 Div as they sat holding on to a hardly won bridgehead over the Garigliano. When 56 Div moved over there, taking, incidentally an ex B.M.R.A. of 5 Div, Lieut.-Colonel W. Zambra, who was C.O. of one of their Field Regiments, they received much sympathy and well wishing from their neighbours. Little then did the latter realize that it would be they who were, less than a month later, to relieve the battered remains of 56 Div.

The take-over was to be a difficult one as 56 Div were still engaged in fierce fighting and the ground was heavy with mud. It was planned that brigades would relieve each other one at a time and that, by and large, all vehicles, guns and equipment were to be taken over *in situ* because of the impracticability of loading and unloading such in a shelled harbour. Furthermore, unwelcome enemy attention and heavy rains would have made it impossible to get guns and vehicles out of their present position. This leaving behind of vehicles that had been with the Division for so many miles was an unpopular decision that had to be faced with resignation. The troops were to be ferried by landing craft to Anzio in relays from Pozzuoli, the ancient little port north of Naples from which St. Paul once sailed.

15 Inf Bde Group went first and took over from 167 Bde Group of 56 Div on 7th March in the early hours of the morning. Command passed at 0250 hrs. and 15 Inf Bde came under command of 56 Div. It was fortunately a comparatively quiet night although shelling and mortaring from both sides hardly ceased and made take-overs very tricky. The Gunners of 92 Fd Regt had changed half a gun detachment at a time and the passing of control by Regimental H.Q. was also done in easy stages. The Brigade Group went straight into what was to be known as the Fortress Area with 1 Green Howards on the right and 1 Y and L on the left, 1 KOYLI being in reserve. Main Brigade H.Q. was midway between the Lateral Road and the Gun Areas in a comparative haven. Almost at once all units set to improve their lot, it being one of the virtues of the British soldier that he is never satisfied with what he has taken over from another British soldier. The soldier who wore the "Y" was no exception, in fact his experience invariably prompted a feeling that what had been handed over to him had much better be started all over again which was not possible at Anzio. This particularly applied to the Gunners who had found themselves in some very unattractive positions along a straight track marked on the map, Gun Alley, and lined with tall poplars that brought down on to them every round aimed at Anzio itself, or so it seemed. They soon moved to alternative positions but were shelled equally heavily for their pains.

During that first night, 15 Inf Bde captured an enemy Postal Orderly and all his mail which was a little hard on the men of the 3rd Battalion The Sturm Regiment, who were opposite them and to whom the Postal Orderly belonged. The next night on the left of the Brigade, by the sea, three Italian saboteurs landed by boat only to be smartly captured by the 36th U.S. Engineer Battalion in that area; two M.E. 109 E's were shot down into the gun area.

On 9th March, 17 Bde Group started to take over from 168 Inf Bde in the area of the Lobster's Claw. As battalions arrived in the harbour they were rushed by truck to the "B" Echelon where they immediately dug in. This was not only against enemy artillery but also against the fragments from the colossal beachhead A.A. barrage that went up at frequent intervals. By the 10th, 15 and 17 Inf Bdes were well organized and used to the methodical German shelling and mortaring. The gunners too, knew when to stop and quietly wait for the midday concentration near Gun Alley. They now got down to counter-bombardment which was to take up a lot of their time and ammunition in the coming months at Anzio. Probably never had the German Artillery been so efficient and numerous as at Anzio and it was used on lines of thought much as had been generated by the British from Alamein onwards.

In the early hours of the 11th, 5 Div took control of the Sector from 56 Div and immediately started planning their part of a projected Corps attack, an attack that never took place. Enemy air activity was greater than the Division had experienced for some time. A raid by seven Italian Torpedo Bombers failed to damage any of the Allied shipping off Anzio and two of the bombers were shot down. The Allied air effort that day was 300 sorties which struck at gun positions, railway and supply centres of the enemy.

The 12th was a very wet day and the rain was so continuously powerful that it quietened down the activities of both sides. Shelling increased in the evening and many Signal Lines were cut. There was an alarm in the Coastal Sector which was largely stopped by D.F. from 156 Fd Regt and 67 Fd Regt, normally part of 1 Div but now grouped under 5 Div as was 4 Medium Regt. On this day 91 Fd Regt took over from 65 Fd Regt of 56 Div.

A prominent house near Fossignano ahead of the Fortress Area, which was flying a Red Cross flag, must have been used as an enemy O.P. as well, according to a report from 1 Y and L, who claimed they had clearly seen an observer at the window during the day, with binoculars. Although visibility was restricted by the weather, it would have to be watched in the future, for it just could not be believed that it was a Medical Orderly looking for casualties.

On the 13th, 2 Northamptons in the "Lobster's Claw" Area together with 6 Seaforth, reported having seen stretcher parties busy at what was to be known as R.A.P. House; the same one as reported by 1 Y and L. It looked suspiciously as though some of them were armed. Throughout the day it was noticed that the activity of small calibre enemy guns firing individually was increasing. They caused many casualties as it was the unexpected round that so often caught the stray man in the open.

During the night 13th/14th, the 91 Field O.P.s took over from 92, this sort of relief was to be of frequent occurrence during the next months and showed how flexible the liaison arrangements really were, although every battalion hated to be without its habitual Gunner.

There were unconfirmed reports, also during the night, that enemy parachutists had landed the other side of the fly-over bridge—all Gun Areas and "B" Echelon were alerted.

Next morning, the 14th, thirty-five enemy F.W. 190 and M.E. 109 attacked the beachhead.

On the night of the 14th/15th, 15 Inf Bde handed over the Fortress Sector to 13 Inf Bde and came back into reserve. By the 15th the General had visited every sub-unit of the divisions in the beachhead with the solitary exception of one of the Green Howards' forward companies that was, in any case, inaccessible by day. This he repeated time and time again until he knew more about parts of the area than those who were in them at the time. 13 Inf Bde had 2 Cameronians on the right, taking over from 1 Green Howards in the Fortress itself, and 2 WILTS on the left. During the day patrols identified prisoners from 65 Inf Div and from 1 Parachute Div and 18 L.A.A. claimed a hit on one of two F.W. 190 that strafed the forward areas.

And so the take-over was completed and 5 Div was firmly in control of what was to be the lynch-pin of the whole defence of the beachhead. From now on it was a question of resisting the stubborn tenacity of the enemy and yielding not an inch of the vital ground that the Division had taken over. Attacks were planned by both British divisions and over on the American Sector, but rarely came to anything. The defence became one of routine; the movement of this battalion to relieve that battalion, a small attack beaten off here and another one beaten off there; of artillery fire and counter-fire; of fire

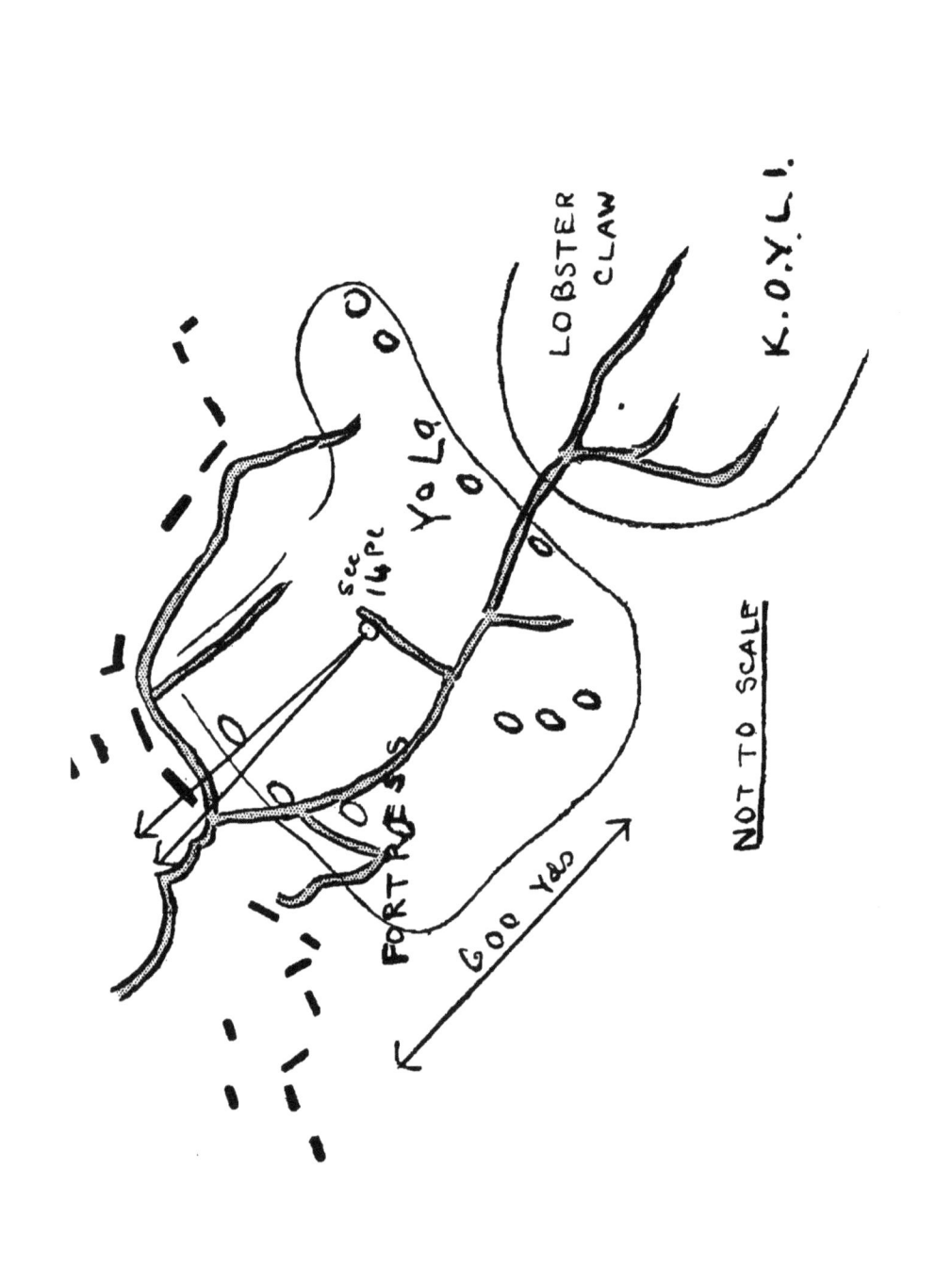

against aircraft; of the bringing up of ammunition, food and water under deadly conditions. The little incidents that occurred during the next two and a half months were many and important when they occurred to whom they occurred at the time. Unfortunately it would take a large volume to chronicle them. Here it is only possible to tell the outline story of that routine and how the Division conquered the enemies of boredom and the fear of the unknown.

The Routine Defensive Battle

Slowly the weather improved and spring came to the beachhead. Despite the terrible beatings that nature had taken for the last two months from a good deal of artillery fire and other man-made horrors, the trees and shrubs began to burst into greens and yellows and the grass grew more vivid in accompaniment. The whole formed a bright contrast against the Mediterranean blues of the sky and the sea. It was a brave sight that defied the war of man and heartened considerably those who lived under the earth of the beachhead. Activities however humdrum, took on a new lease of life, although they followed the same monotonous pattern.

From the end of March to the end of May, behind the façade of attack and counter-attack, shellfire and counter-shellfire, a formidable force was being built up in this the bridgehead for the long awaited break out. The beachhead itself was becoming a vulnerable base, as was shown when every now and then an enemy shell touched off a dump of petrol or ammunition. The whole area, from tented hospitals to mobile bath units, was liable to enemy shellings and it was always the unexpected that lay around the corner. But so far as 5 Div was concerned, those in the front line battle and those who supported it had to follow a well-worn routine pattern from which there could be no real relaxation without having to pay for it with casualties. There were now no elaborately planned attacks or river crossings, nor much opportunity for deep and spectacular patrolling or raiding; all the Division could do was to hold on to "The Fortress" with a grim and undistinguished determination. There were not many divisions that could have played the part at all, none could have played it as well as the reserve division that had learned to be patient in so many different parts of the world.

The task of the Divisional Commander was an immense one and none was better fitted to it in these particular circumstances. He was the first to realize that it was more concerned with the machine than with the battles it was to fight. The machine had implicit confidence in the leadership of its master, and instinctively knew that it had to keep going for some time yet. It was a question once more of maintaining the morale of all ranks under difficult circumstances. It had started subconsciously a long way back, but it was Major-General Gregson-Ellis who, on the Garigliano, encouraged the soldier to maintain his morale for himself and thus provide the real match-winning factor. The soldier who wore the "Y" on his arm had sound confidence not only in his leaders but also in his brothers in arms and in his supporting arms and services. The Infantryman knew that the Gunner was always behind him and that he would exert his every effort to ensure that the enemy was stopped in his tracks, that the Sapper would lose no time in thoroughly clearing the mines in his path or in building the bridge in some miraculous way or other to get him through the difficulties that lay ahead; he knew that the drivers of the RASC would, by means best known to themselves, see that he never lacked ammunition and food, that his mail would come up as soon as it was humanly possible and go back the same sure way; he knew that, when it was possible, he would get beer and cigarettes from the N.A.A.F.I., the Padre or some other good soul, some entertainment from E.N.S.A. or, better still, from fellows like himself, who lived in the atmosphere of the campaign all the time and knew what he liked and about what he was thinking.

And in their turn the Gunners, the Sappers, the Signallers, the RAOC and RASC men and the Military Police, knew that whatever else happened, these Infantrymen would never fail them, would never give ground which could not be regained. Not one of these men would ever let down the traditions of the "Fighting Fifth" or "The Globetrotters" or by whatever name the reserve division was known.

Morale had never been higher than it became at Anzio. If the crossing of the Garigliano saw the peak of the Division's tactical and technical proficiency then the beachhead saw the peak of its morale, experience and powers of endurance. It was now more than two years since the Division had sailed from the United Kingdom and a great deal had happened during those two years, not only to the Division but to those whom it had left at home. There had been a form of warfare carried into the home, not only of the bombs, the black-out, and rationing, but the battle, in some cases, against loyalty to the man overseas. Many were the tragic problems that confronted the Welfare People, the Unit Officer, Padres, Soldiers, Sailors and Airmen's Families Association who with the Women's Voluntary Service did so much for the Division that cannot be recorded here, and yet, despite all this, morale was never higher than in the beachhead where, for many, there was a great deal of time left for thinking of those left at home. Home was becoming much nearer than expected. One realized it never more poignantly than when the B.B.C. broadcast the song of the nightingale relayed from the beachhead, for the nightingale was now beginning to sing almost everywhere except in the Fortress itself. Facilities for welfare were undoubtedly more abundant than in Persia, for instance, but although the problem was fundamentally the same, the approach to it here was different.

It must be remembered that nowhere in the beachhead was there immunity from enemy shellfire, that now more than ever all parts of the Division were in front-line battle together, and felt themselves to be so with a deal of pride. Casualties were regularly suffered by those who had to live in "B" Echelon and by those who had previously spent many tedious hours guarding ammunition dumps and other base installations, or repairing vehicles for the many road moves, or repairing the bodies of the wounded so that they might fight another battle. Every officer and man of the supporting arms and services was now virtually alongside his infantry and this knowledge contributed to the height of morale; this, and imaginative leadership at all levels.

Much was contributed within the unit and with local resources. The good Padre, and there were some really good Padres in the Division, put himself out unostentatiously without counting the cost, not only doing that which was expected of him as part of his job, but turning readily to more mundane tasks, such as baking buns, and delivering them to the forward troops, providing literature other than the Scriptures, helping with letters home, playing games with or just having a drink or a chat over a smoke with those resting from the battle. With very few exceptions the soldier knew he could depend on this.

At Brigade Headquarters they were mostly pre-occupied with fighting the battle and in maintaining that administration necessary to ensure success. Somehow one didn't associate morale with brigade although, let it be said, there were few Brigade Commanders of the Division, at any time, who failed to realize its importance. The few exceptions paid for it dearly.

At Divisional H.Q. a lot could be and was done, because the amount largely depended on the imagination of the Commander. Here again General Gregson-Ellis was a past-master at contriving or inspiring others to contrive something new. Who will ever forget his catapult that threw a mortar bomb, his multi-barrelled mortar and silent mortars. It was he who was the originator of the Division's Derby Sweepstake that gathered in £7,750 in prize money, a contribution of about 7s. 6d. per man in the Division. He encouraged the apparent trivialities of beetle racing, of parties for odd reasons; he started the idea of a concentration of the whole Divisional Artillery at midday on to a target to be chosen by every company who produced a prisoner. As already mentioned he tirelessly visited every sub-unit often in the most dangerous of circumstances and at the most unusual times. He spent hours chatting to the little man and to pinning well earned medals on to officer and man alike. This lead was well taken up at all levels of Command and made for a happy and confident family.

Although it is not possible here fully to chronicle all that went on in the Division during this routine defensive period mention must be made of one or two of the highlights. The Corps attack as planned when the Division arrived in the beachhead, as already mentioned, never took place, but on Sunday, 19th March, a combined effort was made by 6 Seaforth, 2 Cameronians and 9 Commando, who were in the sector and under command of Division, to simulate a more serious threat, to distract attention, and to tidy up the Fortress position. On the right the Seaforth attack, the only position that was to be retained after getting there, failed to get right home; in the centre the Cameronians ran into a similar attack by the Germans which coincided with their plan. "C" Company set off to attack an objective some 150 yards away just as the enemy attacked and surrounded their "B" Company. "C" Company, whose advance was successful were fortuitously diverted by the Battalion Commander to cut off the Germans who had attacked "B" Company. This was not successful, but "C" Company eventually restored "B's" positions and occupied them themselves. The latter had lost one platoon completely. In the middle of their "chinese" attack on the left, 9 Commando ran out of ammunition which was very courageously replaced for them by men of 2 WILTS, across a very open approach. 2 Cameronians alone lost twelve killed, forty-nine wounded and thirty-five missing.

On the 20th there was a spectacular dog fight over the Divisional Area. Spitfires got amongst a superior number of F.W. 190s and M.E. 109s and shot down six of them. In the evening 15 Inf Bde relieved 17 Inf Bde less 6 Seaforth who handed over to 1 Y and L the following night. Three days later 15 Inf Bde took over from 36th United States Engineer Regiment who had been in position for some time and under command of 5 Div. They had done a good job of work, having not been trained in an Infantry rôle.

On the 24th, a bitter blow to the Division was the reduction of 25-pounder ammunition expenditure to 15 rounds per gun per day from 80 rounds per gun per day. This meant a reappraisal of Defensive Fire Tactics and a reduction of counter-bombardment particularly against hostile mortars. The latter reduction was not popular with the infantry. However the value of 25-pounder fire against mortars well dug in the reverse slopes of the wadis was always questionable; indeed even guns firing in the upper register, i.e., with an abnormally high trajectory and consequent steep angle of descent, had not been very effective. This eventually was taken on by brigade mortars; this action proved to be the only real antidote. One of the difficulties with mortars was the lack of indication from where they could be firing; lack of observation generally being a great handicap in the beachhead. The only way to get the necessary height was to resort to towers, those already in being on Lorenzo or Anastasio, or specially made ones of tubular steel scaffolding which had to be concealed in the woods to the south of the Lateral Road. In all these cases the towers were too far back to be really effective. The other alternative was the air O.P.—the Auster aircraft—which did a wonderful job of work for the

Division in the beachhead. But they found it hard to spot mortars firing during the short time they could be watching. Frequently they were shot at by German 88-mm. flak guns and attacked by fighters. Their landing strip was under shellfire and when not being shelled was more often than not being used as a football pitch. So thick was the air with shelling that one pilot, Captain Aitchison, ran into friendly artillery fire and was blown to pieces. They led a particularly hazardous life at Anzio but never once slackened their efforts to counter the disadvantage of observation against the Division.

Having been absent, through no fault of their own, on the only occasion when tanks got among the Infantry on the Garigliano, the 52 A Tk Regt were in position and more than ready and eager for German tanks to attack down the Coastal Road. They waited in vain but never relaxed their vigilance. They were certainly having an unlucky war, being the first Territorial A Tk Regt to go overseas, they had had to be mostly content with their secondary rôle, in those days it was a L.M.G. A.A. rôle. They were the first A Tk Regt in the Army to have sixty-four guns. In Central Italy, however, for lack of opposition from German tanks, they had to resort to another secondary rôle; that of pioneering, and two of their batteries were trained as Sappers for Bailey Bridging. Whatever they were asked to do, they did well and readily.

On Friday, 31st March, a fierce attack was put in against 2 RSF in the Fortress; the right-hand company was scattered temporarily and had to be helped out by a Company of 6 Seaforth who restored the position. No ground was given up nor was it the following night when a similar attack was made against 1 KOYLI's right-hand Company (Captain Deedes). In an attempt to intimidate any possible mutual support this time, the next door battalion, 1 Y and L were severely shot at and the enemy advanced with flame throwers. Forgetting any restriction on ammunition expenditure in such an emergency, the Div Arty made up for lost time and helped to achieve a solid defence. 1 KOYLI had few casualties and amongst other things captured two of the flame throwers.

On Monday, 3rd April, a shower of exotic propaganda leaflets were fired at 1 Green Howards. Such artistic works as the drawing of the woman undressing whilst an American stands by over the caption "While you die . . ." An agonized woman's face "London blitzed again". A rather more intimate variation of the woman and the American entitled "You Americans are so different". "The road to Rome is paved with skulls" and many other lurid efforts which were promptly picked up and sent home by the soldiers after a good laugh; not the effect hoped for by their German originators.

On the same day four Germans arrived opposite 1 KOYLI bearing a Red Cross Flag and purporting to bury their dead. When it was obvious that they were paying rather more than the usual attention to the defensive lay-out they were promptly captured and found to have hand grenades in their pockets. Next day the Commander of German 4th Parachute Division, whose men they were, sent over a demand for their return, in mortar shells, quoting at length, the Geneva Convention. No time was wasted by the G.O.C. in replying with 400 copies of a terse but apt reply delivered by 25-pounder shell and nothing more was heard of the incident.

On Wednesday, 12th April, 18 LAA repeated their feat in Sicily and shot down eight enemy planes. On 17th, 6 Seaforth, in the Fortress, beat off a series of small but persistent attacks against their right hand platoon. On 20th, Brigadier A. Finlaison, who had been commanding 2 Cameronians took over command of 17 Inf Bde. Five days later 5 Recce Regt, who had just arrived in the beachhead, took up position as Infantry at La Cogna.

On the 30th April another determined German attack on the Fortress overran a platoon of 2 Northamptons, then in residence. A quickly mounted counterattack, in the afternoon, was not successful. It was decided that 6 Seaforth should make another attack after midnight on 1st May, but again this was not a success. It was then planned to relieve the Northamptons with the Seaforth that night so that the former could mount a proper attack the following night. Whilst the relief was being carried out further determined local attacks were put in against 2 R INNISKS and 2 RSF as well as against 2 Northamptons, as they were about to move back. All the attacks were soundly thrashed and the Irishmen took a number of prisoners among whom was one who gave away the headquarters of 4th Parachute Div. Just after midnight, on the following night, the 3rd, "A" Company of the Northamptons put in a good and well-led attack which was unlucky not to take its objective. A conference between the G.O.C. and Brigadier Finlaison agreed that it would not be practicable to go on attacking in an attempt to get back the small position of the Fortress that had been lost, it being of no more than local importance. By now all battalions were getting very thin on the ground and reinforcements were not coming through as regularly or as fully as they might.

The Corps Commander, General Truscott, who had taken over from General Lucas, decided that the Fortress Area must be restored; a plan was discussed but was abandoned as being too expensive. His attitude underlined the importance of this key defensive position all the more.

On 6th May the Army Commander, General Mark Clark, paid another visit to the Division and was complimentary about all that he saw including the carefully contrived dummy sergeant at the salute near his dummy A.A. gun position on the drive out of Divisional H.Q. General Clark was not the first senior officer to be taken in to the extent of returning the salute.

There was no real "rest" area in the beachhead, but as battalions completed their tours in the worst sectors such as the "Fortress" and the "Lobster's Claw" it was endeavoured to get them to their "B" Echelons. Here they could at least relax although "B" Echelon was no haven of peace, being surrounded by such vulnerable targets as air O.P. landing strips and ammunition dumps. Here battalions came back to dip into the N.A.A.F.I. rations of beer and spirits that had been carefully kept for them whilst they had been fighting, and had some very successful parties. By day, when they had cleaned themselves in the mobile baths, just down the road, they set about cleaning their clothes, weapons and equipment, checking their kit and household goods. Letters were written and read as was the gossip in the local paper from home, always of interest however old it was. In between this they ate and slept as soundly as any very tired person could and did with an eternal cacophony going on around them. On special occasions unit sports and gymkhanas were held with bottles of beer for prizes. The enemy might have been a thousand miles away for all the effect they caused even when they shelled the race track or football field or playfully splashed the hardy bathers in the sea. The mobile cinema gave many happy performances and the operator's complaint was only that his performances were often spoiled by flare bombs dropped by the enemy to penetrate the

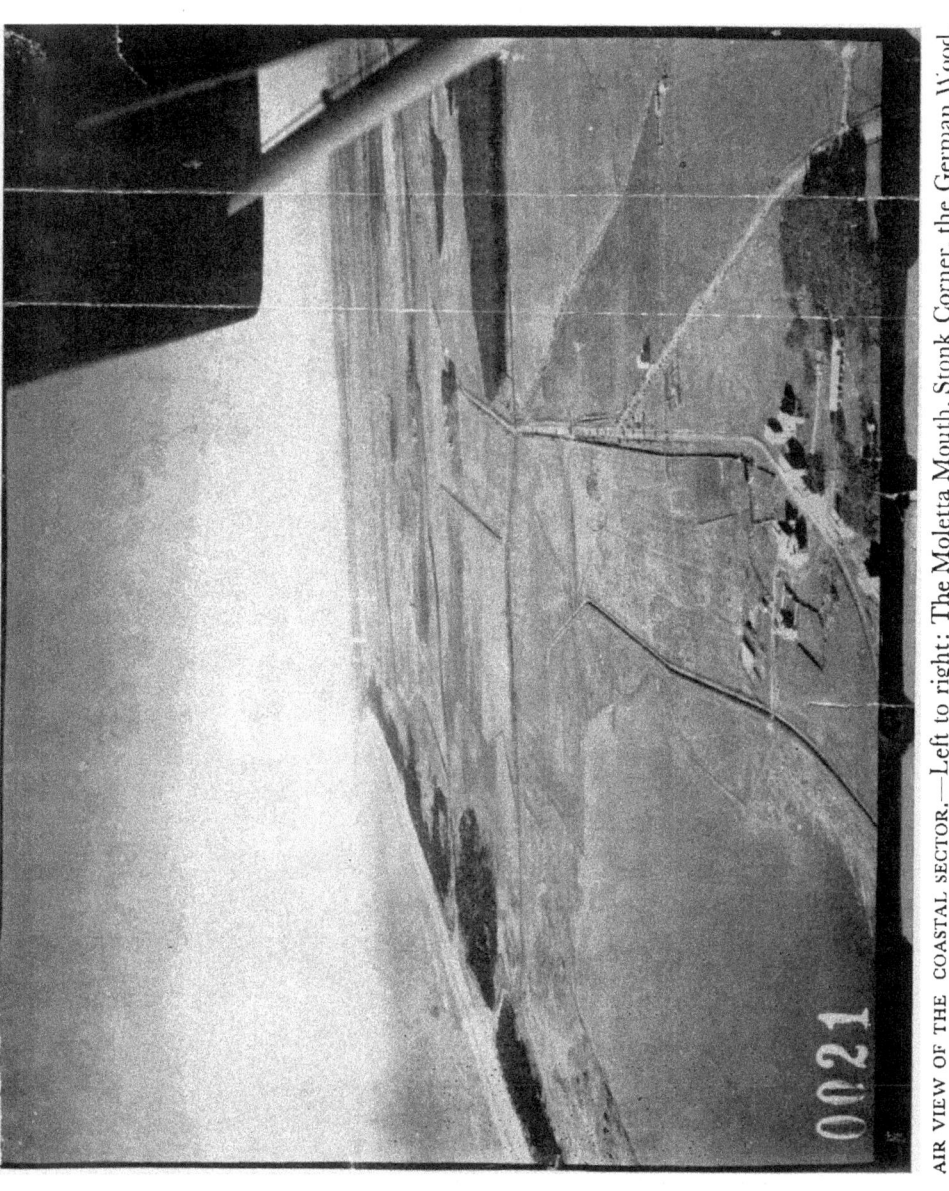

AIR VIEW OF THE COASTAL SECTOR.—Left to right: The Moletta Mouth, Stonk Corner, the German Wood.

Sappers of 245 Company R.E. building a wired log bridge over the Moletta.

MOLETTA.—Stretcher bearers return with one of the many wounded.

ANZIO: The three Brigade Commanders.
Top: left to right, Brigadier Campbell, Brigadier Dudley-Ward, Brigadier Whitfield.

CONFERENCE AT DIVISIONAL HEADQUARTERS.—Left to right, Lieut.-Colonel Pye, the G.O.C., Brigadier Whitfield, Brigadier Dudley-Ward, Brigadier Campbell (both sitting), Lieut.-Colonel Turpin (A.-Q.)

Major-General Gregson-Ellis decorates Sergeant Mumford of the 92nd Field Regiment with the Military Medal.

Lunchtime scene at "Leicester Square", outside the cave headquarters of 92nd Field Regiment.

A Patrol of the Royal Inniskilling Fusiliers in the early days of the Bridgehead.

C.Q.M.S. Sutton collects his winnings from the "Tote" of the Anzio Turf Club organized by the Green Howards when out of the line.

The mortar bomb-throwing catapult, an inspiration of Major-General Gregson-Ellis, shown on its trials. The workshops motto was well known throughout the Division to be not far from the truth.

ST. PATRICK'S DAY.—A rum issue from R.S.M. Kilduff and pipe music from Corporal Niland for the Royal Inniskilling Fusiliers as they come out of a forward position.
Private Peter G. Caraberis of Brooklyn, New York, is given instruction by Pipe Major Reach of the Seaforth.

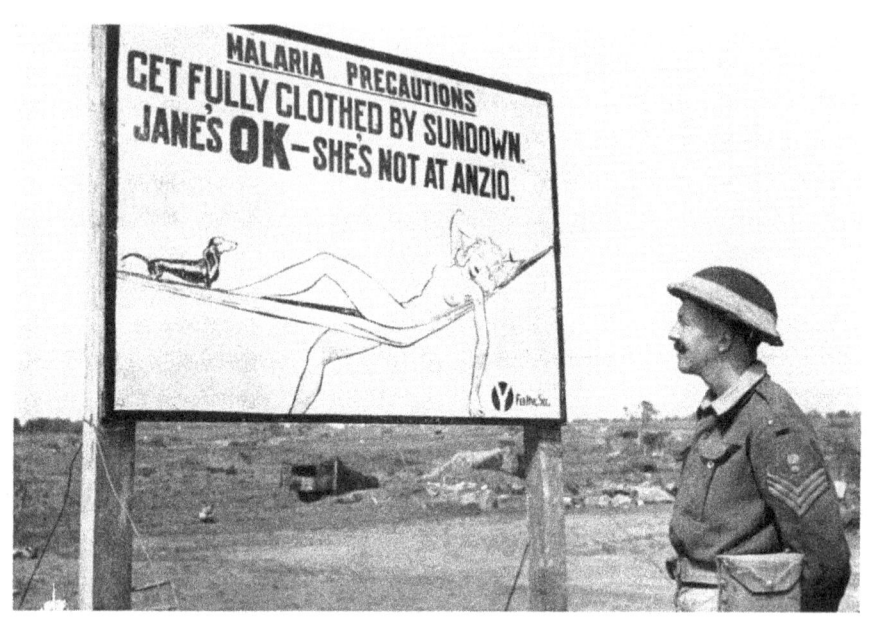

Jane plays her part in the Divisional anti-malaria campaign.

Mealtime at one of the gun pits in Gun Alley.

A Vickers Machine Gun of 7 Cheshire manned by Private Hoyland in the La Fossa area.

The Padre of 7 Cheshire leaves his frontline rectory.

ANZIO.—156th Field Regiment gunner goes back into khaki-drill soon after arriving in "B" Echelon area.

Green Howards moving up one of the forward wadis.

THE BREAK-OUT ACROSS THE MOLETTA.—Captain E. S. Roberts, M.C., of "C" Company 1st Battalion Green Howards, briefs his officers, from left to right, Captain Driscoll, Lieutenant Foster and Lieutenant Ryrie.

The troops move up to the Moletta.

MOLETTA.—Private Johnson and L/Corporal Hyman prepare to support the attack with one of the mortars of 17th Inf Brigade Support Company.

MOLETTA.—Two captured German paratroopers bring back a Green Howard who has been blown up on a mine.

Empty cases of just part of the mortar ammunition expended in the attack.

ANZIO: THE FORTRESS.

R.M.O. of 156 Field Regiment gives a morphia injection to an air raid casualty in the gun area.

General Alexander meets Captain Wedgbury of the York and Lancaster Regiment in the middle of the town of Anzio, to present him with his Military Cross.

darkness. Concert parties, professional and local talent, gave many shows that were much appreciated. The pipe bands of the Division went to play to the American Divisions, to much applause, whilst American bands, also much applauded, came to entertain battalions at rest; other Americans came round with items from their stores which they offered to exchange for any non-drinker's whisky ration.

In other branches of entertaining, enterprising amateurs had built themselves miniature radio sets in match boxes and beer bottles, they could at least listen to "Sally" from Rome, the German Propaganda Girl who sang with a good band and invited the Allies to come and join her for the night in Rome. Unit and formation newssheets flooded the free market with local gossip as well as their own outlook on things of more importance. To name a few, these were "The Beachhead News", "The Divisional News Sheet", "The Wadi Gazette", "The Steelback", "Lowdown" and others. They in their way did much towards the general maintenance of morale but unfortunately they had to be curbed before long, for fear of security, among other things. The leaflet war was waged by both sides and covered all fields, delicate and indelicate.

Beetle racing became very fashionable, owners having their "runners" numbered, registered and even painted in their colours. A totalisator was operated and serious contentions evolved around the various runners. The private "bookmakers" clubbed together to buy a notorious winner and publicly stamp it to death aware that the R.S.P.C.A. was unlikely to have inspectors in the beachhead. There was a lot of suspected substitution and foul play that would have shocked the Jockey Club of Beetle Racing had they been able to be present, but by and large a lot of innocent fun was had by all, particularly when a famous insect called "Mae West", whilst well in the lead and carrying a lot of money, as well as weight, rolled over on her back and passed out amidst rude remarks from her backers.

Meanwhile the grim struggle in the Fortress and the "Lobster's Claw" went on for each battalion as it came back from rest. But there was good news of the attack going on on the main front around Cassino and it was now getting nearer the time for the beachhead to break out in an attempt to loosen the enemy grip elsewhere. There were signs that the indomitable

4 Parachute Division, opposite 5 Div, were tiring and were probably even more depleted. By and large they had fought well and fairly. The actual break out was going to be a hard nut to crack. The Divisional Plan was for the Green Howards to attack across the Moletta River under the command of 17 Inf Bde who would mount the attack. At the same time, as soon as it was possible, it was desirable to fall back from the expensive Fortress to positions then being prepared some 300 yards to the rear. To create doubt as to where the attack was coming many dummy gun positions were built and some realistic rubber tanks were blown up in fake assembly areas. It was hoped that the Germans would not notice the odd one deflate itself when punctured by a shell splinter.

On 22nd May, 5 Div. said good-bye to United States VI Corps being now directly under command of 5 Army. At the Fortress, 15 Inf Bde, less 1 Green Howards earmarked for Operation "Wolf", as the break out was to be called, were preparing to move back a little from the Fortress. 1 Y and L were preparing to advance on the right flank towards the Buonriposo Ridge. It should be recorded that beside the battalions quite a lot of other units within the Division had been taking their share in the forward areas. The Reconnaissance Regt., as already mentioned, had been manning La Cogna. Also in the line at various times and places were all the MG platoons of 7 Cheshire. For the break out, these forty-eight Vickers guns were reinforced by eight extra Vickers, thirty-six American Browning guns presented personally by General Mark Clark and over twelve Brens. Everybody in 7 Cheshire, with the exception of the Padre, became a gun number for the occasion. The Royal Electrical and Mechanical Engineers, and the Divisional Defence Platoon also played their parts. It should also be recorded that a very elaborate Defence in Depth Plan had kept these and other units occupied in planning a series of Stop Lines should the forward troops have been overrun, on the principle that no withdrawal would be permitted. The two Divisional stop lines were known as "Blenk" Line manned by Sappers, 192 Anti-Tank Battery and a Company of 7 Cheshire, all commanded by the C.R.E., Lieut.-Colonel K. H. Osborne; and "Silver" Line manned by H.Q. 5 Div including H.Q. of attached arms and services, all commanded by Lieut.-Colonel C. S. Durtnell, Commander

7 Cheshire. Very detailed plans were made for each of these positions, plans which were rehearsed but never put into action.

The Break-out and Advances on Rome

The Battle for Rome started on 11th May with General Alexander's intention of destroying the right wing of the German Tenth Army and to drive what remained of it, together with the German Fourteenth Army North of Rome, up to the Rimini-Pisa Line "inflicting the maximum losses on him in the process". The capture of Rome, so desperately held by the Germans throughout the winter, would prove a great symbolic victory for the Allies especially if it could be achieved before 21 Army Group was launched across the Channel into Normandy. The Allies now had an invaluable bridgehead across the Garigliano, access to the Liri Valley, and a foothold in Anzio which threatened the German lines of communication. General Alexander had re-grouped his armies so that 8 Army was poised in the centre for the major attack whilst 5 Army, reinforced by the French Expeditionary Corps, would be responsible for the long front between 8 Army and the Tyrrhenian Sea. The Adriatic Sector was to be a very thinly held Corps Front. Behind the Gustav Line, the Hitler Line had been rapidly built. This was manned by General von Vietingoff's 10 Army. General von Mackeson's 14 Army was still containing VI Corps in the Anzio Bridgehead.

The plan started with a cover plan in the form of a much heralded dummy landing around Civita Vecchia, north of Rome, to try and make the enemy thin out his main Liri Valley positions. At the same time 5 Army went out of its way to give the enemy the impression that they were prepared to sit where they were until the end of the war if necessary. Meanwhile 8 Army led by the Polish Corps was to attack north of Cassino and join forces with XIII Corps west of Cassino on Highway 6 and come in on the Monastery from the north. 5 Army were to secure the Ausonia defile and advance parallel to 8 Army on Highway 6. On and after the fourth day of their operations the VI Corps at Anzio, at twenty-four hours notice, was to break out towards Valmontone to cut Highway 6 ahead of the other armies, and behind the Germans.

When the guns thundered out on 11th May they caught the

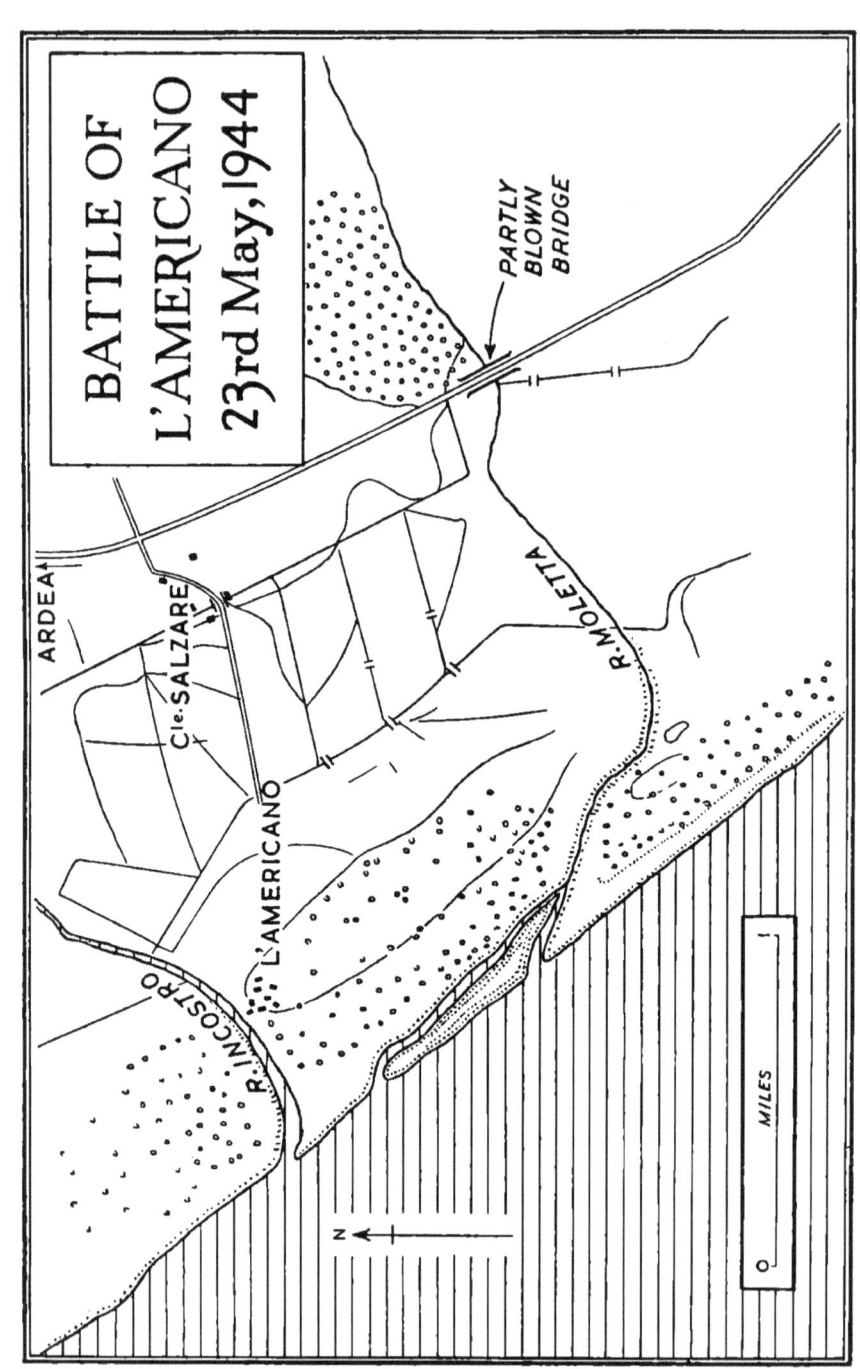

Germans completely by surprise, as they had not expected a major battle for at least another fortnight. The stories of these battles belong elsewhere; of the Poles at Cassino; of XIII Corps crossing the Rapido River and fighting in the Liri Valley; of the French Corps's magnificent advance over the mountains on the left flank; of the American II Corps coastal advance up to Anzio and of the Canadians at Pontecorvo.

When 5 Army had got as far as Itri and Monte Grando, General Alexander decided to push the American II Corps up towards the beachhead which was now to break out. The enemy against VI Corps was now 4 Parachute Division opposite 5 Div, 65 Grenadier Div astride the Albano road and facing 1 Div, and 3 Panzer Grenadier Division, 362 Grenadier Div and 71 Light Div, with various other troops, opposite the American 45 and 34 Divs and the 36 Engr Combat Regt which had recently been under command of 5 Div. The American 3 Div, and 1 Armoured Div were behind them in reserve and 36 Div was about complete in the bridgehead. The main battle against Valmontone was to be an American one. 1 and 5 Divs would have only minor diversionary attacks to make and were not to be used north of the Tiber. 5 Div was to strike the first blow of all. This was known as operation "Wolf" and was mounted by 17 Inf Bde but carried out by 1 Green Howards of 15 Inf Bde and attached troops.

Operation "Wolf"

Operation "Wolf" was really little more than a battalion raid on the extreme left flank, aimed to keep 4th Parachute Division from influencing the American outbreak to the east, timed to start on the 23rd May. The enemy was now weak on the ground, but was still strong enough to make himself felt from his well developed defensive positions. He also had what benefit there was to be gained from observation of the battlefield. This and their stubborn tenacity, helped the Germans to make the break out from the beachhead, both in the case of this preliminary operation "Wolf", and in the later American drive, a fierce prolonged struggle. Enormous casualties were caused to the Allies who were robbed of much of the kudos of eventual victory, won by sheer weight of numbers and superiority of arms that bulldozed the eventual way to Highways 6 and 7.

The plan for operation "Wolf" was a simple one. The Moletta even at its mouth was not a formidable obstacle and the water then was not deep. A start line had to be secured and a base set up on the south bank by 2 Northamptons. 1 Green Howards were then to pass through and advance along the dunes to L'Americano, an enemy held farm on the next river, northwards, the Foce, and about 2,000 yards away. This achieved, they were then to return to base.

The initial assault started with the Sappers of 38 Company gapping the minefields at 0330 hrs. on the 23rd May. Here difficulties were met right away. The Sapper Gapping Party struck mines that killed their officer and a member of 12 Platoon, Green Howards, detailed to assist them, wounding several others. This brought down intensive enemy mortar and artillery D.F. which never ceased until the operation was concluded. "D" Company crossed the Moletta and the start line, on the north side, at 0447 hrs. and captured their objective, a M.G. position on the west edge of the position, by 0505 hrs. under a standing barrage from the Divisional Artillery which moved on at 0613 hrs. At 0700 hrs., 18 Platoon of "D" Company cleared the enemy Spandau post and consolidated its position which was in close scrub and therefore gave limited visibility. Several odd Germans were mopped up in this process. At 1000 hrs. 11 Platoon of 7 Cheshire got their machine guns up but were unable to establish them owing to pockets of enemy still being in their area. They were put down in the area of another platoon and half a platoon were sent from "B" Company to make up the losses of "D" Company. At midday a special carrier party delivered rations, water, wire and ammunition to the Forward Company.

At 0600 hrs. "C" Company had crossed the Moletta and prepared to move up to the assistance of "D" Company. It immediately ran into mines which played great havoc, and tried to go through "D" Company to L'Americano. By now the enemy were fully alerted and were particularly active from the long strip of wood to the east of the dunes. The tanks managed to keep up with the Infantry but one of them was hit in the engine.

At 0924 hrs. "C" Company made their assault with an Artillery Fire plan of which smoke, to blind the wood on the right flank, was a feature. Helped by other companies shooting

The British cemetery at Anzio in which the Divisional dead are buried, seen at the time of the break-out from the Bridgehead.

The Divisional Pipers play at the Colosseum in Rome.

The Fortress after the battle.

when they could see through the dunes, they carried the objective with great difficulty. In so doing, they suffered losses from German rifle and MG fire and from grenades thrown from the houses. One section of 13 Platoon including the officer in command were all killed by machine-gun fire whilst trying to reinforce the objective.

"C" Company were on their objective but desperately hanging on against tremendous odds. At 0930 hrs. the C.O. ordered them to hold on and the artillery started a curtain of fire, as at Minturno, which was to last for hours on end. Some of the enemy were seen to be infiltrating down the river but were spotted and dealt with by the gunners. At 1130 hrs., after an uncomfortable journey, Captain Howell delivered fifteen reinforcements to the beleaguered "C" Company, and one carrier got up with wire and ammunition, so that the position could be consolidated. They were being heavily shelled whilst doing so and two were killed while digging. This position was about 400 yards broad and about 600 yards ahead of the intermediate "D" Company.

At 1238 hrs. the enemy started a thick smoke screen around L'Americano on the Foce River and firing increased. The G.O.C. and Brigadier Finlaison arrived for a conference with Lieut.-Colonel Perreau at 1400 hours and decided that two platoons of Northamptons from the south bank should go to reinforce "C" Company, who must drive the enemy across the Foce. The two platoons were to be supported by five tanks from 46 R. Tanks and F.O.O.s from Field and Medium Regiments. This party was not to attack but was to infiltrate whilst the guns dealt with a counterattack which was obviously building up behind the enemy smoke. This attack did come in from the right flank with much shouting and automatic fire; a further party got round the sea flank and the Green Howard-Northampton positions became a salient assailed on all sides. "C" Company were soon overrun and survivors made their way back to "D" Company who were now attacked from the left; they were now less than seventy strong and were again attacked this time from the front. This threat was beaten off by the fire of all calibre weapons particularly of the Cheshire machine gunners, and the enemy withdrew for the night. Shelling was intensive from now on and a covering position commanded by Major C. S. Scrope and a scratch force of "C" Company survivors and some men of 2 Northamptons was formed behind "D" Company on the north bank of the Moletta. At 0415 hrs. it was planned to withdraw "D" Company from the north bank but they were then out of touch with Battalion and this withdrawal eventually took place at 0900 hrs. covered by 2 Northamptons. The enemy followed it up to grenade range but were beaten off in a very close-quarters battle. The Divisional Artillery still fired away almost ceaselessly, causing tremendous casualties to the advancing enemy. Within a short time all were safely across the Moletta and the noise of battle died away.

Whatever this small engagement achieved tactically, at the expense of casualties to the Green Howards (six officers and 149 other ranks), it seemed to show how well all arms in the Division could support each other. Gallant efforts were made to lay cable up to the forward companies and each time it was shelled and cut, repair detachments were lost on mines. Radio was erratic but some gallant operators, some of whom were doing other jobs such as mortar detachment at the same time, saw that the vital links were kept open. The tanks of 46 R. Tanks gave first-class support throughout. Before the carriers got up they moved ammunition to forward positions, then sent back valuable information on their own. Despite mines they never failed to go where they were wanted and in doing so lost two tanks burned out and two ditched. The Gunners fired more than 50,000 rounds, firstly to explode mines and cut wire, then to cover the advance and finally to ward off counter-attack. The machine gunners had some really good shots and rose to the occasion. The Sappers had initial misfortune when they ran into minefields which had only been laid a few hours previously but never ceased to try and clear the way for the Infantry.

At 0545 hrs. on the 23rd, whilst 5 Div were holding 4 Parachute Division on the Moletta, the expected grand barrage of shells and bombs opened up the way for VI Corps who were, nevertheless, to have to fight for every inch of it. It took the 3rd U.S. Division three days to capture Cisterna from the remnants of 362 Grenadier Division who still held their ground around Velletri. The Allied Air Force were causing colossal chaos among the German troops trying to regroup and move by road. On the 26th, 34 and 45 Divs switched towards

Rome while 3 U.S. Division continued on the original axis to Valmontone. Here the Hermann Goering Division, who had dogged 5 Div throughout the war, stood so brilliantly that the major part of the German Tank Army was able to withdraw behind it.

1 British Div meantime had started to move forward and slightly toward the new American advance. On the 24th plans were made for 5 Div to take over 1 Div's front as well as its own. At the same time it became possible to release the pressure in the Fortress Area and to pull back some 300 yards to positions already prepared. This was a move that the Divisional Commander would dearly have liked to have been able to do before, but such was the importance of the Fortress that to have abandoned it would have given the enemy a chance of breaking in to the Allied Perimeter. It cost the Division almost a thousand lives to hold the Fortress, a small apparently insignificant piece of ground, but it was held with the most commendable and gallant determination.

On the 25th the Advancing American II Corps linked up with the beachhead which was now technically relieved. Patrolling became active but the Germans showed no signs of relenting in front of the Division. On Saturday 27th, 15 Inf Bde took over the area of 3 Inf Bde of 1 Div which was immediately around the main Albano-Anzio road in the neighbourhood of the fly-over bridge. This was not used for long as an O.P. as the brigade advanced slowly that day with 1 Y and L probing across the Buonriposo Ridge up the familiar road of derelict houses and burnt out tanks that had been the right hand boundary of the Divisional Front for so long. 17 Inf Bde planned to probe forward on the left with minor attacks the following day. One of these raids brought tragedy to 2 RSF who were caught by their own box barrage just as they were on the enemy wire, waiting to break through; they suffered many casualties but did not lose confidence in their gunners, so great had been the support during the last eleven months. It was symbolic however of a tired and much overworked machine that now needed rest and a change of oil. On the right 1 Y and L, under the merciless driving of Lieut.-Colonel R. J. Kaulback, were going ahead extremely well. The experienced parachutists of 4 Parachute Division were still full of fight and individual skill and mines were a prolific deterrent. To their left 1 KOYLI were having a tougher time and undoubtedly were up against the enemy's hard core; the positions from which the enemy had fought so ruggedly for the last months.

Gradually the defences around the enemy centre of Ardea were being entered and this was confirmed by the increase in tempo of enemy shelling. 1 Green Howards, now reinforced with very inexperienced troops, were counterattacked and driven out of a position they had won in the early hours of the 31st. The forward companies of 6 Seaforth and 2 Northamptons, further to the left, had also to be reinforced. The unfitness of troops who had sat in holes for most of the winter, was now beginning to take its toll, but the indomitable spirit of "The Globetrotters" carried them even when their feet advised them not to go. The going was hard and rough everywhere, against the succession of wadis that ran across the front, and devoid of tracks, particularly in the centre, although on the right, use was made of a railway cutting that ran from south-east to north-west.

At last observation was swinging round to the Division's advantage and the pattern of what lay ahead was a little less a matter of conjecture.

In the early hours of the 1st June, one complete Company of 6 Seaforth was practically annihilated by an unexpected clash in the night. This was further evidence of the need for rest and refitting if ever there was any. Contact was kept with 1 Div on the right and many plans were made for combined attacks; none of them materialized although the two Divisional Artilleries were able to help each other. 5 Div Artillery was finding it hard to produce its erstwhile mobility, and on one occasion was so ashamed of the barrage it had evolved for an attack that it decided to fire it again just to show that it could do better, given favourable conditions.

The Battle for Ardea

On 3rd June in the early afternoon 1 Y and L mounted a good attack against point 55 which coincided with an equally good one by 2 WILTS on their left. In both cases they suffered minimum casualties and staved off some pretty desperate counterattacks.

The attack of 2 WILTS was the highlight of the Anzio

Sergeant Maurice Albert Wyndham Rogers, V.C. The Wiltshire Regiment (Duke of Edinburgh's).

Finale, it also brought the one and only V.C. to the Division. 4 Parachute Division had organized a very strong position on the high ground north-west of Ardea. Troops on either flank of 2 WILTS were completely pinned down and so they attacked the two main enemy centres each with a company. "C" Company was directed on to Point 51 and "D" Company on to Point 57. Both advances were held up short of the objectives by heavy casualties. The only reserve by now left to the Battalion Commander was the dismounted Carrier Platoon. This was immediately ordered to capture the north-east Spur running out of Ardea supported by a troop of 46 R. Tanks. This platoon was led by Sergeant Rogers, M.M., and Corporals Boyland and Cuddle with such gallantry that all objectives were taken after all the N.C.O.s had been killed.

The Special Order of the day later issued by the General gives an account of this supremely gallant occasion.

"His Majesty The King has been graciously pleased to approve the posthumous award of the Victoria Cross to:

"No. 5568932 Sergeant Maurice Albert Wyndham Rogers, The Wiltshire Regiment (Duke of Edinburgh's) (Plaistow).

"In Italy a Battalion of the Wiltshire Regiment was ordered to attack high ground held by the enemy.

"The leading Company had taken their first objective but were unable to reach their final objective owing to heavy enemy fire, and casualties. The Carrier Platoon, dismounted were ordered to capture the final objective, supported by fire from the Company and a troop of tanks.

"The objective was wired and mined and strongly defended by the enemy. The Carrier Platoon advanced through machine gun and mortar fire until they reached the enemy's wire, which was 70 yards from their objective. At this point the Platoon was under the intense fire of seven machine guns firing at ranges from 50 to 100 yards, and sustained a number of casualties. The Platoon, checked by the enemy's wire and the intensity of his machine gun fire, took cover and returned the fire preparatory to gapping the wire. Sgt. Rogers, the Platoon Sergeant, without hesitation continued to advance alone, firing his Thompson sub-machine gun. He got through the enemy's wire, ran across the minefield and destroyed two of the enemy machine gun posts with his Thompson sub-machine gun and hand grenades. By now, Sergeant Rogers was 100

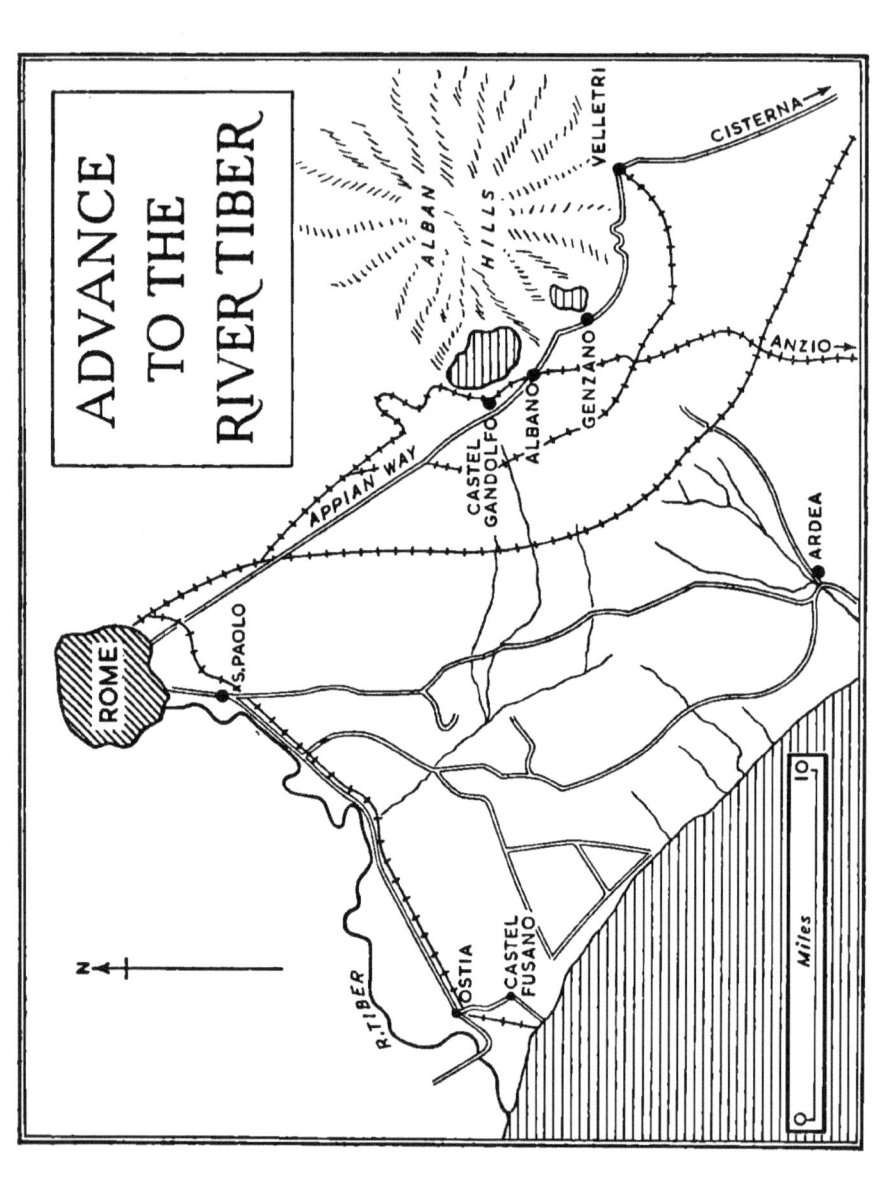

yards ahead of his Platoon and had penetrated 30 yards inside the enemy's defences.

"He had drawn on to himself the fire of nearly all the enemy's machine guns and had thrown their defences into confusion.

"Inspired by the example of Sergeant Rogers, the Platoon breached the enemy's wire and began the assault. Still alone and penetrating deeper into the enemy position, Sergeant Rogers, while attempting to silence a third machine gun post was blown off his feet by a grenade which burst beside him and wounded him in the leg.

"Nothing daunted, he stood up and still firing his Thompson sub-machine gun, ran on towards the enemy post. He was shot and killed at point blank range.

"This N.C.O.'s undaunted determination, fearless devotion to duty and superb courage carried his Platoon on to their objective in face of a determined enemy in a strongly defended position. The great gallantry and heroic self-sacrifice of Sergeant Rogers were in the highest traditions of the British Army."

This award was a fitting culmination to this great example of what could happen even after months of monotonous existence.

Advance to the Tiber

Sunday 4th June saw the end of 4 Parachute Division's opposition and the 5 Recce Regt went through in the traditional rôle that had been denied it since the chase up Southern Italy of nine months ago. In the beachhead they had played their part but as with the 52 A Tk Regt there could be nothing so irksome as being unable to carry out the rôle for which they had been trained. They cleared away what little opposition there remained and reached the banks of the Tiber, the first Allied Troops to do so, before dark that night. A few days previously it had been piously hoped that they would come up to the Tiber in Rome itself. There had been a certain amount of playful jostling among Divisions for place of first into Rome, and the Divisional Provost had spent the last week or so producing magnificent signs to the effect that "Y" Division welcomed all and sundry to Rome. These were put into a special truck which was to have driven with the General's Tactical

Party sweeping on behind the forward squadrons of the 5 Recce Regt.

There were many other stories told of that hectic chase to the Tiber. Whilst 15 Inf Bde were still fighting around point 55 the Line Laying Truck of an O.P. Party of 92 Fd Regt was instructed to go on laying its cable up a certain axis until it found the O.P. which was moving very frequently. The party got so immersed in their work that they did not notice that they had outstripped the O.P. Party and indeed the Forward Troops, until when they stopped to tie back the wire, they dropped on to a German Machine Gun Detachment. The latter were so surprised that the Signallers managed to get away down the ditch just as their truck was hit and burst into flames. A very shaken detachment eventually got back into friendly country.

On Monday, 5th June, Divisional H.Q. moved up to the park of Castel Fusano. The General learned that the Division was to be withdrawn and sent back to the Middle East for refitting whilst 1 Div was to go on northwards past Rome.

The Battle for Rome was now at an end. The withdrawal of the major part of the German 10 and 14 Armies had been made through Rome during the night of the 3rd and 4th June. This withdrawal was covered in the Alban Hills by the 4 Parachute Division who fell back on to prepared positions after their tussle with 5 Div at Ardea. This small rearguard kept contact with the American Reconnaissance Columns moving along Highways 6 and 7 and only checked them for a short time just south-east of the City outskirts. As the Germans passed out of Rome, some of them in a bad way and in improvised transport of a great variety, the real opposition to the advancing Allies lay in the wildly excited crowds half delirious in the approved Italian manner. By midnight of Sunday the 4th, however, the bridges on the Tiber were secured at the same time as 5 Recce Regt arrived at the river near Ostia Antica. The 88 Div, who had taken over the Minturno Sector from 5 Div in February, were now the first into Rome.

The wild scenes in Rome continued for some forty-eight hours but the advance had to go on to maintain contact with the German armies fast falling back on to the next line on the Arno. On the 6th June, the news of the Allied landings in North-West Europe took the sting out of the Roman triumph.

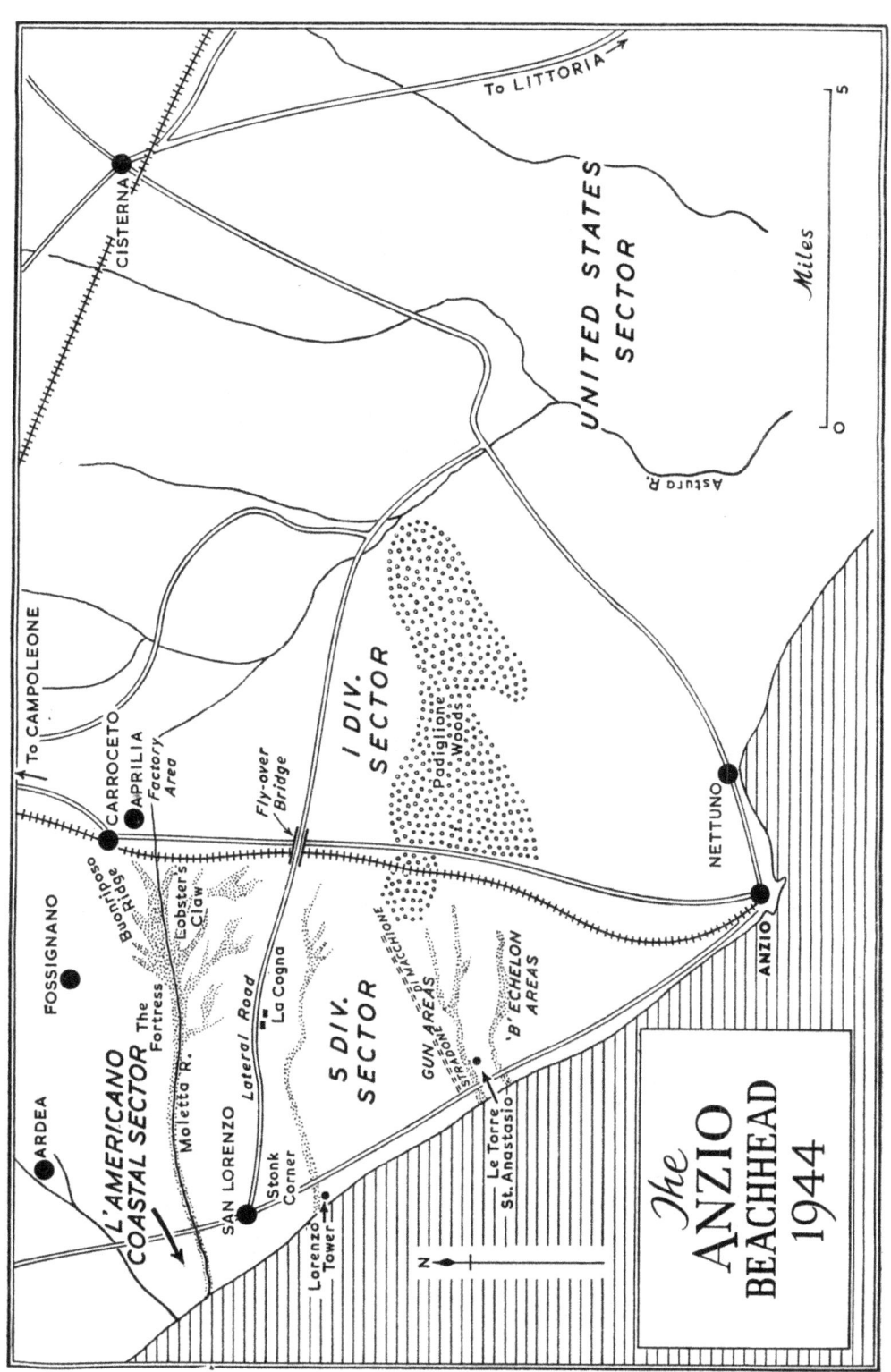

Although denied entry into Rome, 5 Div, on the extreme left wing of the battle, had played a noble and very positive part in the ultimate victory.

The price paid for this achievement was not inconsiderable, 155 officers and 2,838 men had become casualties since the Division landed at Anzio into what the Americans so picturesquely called "The Hatbox of Hell".

A fitting tribute was paid by The Army Commander, in a letter to the G.O.C. dated 20th June:—

"It is with profound regret that I must now say farewell to the Officers and Men of the Fifth British Division.

"The complete harmony and co-operation which have constantly existed between British and American Units within Fifth Army have given me one of the greatest satisfactions of my Command. Truly Fifth Army has been symbolic of the entire United Nations War Effort as well as of the future relations between our countries, which will ensure a better and more stable peace.

"The part played by The British Fifth Division in the consolidation of the Beachhead, the gruelling months of fighting which ensued and the Division's participation in the operations resulting in the final break out are so well known that they need no emphasis at this time.

"I am deeply grateful to your Division, as well as to yourself, for the way in which you carried your share of the burden. I am proud to have had your Division under my command, and as you depart for new undertakings, I wish to extend my congratulations for a job performed in a superior manner and my heartfelt good wishes for your future success.

"Sincerely yours,

"(signed) Mark W. Clark.
"Lieutenant General, U.S.A.
"Commanding."

CHAPTER THIRTEEN

THE MIDDLE EAST REVISITED

In which 5th Division bids farewell to the Roman Campagna, concentrates north of Naples and sails again for the Middle East. In which reinforcements are absorbed, equipment, guns and vehicles replaced once more, and intensive training is resumed. In which Advance Parties of the Division sail for Italy in November and are just about to take over from 4th Division on the Adriatic Sector of Eighth Army when they are recalled in time to rejoin the Division for Christmas in Palestine.

The move back again

A few men from the Division found their way into Rome on 6th June, whilst the American columns were pouring northwards, but Rome was put out of bounds to the Division generally. This caused a lot of heartaches to those who had fought their way from Sicily, always being told that they were on their way to Rome. General Gregson-Ellis was as much aware of this as anyone else was. He fought a valiant battle for the order to be rescinded and, while this was *sub judice*, permitted certain people to go while they could and particularly those who were going on the advance parties. The general feeling though, was one of frustration rather than of resentment. Not only had they been banned from seeing Rome but also the battle in North-West Europe had started without "The Globetrotters" and there was no *Queen Mary*, off Ostia, to take them home.

There were exceptions for the privileged, however, for on Monday, 12th June, at ten o'clock in the morning, a 5 Div Mass was celebrated in St. Peter's Basilica and the Pope honoured the Division by holding a large audience afterwards. The Pipers of the Inniskilling Fusiliers played at this audience and were so carried away by the occasion that they gave three cheers for the Pope which caused a few embarrassing moments to those who were there.

Senior Commanders, 1944.

Unit Commanders, 1944.

The road to Tiberius.

The Gateway from which St Paul escaped from Damascus.

Egypt-Palestine Frontier.

Six Columns of Jupiter, Baalbeck.

Two days prior to this the massed Pipers of the Division, about fifty strong, played and marched between the Colosseum and the Piazza Venezia, which was a great novelty for the Italians and a tremendous boost to morale in all quarters. Pipe Major Macconnachie's "The Roads that Lead to Rome" was played on this occasion for the first time.

But these glimpses were all that 5 Div got of The Eternal City; the Division had been concentrated around Castel Fusano, Castel Porziano, and Ostia. The area had once been lovely parkland with Ostia as the Roman Brighton, but now it was barricaded and heavily mined as the Germans had expected landings there from the sea. The gunners were concentrated around Anzio again and all moved down to the area north-east of Naples with Divisional Headquarters at Pignaturo. The advance parties set off and sailed to Alexandria, where they entrained for Cairo. At Mena Barracks, near the Pyramids, they started to take over from 56 Div whom they had relieved in Anzio. This time the roles were reversed, for the London Division, after a few months refitting and training, were to return to rejoin 8 Army on its trek into Northern Italy. 5 Div was to follow this cycle coming back under command of 8 Army later still.

Before leaving Italy the G.O.C. received a letter from Lieut.-General Sir Oliver Leese, who was then commanding 8 Army, welcoming the Division back to the Army:—

"I would like to take this opportunity to welcome your Division to the Eighth Army. We all look forward to the day when you rejoin us after your well-earned period of rest in the Middle East.

"The 5th Division has seen much fighting in the Eighth Army. I well remember when you landed in Sicily and fought alongside 30 Corps in the Catania Plain. I then watched your Division in their operation across the Straits of Messina. When I returned to the Eighth Army in the New Year I heard great stories of the Fifth Division's fights up to the Sangro Line. It was a great regret to the Eighth Army that you then left us to join the Fifth Army. We followed there your epic fight on the Garigliano. Since then, we have watched with the greatest admiration your tough battles in the Anzio Beachhead.

"I would like to refer to the previous record of your Division

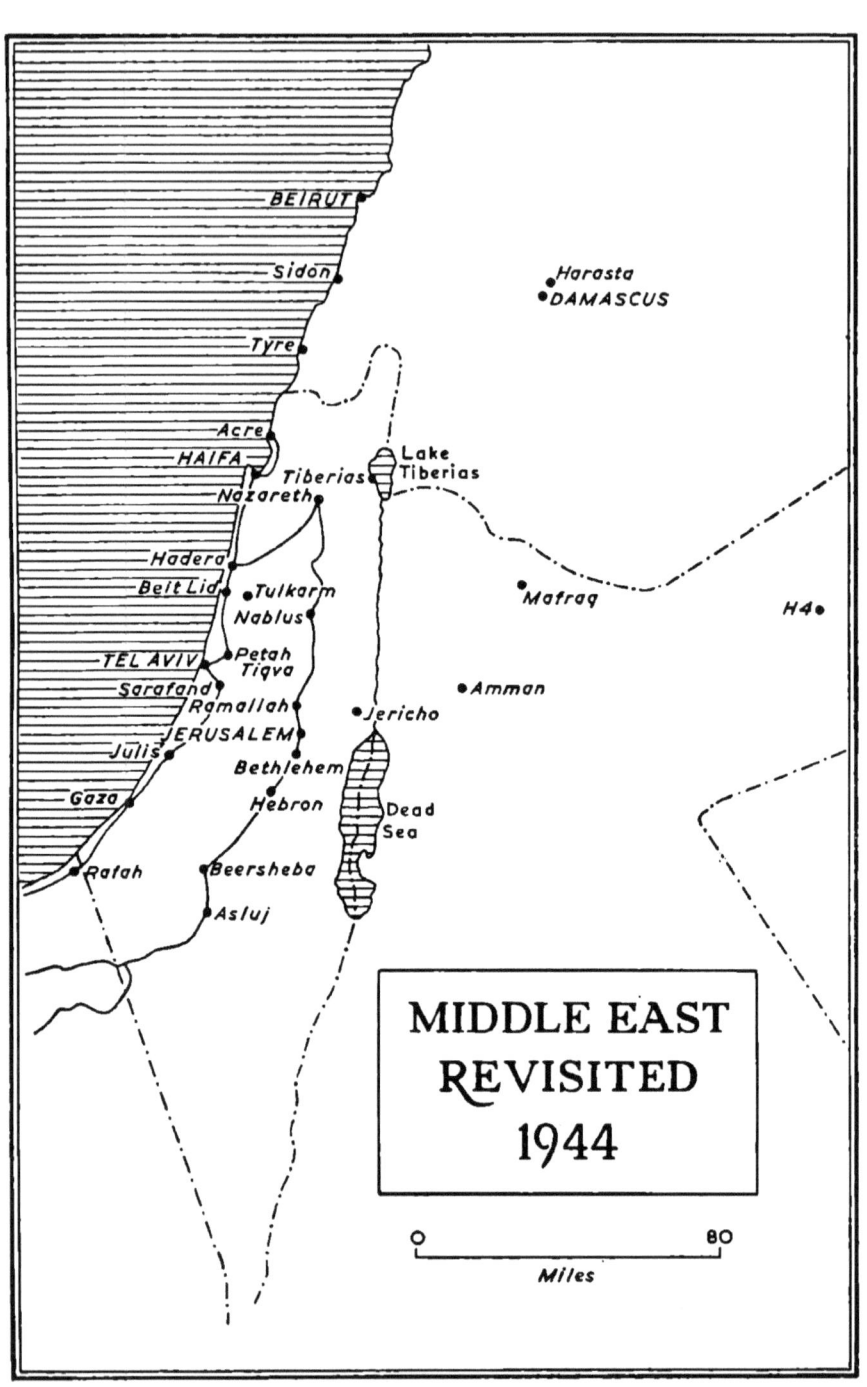

before they joined the Eighth Army, it must be unique. In 1940 you took part in the heaviest fighting in France, while one of your Brigades was in Norway. You then sent a Brigade to Madagascar. After this, the Division saw service in India and in the Middle East. It is indeed a wonderful record, of which you may be very proud.

"I would be grateful if you would tell all ranks of your Division how glad we are that you are returning to the Eighth Army. Many tasks lie ahead of us on the road to Victory and we are glad that the 5th Division will march with us."

The equipment taken over from 56 Div was nearly new and in good condition, the vehicles and guns being painted in desert sand colour. A few "restful" evenings were spent in Cairo and the main bodies arrived at Port Said. The Division then moved by convoy up to Palestine, and later into Syria.

Training in Palestine and Syria

For eleven months the Division had been almost continuously in action after a long period of training. Units in turn, it is true, had a few days' rest here and there, but the Divisional Staff Officers and Divisional Units such as the Gunners, Sappers and Machine Gunners had been in action all the time or else moving from one position to another. The RASC Drivers had driven many thousands of miles more than the Division as a whole had actually travelled and the other services had had but little rest except possibly for those who had to be left behind as rear details at, for instance, Castellemare, near Naples, when the rest of the Division was fighting at Anzio. Some of the fighting soldiers also had periods of respite on courses, in hospital, and at the Divisional Battle School, which was run near Foggia all the time the Division had been fighting in Fifth Army. But by and large the Division was very tired and sadly depleted of the trained men with which it went into Sicily. This was evident from the shaky performance given by some, when the Division got up out of its holes in the ground to advance to Tiber. There was only one thing to be done and that was to start all over again and build up a fresh Division embodying all the spirit and experience of the old one.

This then was the object and theme of training in Palestine and Syria during the next six months. Very little time was left for initial relaxation, much of which was obtained on the voyage from Italy to Egypt, and straight away training went to the mechanics of elementary soldiering. However much of a veteran he might now consider himself, not a single man was too proud to start his soldiering all over again. It took a very little longer this way and produced every bit as good a result when required.

Most units had passed through Palestine during their previous tour in the Middle East; now they were to work there at some length and admire the brave effort that this small new nation was putting into reclaiming the desert into its collective farms and at the same time, keeping itself strong enough to prevent any over-exuberant neighbour from trespassing. Camps were situated from the Er Rama area in the north, near the Syrian border, to Julis, near Gaza in the south, or, as it might be said, from Dan to Beersheba.

Divisional H.Q. was established at Hadera early in July and units were in part-hutted and part-tented camps stretching up to the Carmel foothills and in among the Jewish villages where the troops freely mixed in the continental type cafés. There was pleasant bathing on the coast which was very near to the camp, there were trips into Tel Aviv and Jerusalem, there were camp cinemas and theatres for concerts and dances, the climate was wonderful and training was hard but not severe; yet the soldier who wore the "Y", by now quickly acclimatized to anything, soon became bored with spending money and became anxious to get back to Italy.

A new language had now to be mastered or mastered enough at least to be able to ask a local girl to dance ["Kif Halak?" (How are you); "Ilhamdilla Maesut" (Very well, thank you); "Ana Inglizi" (I am an Englishman), as if that were not obvious]; but the experienced soldier was now not to be daunted by the cosmopolitan population of Palestine. The local population were in fact, extremely kind to the soldiers of 5 Div and nowhere more so than in the "Ark" at Tel Aviv; here was a real Soldiers Club run efficiently and generously, some of the Division's concert parties and soloists returned the hospitality by giving their services for special performances.

Visits were arranged to some of the Jewish settlements each of which were run communally striving to become entirely self-supporting on an agricultural and dairy farming basis.

How departmental committees ran the various activities of the settlement; how everybody worked for nothing but the necessities of physical and mental well-being, were studied with interest. Visitors were shown everything and entertained in the evening to a good meal and to some folk dancing followed by a style of dancing with which they were more familiar.

In the middle of September, the Divisional Artillery went to practice camp at Harasta, near Damascus, and there quickly proved that they had got back all the old magic of Damascus. Exercise "Harass", a formation exercise set by 9 Army under whose command the Division was then, tested everybody fully, particularly in rapid movement and deployment, an art for which there had not been much scope in either the Gargliano or Anzio battles. Division set three appropriately named exercises for brigades known as "Matthew", "Mark" and "Luke", these again were to practise mobility using vehicles as well as feet. On "Matthew" Brigadier C. T. Huxley who had taken over 15 Inf Bde from Brigadier J. Y. Whitfield, was getting a little frustrated by what he considered to be unfair machinations on the part of the umpires and Directing Staff. He was particularly exasperated when he was informed over the radio whilst talking to one of his battalion commanders, that the latter had been held up by a lot of imaginary "Tiger" tanks invented by the umpires. His prompt reply was to the effect that "Those —— the Gods are responsible for this" when he was interrupted over the air by a familiar voice proclaiming "This is a God speaking, you asked for it and now you're going to get it"; and the Tigers multiplied almost visibly. Fortunately for the delayed battalion, God smote the Tigers with a ball of fire and the exercise was continued.

Entertainment took on the usual pattern but in this period the quality and quantity of sport within the Division was never so high. Football had always been played within and between units and the Division had some useful players, among them Pte. Mannion of the Green Howards, the England and Middlesbrough player and Pte. Saga of the R.A.S.C. who had kept goal for England. Cricket had been hotly pursued by the Green Howards in particular and some opponents were found from within the Division for the battalion side that once included Lieutenant Norman Yardley and Captain Hedley Verity. But now fresh fields were entered. Hockey was taken up with great enthusiasm, as was cross country running, competition swimming and even cycle racing. The Divisional cyclists, who quite appropriately, called themselves "The Wanderers", did well to win an all Palestine race. Tennis, Boxing and Rugger had their enthusiasts, the latter being taken extremely seriously. There were, however, lighter forms of sport ranging from gymkhanas, skill at arms and other fancy events, to inter-unit officers football matches, which proved fair game for the sarcastic tongues of the spectators.

On one occasion when a battalion side was playing its affiliated Gunner officers one of the latter made a spectacularly uncontrolled shot at goal. An Infantry officer, wishing to show his knowledge of gunnery shouted "Shot one", quick as lightning came the cockney voice of a spectator "Unobserved".

The Padres of the Division took the opportunity of organizing many pilgrimages, all of which were well attended, to places of Biblical interest. Nazareth, Bethlehem, Jericho, Acre, Tiberias, Lake Galilee and Jerusalem were all visited. The latter appeared to overdo the commercial aspect of religion to an unappetizing degree, but it was a great experience for so many members of the Division to have the Bible brought so vividly to life before their eyes. Although the modern Jewish population was apt to sport very racy clothing, there was still enough of the old-style Arab against the background that has hardly ever changed through the centuries, to complete the timeless illusion in most places. In Damascus, in Syria, particularly was this so, the Suk or market place cannot have changed at all, and the surrounding countryside must have been exactly as St. Paul saw it when he made his escape from the city walls.

Whilst in Damascus in September, some of the Division were at "The Cercle" or French Officers' Club, when the liberation of Paris was celebrated. Against the background of the fiery double-barred Cross of Lorraine, lit by electric light in the hillside, it was an occasion chiefly memorable for the celebration by the English rather than by the French, who remained slightly aloof at the "Droshki" race organized by some well known Divisional characters; a race that ended up in the goldfish pool and fountain at the entrance to the ballroom. From Syria many members of the Division revisited the wonderful Leave Centre of Beirut, perhaps the most magnificent leave centre ever encountered by the Division on its many travels.

Advance Parties to Italy and Back

This six months break was truly a memorable one of hard training, sport and pleasure which was much appreciated, and although the Division had now been away from home for two and a half years, morale, for the reasons referred to elsewhere, was extremely high again and the earlier sentiments of wanting to get on with the job and take further steps nearer home, were now predominant. When, in November, it was suddenly announced that 5 Div was about to go back to Italy to rejoin 8 Army in the Rimini Sector, there was a great uplift of interest and excitement. Advance parties under the command of Lieut.-Colonel I. G. H. Leake, Commander of Divisional R.E.M.E., left Haifa shortly afterwards on a Canadian lake steamer. The Eastern Mediterranean once more obliged with its alarmingly sudden tempests and the flat-bottomed boat proved a great conserver of none too appetizing feeding arrangements, even on a level sea. A few days were spent in Transit Camp at Taranto and then the whole party moved by train up to Pescara on the Adriatic Coast, a few miles north of Ortona, the farthest north that the Division got about eleven months previously. This rail journey was one of the coldest in conditions of great discomfort where a shave could only be got by extracting hot water from the engine-driver—at a price. The "carriages" provided were open cattle trucks, very draughty and bumpy.

At Pescara the advance parties took over vehicles from 4 Div who were on their way back to the Middle East after some hard fighting. 4 Div then departed for Bari and Taranto, and 5 Div advance parties waited with the vehicles for the main parties to arrive from Haifa. They waited in vain. A division was urgently wanted in Greece and it was decided that this was a task for the reserve division. Plans were made to bring them direct from the Middle East to Greece and the guns and vehicles were to be shipped from Bari and Taranto. Almost immediately it was realized that it would take too long to effect such a move, even with the swift-footed "Globetrotters", and instead 4 Div were diverted to Athens. 5 Div advance parties then had to make a dash south as quickly as possible to hand back the vehicles to 4 Div. This was a move to be remembered. Weather and road conditions were appalling and there were not really enough drivers to go round. To counter this a little judicious towing was employed, and all those motor cyclists who could drive four wheeled vehicles hoisted their motor cycles on to lorries, and lent a hand. The hand-back was completed in time and after a few days further waiting in the Taranto Transit Camp, the thwarted advance parties eventually set sail for Alexandria, escorting German prisoners recently captured in the north. Some of the latter insisted on dragging a Christmas tree on board one ship the *Bergensfjord* quite determined to celebrate *Weinacht*, wherever they might be, in the traditional manner.

And so, just a few days before Christmas, the advance parties returned to much applause from those who had stayed in Palestine. This was to be the fifth Christmas of the war and the third away from home. It was a good one and the very best was made of local facilities. Again local hospitality rose to the occasion in Jaffa, where the English Club was particularly kind, and in Tel-Aviv. But perhaps the greatest memory for some of the Division was carol singing in the fields of Bethlehem which made up for a lot of other things missed.

Almost immediately after Christmas the call back to 8 Army came again. There had now emerged almost a new Division, the Commander of which was Major-General R. A. Hull (later General Sir Richard Hull, K.C.B., D.S.O.). Of the senior commanders who fought with the Division only the C.R.A., Brigadier Buffey, remained in command.

Nevertheless the imprint of the "Y" was unmistakably there. The breath of fresh air that had been breathed on the Division in the Middle East had revived it and prepared it again for resuming the journey, a journey that was to turn out to be nearer home and a good deal longer than expected.

CHAPTER FOURTEEN

RETURN TO NORTH-WEST EUROPE
THE END OF THE JOURNEY

In which 5th Division, having regained its former strength, prepares to return to Italy to take its place once more in the Eighth Army. In which having got as far as Salerno and while preparing to take over from the New Zealand Division on the Faenza Sector, the Division is suddenly switched on to Operation "Goldflake" which entails a move to 21 Army Group in North-West Europe.

The Move into Italy and France

The Division, after a bountiful Christmas, was ready once more to join 8 Army, now in Northern Italy. The false alarm when 4 Div eventually went to Greece only left a short breathing space before orders were received for a return to Italy. Once more the advance parties went ahead and when they reached Italy were sent up to the Faenza area, where 8 Army were then engaged, ready to take over from the New Zealand Division. Once more last minute preparations were made by all units but by this time these were practically automatic and needed little but reminder from the Divisional Staff. Once more the vehicles and guns, the good ones taken from 56 Div in Egypt some six months previously, were to be left behind, to the bitter disappointment of their crews. The Division was to embark at Haifa and sail for Taranto from where it would entrain for the north.

The sea voyage was noteworthy only for the roughness which can be suddenly whipped up in the Eastern Mediterranean, and which the advance parties had already experienced on their last trip to Italy. The train journey, however, took the Division to Salerno, on the west coast of Italy, where it was camped around the airfield and about where 5 Army had had such heavy battles in September of the previous year. Everything was tremendously secure again and only the most important or dishonest people got out of the camp. It was soon realized, from long experience, that something more than a normal relief was about to take place. This was confirmed when the advance parties returned from Northern Italy to their units. Once more Divisional advance parties had set out on a false errand.

It was learned that the Division was to become part of "Operation Goldflake". This was a move, mostly of Canadian troops, from the Italian theatre to 21 Army Group in North-West Europe where they were to be ready to exploit the crossing of the Rhine due to take place in the Spring. It was said at the time that General Montgomery had asked for 5 Div as he had promised he would when he left Italy; as far as the troops were concerned it was a move in the right direction, although by now there were many cynics who still expected to find themselves in the Pacific theatre, the only theatre in which the "Y" had not yet been seen.

The weather at Salerno was bitterly cold and comfort was conspicuous by its absence. It was not long before embarkation took place, in the utmost secrecy, at Naples; and some units of the Division found themselves in brand new American troopships where life revolved around a continuous "chow line" of black coffee, waffles and bacon! The voyage was not to be a long one. At Marseilles units disembarked and were taken up to the most exposed transit camp there ever was and which made Persia seem like a cosy parlour. This was the transit camp at L'Etang de Berre, to the north-west of Marseilles. Visits to Marseilles were out of order, but mercifully, the stay there was not a long one. Soon the troops were put in cattle trucks (once more 40 *hommes ou* 8 *chevaux*) and then started another epic "Y" journey, this time across the length of France from south to north. It lasted some few days and consisted of trying to keep warm huddled together in draughty railway trucks, punctuated by welcome stops of about an hour a time when legs could be stretched and hot meals, albeit American ones, enjoyed in peace without having to peel the potatoes or wash up the mess tins afterwards.

The trucks rumbled along up the Rhône Valley, through Lyons, Laon, across the frontier into Belgium at Mons where the climate became a little milder and even foggy. Here the rail journey came to an end at Sotteghem; the advance parties met the trains with the tremendous news that there was to be immediate *U.K. Leave* for all ranks. This had been made possible by other Divisions of 21 Army Group forgoing their vacancies, a fact much appreciated by 5 Div as it had been abroad almost exactly three years. Some of the advance parties had already gone home and almost as great a joy was the welcome by Belgian families of men billeted on them. For the last three years accommodation had been nothing but huts, tents, sangars or ditches for habitation and now the warm feeling of a lived-in home came like a breath of fresh air.

Divisional Headquarters was at Ghent and the rest of the Division was spread around the area. So good had been security that the Germans had no idea that the Division had joined B.A.O.R. until contact was eventually made with them. Those not on leave drew up vehicles and guns and got them ready for the final battles. The guns were calibrated from positions outside Dunkirk almost exactly from where the last rounds were fired in 1940. This time, however, they pointed into Dunkirk on to the defiant German garrison.

At Ghent, all in the Division were sorry to say goodbye to Brigadier W. Buffey who was evacuated into hospital. He had been C.R.A. since the initial invasion of Sicily and who had served with 5 Div since the outbreak of war. His place was taken by Brig. H. C. Phillips.

It was whilst the Division was at Ghent that they watched the armada of troop-carrying aircraft and gliders taking 6 Airborne Div into battle across the Rhine. There were many who thought that the Division had been sent for to help cross the Rhine and were therefore surprised to see this and realize that the Rhine had already been crossed. Within a matter of weeks, part of the Division was to fight under command of the Airborne Division on the River Elbe.

The Advance to the Elbe

As soon as the battle had moved towards Hanover, and the bridges were cleared, 5 Div moved up to take its place in VIII Corps (Lieut.-General Sir Evelyn Barker) which had just successfully crossed the river Aller at Celle and was moving towards Luneburg heath. A strong German army was still fighting in the Ruhr, so the route had to skirt this and proceed through Xanten, Essen, and Osnabrück to Hanover. After crossing Xanten bridge the route lay through the landing zones of 6 Airborne Div so recently dropped across the Rhine. Here were still the damaged gliders and hanging parachutes

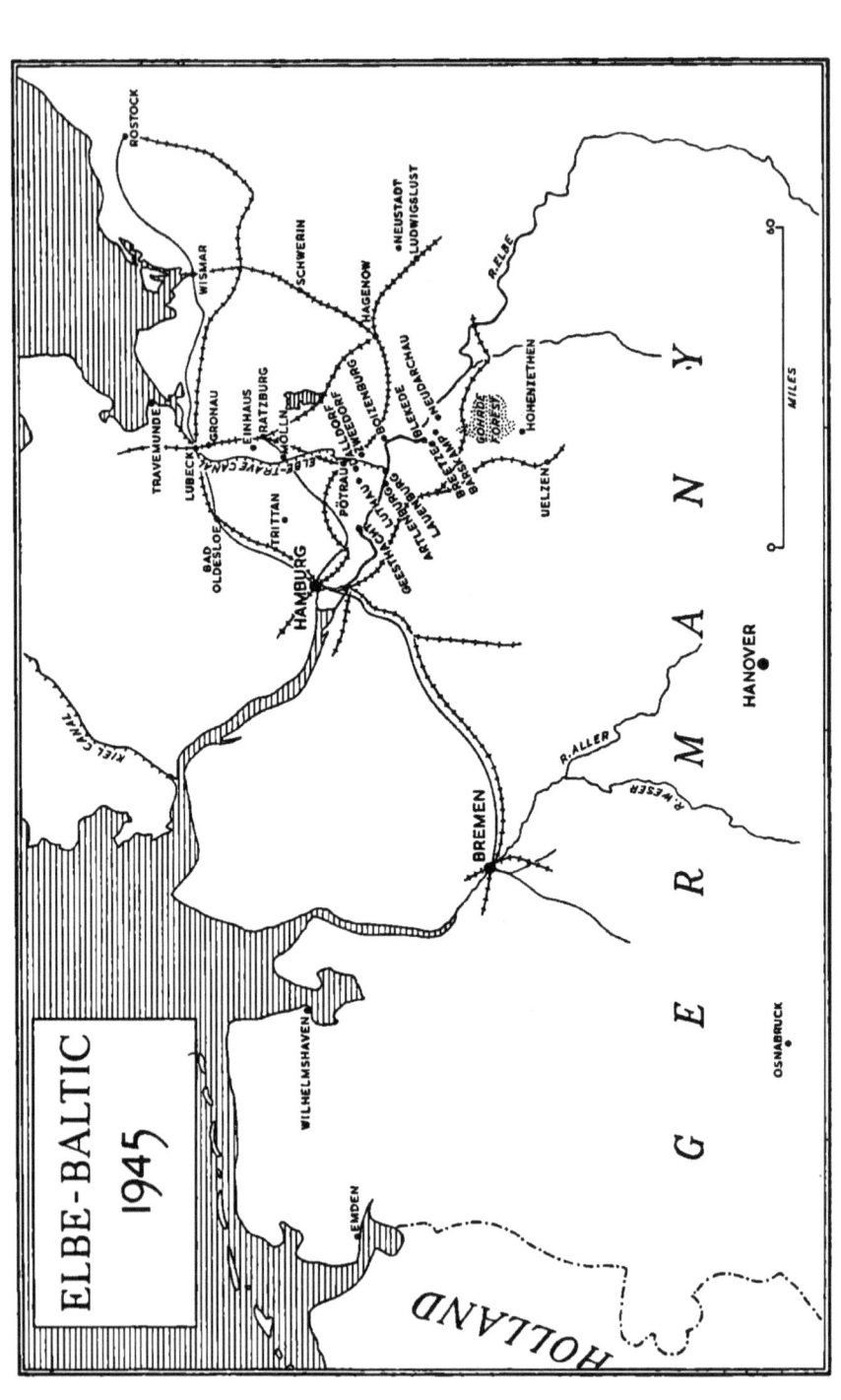

that the Division saw when it landed in Sicily. There was hardly a road that could be traced in its original form in Essen, so heavy had been the bombardment by the R.A.F. The way had to be picked out, avoiding the craters and ruins, in very rough conditions.

The Division was concentrating south of Uelzen between the 16th and 19th April and had orders to be prepared to pass through 6 Airborne Division on 20th April on the general axis Uelzen-Zerten-Neudarchau; to establish itself on the west bank of the Elbe, between Neudarchau and Bleckede; and to take over the latter town from 15 Scottish Div. This move up to the river took a further three days. The advance was through fairly thick forest in which small parties fought with enemy small parties. The German Army, now practically broken, was joined by the Volksturm, the Navy and all manner of determined and patriotic Germans of both sexes martialled with any available weapons and grouped, as only the Germans knew how, in mixed formations.

The advance waited on 30th April with 5 Div on the extreme right of VIII Corps. 17 Inf Bde (Brigadier C. B. Fairbanks, later, Major-General C. B. Fairbanks, C.B., C.B.E.) on the right and 13 Inf Bde (Brigadier W. H. Lambert, later Major-General W. H. Lambert, C.B., C.B.E.) on the left with 15 Inf Bde (Brigadier C. Huxley) in reserve. On the left of 13 Inf Bde was 15 Scottish Div. On the next day 13 Inf Bde captured Barskamp and was astride the railway just south of Bleckede. 2 Cameronians supported by tanks of 4 Gren Gds advanced in vehicles with "C" company in the lead, riding on the tanks. At first it was only opposed by some sniping from a wood to the north-west of the village of Breetze. After nearly three hours the head of the column came to the outskirts of Bleckede and here met with stubborn resistance. "C" company attacked supported by the tanks but they were unable to advance against strong small-arms fire from the town. They suffered a few casualties before digging in. The Battalion Commander immediately ordered the rest of the battalion to debus, and moved his Headquarters up to "C" company's area in order to prepare for a full scale battalion attack on Bleckede. This attack was put in at 1245 hrs. with "A" company on the right, "B" in the centre and "D" on the left, again with the support of the tanks. Again they started well but resistance was obviously very strong and the attack came to a halt soon afterwards with several casualties, "D" company having to withdraw slightly on the left. The Company Commander (Major W. A. Craw) was wounded as was his successor (Lieutenant Johnson) just as he was taking over; the remaining officer in the company was also wounded leaving C.S.M. McArthur in command. Several gallant and audacious attempts were made to get on ahead but heavy fire caused them serious casualties every time they moved. One complete platoon of "D" company was cut off and missing. At 1730 hrs. the Battalion Commander resolved he could go no farther that night and ordered the companies to consolidate where they stood. They were being heavily shelled from across the river, throughout the night, but digging had been effective enough to prevent serious casualties.

The Germans, however, realizing they were up against an organized attack, withdrew during the night and, when the Cameronians renewed the attack with "C" company in the morning, there was hardly any reply from the enemy. "A" company passed through "C" company and had secured their objective within three hours. Large numbers of Germans had waited behind to surrender rather than cross the river to fight again. For their reward, 2 Cameronians captured a large dump of Champagne and other wine which was thrown open to the Division.

On Friday, 20th April, at 0600 hrs. in heavy rain, 17 Inf Bde on the right flank of 13 Inf Bde attacked through the Göhrde Forest with 6 Seaforth on the left and 2 RSF on the right. 5 Recce Regt led both battalions which were also supported by the tanks of 4 Gren Gds as well as 156 Fd Regt. 2 RSF, riding on the tanks, first contacted the enemy at Bankowitz where they were also shelled. They met stiff opposition at Hohenzethen where the C.O. (Lieut.-Colonel Maxwell) was forced to mount a Battalion attack with a strong fireplan. This attack was successful and fifty prisoners were taken, but some persistent opposition remained beyond the village. This was mostly from sniping and the Grenadiers took several tanks by bazooka. The process of mopping up towards the river line was a laborious one as the opposition was hard to locate. To add to the Battalion's troubles, when it finally reached Neu Dachau it was shelled both by the Germans across the river and by the Americans from the south!

Neu Dachau was garrisoned by about 300 troops mostly of the Luftwaffe. As at Bleckede they put up stiff resistance until nightfall when they withdrew or surrendered next morning. This cleared the area to the river.

The enemy on the other side of the river was now believed to consist mainly of a Police Battalion together with Naval and Air Force oddments. There were so many identifications as to make the picture a very obscure one, which had to be admitted by Captain K. H. Spencer, the Divisional Intelligence Officer. It should be commented that throughout the campaign in Italy, the Divisional Intelligence Staff had always presented the enemy situation more accurately than would have been considered possible. The best information had always been extracted from patrols which had always been a strong point within the Division. They now had too much information that was quite useless. The enemy position was invariably beyond repair although there was still fight left in the tail. A letter was picked up in Neu Dachau written by an officer's mother in Hamburg and addressed to her son in the field, some ten days previously; an extract read, "Christa has just returned from Bremen in a truck. Her husband has not yet been sent to the front, so you see we still have reserves."

The Crossing of the Elbe and on to Lübeck

Operation "Enterprise", the crossing of the River Elbe, had been in the planning stages for the past fortnight. The opposition was known to be scrappy with some 300 A.A. guns of light and heavy calibre in support along the river line; behind the mixed and loosely controlled battalions was the 245th Infantry Division. The river, however, was a formidable obstacle, being 300 yds. wide from a steep wooded escarpment, behind which was the town of Lauenburg, to the dead flat and open marshland on the south side. Somewhat reminiscent of the situation on the Garigliano, but this time the assault was not to be undertaken by 5 Div.

The object of the operation was to secure a bridgehead across the Elbe so that XII Corps and XVIII United States Corps could pass through. This plan had to be altered as XII Corps were too far behind and XVIII Corps decided to cross farther to the east. The final Corps plan was to secure, by phases, a bridgehead over the Elbe to include Pötrau–Scwarzenbeck–Brunstorf–Dassendorf.

The plan was in five phases.

Phase I: 15 (S) Div. and one commando brigade to get initial bridgehead at Lauenburg and Artlenburg. To cover bridging and to secure intact bridges over the Elbe–Trave Canal to the east of Lauenburg.

Phases II and III: 15 (S) Div. to extend the bridgehead farther to include Dalldorf, Luthau and to the east of Geesthacht.

Phase IV: 15 (S) Div to consolidate, re-group and hand over eastern sector of bridgehead to 5 Airborne Div who would then extend it farther to include Nostorf and Zweedorf.

Phase V: 6 Airborne Div on right to secure final limit of the bridgehead using 15 Inf Bde of 5 Div to secure that part of their bridgehead west of Elbe–Trave Canal. To seize two bridges some eight miles north of Lauenberg over the canal. 15 (S) Div to secure final limit of the bridgehead on left of 6 Airborne Div clearing Geesthacht.

The break-out was to be carried out by 5 Div on the right who were to be directed via Mölln on Lubeck and 11 Armoured Div on the left directed via Trittan on Bad Oldesloe to dominate all roads leading out of Lubeck to the north and north-west.

6 Airborne Div was to fan out to the east and come under command XVIII U.S. Airborne Corps in an attempt to line up with the Russians' advance from the east of Prussia.

"D" Day was on 29th April, to forestall refugees blocking the roads. Much bridging had to be brought up to the river bank and ammunition to be dumped for the large-scale fireplan "Cossack" that was to be fired in Sp. of the assault and in which the Divisional Artillery (Brigadier H. C. Phillips) fired 222 rounds per gun.

The crossing went according to plan although stormy weather caused the heavy air bombardment that had been planned to be cancelled. Opposition, as expected, was slight and the bridge over the Elbe–Trave Canal was captured intact, although damaged. It is believed that the accurate firing of the new close proximity fuses, used here by the Divisional Gunners for the first time, and fired by a battery of 156 Fd Regt over this bridge, played a big part in the success, as the

Major-General R. A. Hull, C.B., D.S.O.

German demolition party were all found dead in the area; killed by shellfire before they could blow the bridge.

1 Commando took the Lauenburg Sector and 44 Inf Bde of 15 (S) Div the Artlenburg Sector. 46 and 227 Inf Bdes followed up, the former moving north from Lauenburg. At the end of the day this brigade was in contact with the enemy in Dalldorf. The Class 9 bridge to be used by 5 Div was completed despite enemy air activity by the evening. Enemy artillery was also fairly active, 88 mm. flak guns particularly harassed the bridging sites.

5 Div., having been relieved in the Bleckede–Neu Dachau Sector by 82 United States Airborne Div under command of 9 United States Army, had concentrated in an area immediately south of the Class 9 bridge, opposite Lauenburg. The Division's break-out operation was known as operation "Volcano" a continuation of "Enterprise". It was to go ahead without a pause after the initial bridgehead had been secured.

On 30th, 15 Scottish Div extended its bridgehead and 6 Airborne Div relieved 15 Scottish Div in the right hand sector. The two break-out divisions were now ready to move.

Just after midday 5 Airborne Div was given full use of the Class 9 bridge and the 3 Parachute Bde went over, followed by 15 Inf Bde. The former moved to the east of the bridgehead. 15 Inf Bde relieved 46 Inf Bde and 1 Commando Bde in the area of Dalldorf and immediately west of the Elbe–Trave Canal. 15 Inf Bde was still under command 6 Airborne Div, now halted near Boizenburg.

The planned break-out, following the good initial progress, was now speeded up by the Corps Commanders. Just before midnight on 30th April/1st May, 11 Armoured Div started across the Class 40 bridge at Artlenburg on the left, ready to break out on the morning of the 1st May. On the right 5 Div completed its concentration (after its 2,921 odd vehicles had crossed the bridge) and resumed command of 15 Inf Bde. Its further advance, however, was held up until the next day, 2nd May, so as to give time for 6 Airborne Div to get clear to the east of the Elbe–Trave Canal, where it was now going well towards the advancing Russians. The advance on the left was slowed down by heavy opposition in Schwarzenbeck and at a demolished bridge at Sahme.

Orders were received by Major-General R. A. Hull to

advance as ordered on the 2nd to Lübeck using the Royals to screen the exposed eastern flank over the Elbe–Trave Canal and so keep touch with the XVIII United States Airborne Corps. This advance went to plan when 2 WILTS, leading 13 Inf Bde, passed through 15 Inf Bde after the latter's severe battle for the railway junction of Pötrau the day before.

2 WILTS cleared Mölln by 1100 hrs., after some scattered resistance. By 1300 hrs. they had a company in Ratzeburg and were just south of Einhaus, 3 miles farther north-west. They continued to advance during the afternoon and by midnight had reached Grosse Gronau only 5 miles from Lübeck. 2 Cameronians mounted in M.T. made for Mölln, and took up defensive positions around the town, which was being almost overrun by the steady flow of prisoners, both Germans and Allied returning to the fold. 5 Essex, who had taken the place of 2 R INNISKS released to the Irish Bde in the Middle East, took up similar positions at Ratzeburg and 17 Inf Bde passed their battalions through Mölln by nightfall. The Royals maintained contact with 6 Airborne Div on their right and thus with the Americans.

On the left, 11 Armoured Div were slowed down by heavy rain undermining the roads and by heavy traffic, but resumed the advance next day.

The Army Commander, General Dempsey, who had commanded 13 Inf Bde in 1940, and XIII Corps when 5 Div were in it in Sicily and Italy, told the Corps Commander that the quick capture of Lübeck might result in the Germans now in Schleswig-Holstein surrendering without further ado. Although 11 Armoured Div just got ahead of 5 Div into Lübeck there was not much in it and the latter had received the surrender of General Sanders and the complete 245 Inf Div, a total of about 16,000 prisoners in all. In Lübeck on the 3rd of May, the entire staff of the German XXVII Corps arrived at Battalion Headquarters of 2 Cameronians and surrendered. Hostilities ceased at 0800 hrs. on 5th May.

Here are some extracts from the Divisional Intelligence Summaries of the last few days:—

30th April

Today has been largely spent in building up the bridgehead and in a limited expansion, chiefly to the north-west and east.

245 Jaeger Division surrendering to 7 Cheshire.

2 WILTS on the outskirts of Lübeck.

The Wiltshires round up the last effective German opposition to be met by the Division.

The exact degree of preparations for battle of 245th Division is not known, although it appears that they are very much below strength and that the Division as a whole had by no means completed the process of reforming.

That so much of the limited reserve available has been committed on the second day of the battle suggests that the enemy is fighting the battle of Hamburg now and thinks that we are also. More reserves he undoubtedly will produce at Hamburg and at Lübeck but his present behaviour is indicative of a fundamental inadequacy both in quality and quantity of troops which no amount of improvised battle groups can remedy.

A swimming saboteur was fished out of the Elbe today—believe he did no damage. This, however, serves as a useful reminder that sabotage still is one of the enemy's weapons ineffective though it invariably is.

The enemy air effort was again high today. No substantial damage has been reported and twenty-two planes are claimed as destroyed.

2nd May

Considerable advances have been made during the past 36 hrs. against opposition which has varied between facile surrender in the Boizenburg area, stubborn defence in the Pötrau–Buchen area, and withdrawal behind mines and demolitions on the left.

Civilian comment that Mölln will not be defended owing to the large number of hospitals in the town is doubtless inspired by wishful thinking.

Later

Our advance from Büchen to Mölln proceeded with negligible opposition. Mölln itself was not defended, and the canal bridge was not blown. Our own advance continued to Gronau and by this time 13 Inf Brigade had taken some 2,000 prisoners of war.

The unconditional surrender of all the enemy armies in Italy which embrace in their operational command a considerable area of Southern Austria, means the virtual end of the National Redoubt.

Hitler's death is now accepted. As General Dittmar recently said, once Hitler was dead, all further enemy resistance would rapidly disintegrate. For once the radio commentator's forecast appears to have been accurate.

F.D.–S*

3rd May

The occupation of Lübeck was completed by our troops around midday today and we have since advanced beyond to Travemünde and Neustadt against no opposition.

The main problem today has not been opposition but the purely administrative problems of evacuation and organization of the many thousands of prisoners of war who were found in Lübeck and who are still arriving in large numbers from the right flank. There is no fight left in these troops and the general attitude is one of ingratiating servility.

The Divisional cage tonight with bonfires, accordions and community singing presented a scene more like Bank Holiday on Hampstead Heath than a prisoner of war camp.

The senior officers taken during the day were a mixture of the old regular soldier and the younger more arrogant Nazi type and came from a variety of miscellaneous appointments.

With little more fighting to be done on the right flank and the link up with the Russians now firm on the road Wismar–Rostock, with the surrender of Hamburg and adjoining area at midday today, the question of greatest importance at the moment is the enemy's intention in the Schleswig-Holstein peninsula. Sufficient troops are certainly available to the enemy to put up a brief defence of the Kiel area, but more than this he is in no position to attempt. However, with the snowball effect of successive surrenders in Italy, Lübeck, and Hamburg combined with the death of Hitler and the loss of Berlin, it is doubted if Admiral Doenitz will be able to reman his Kiel Navies and disillusioned Wehrmacht troops even to this final effort.

And so was recorded the last "mad mile" of a long and full journey. The Division did not stay long in Lübeck. Contact, in conjunction with 6 Airborne Div, was made with the Russians in the Schwerin–Ludwigslust–Magdeburg areas and as these parts were scheduled to become part of the Russian Zone of Germany the Division had to withdraw gracefully and cautiously to around Brunswick and the Harz Mountains. Here, in common with the rest of the British Army, it supported the Control Commission, and at the same time returned most of its faithful soldiers to civilian life. Finally then came a day when the banner with the device of the "Y" was hung up, but that is part of another story altogether.

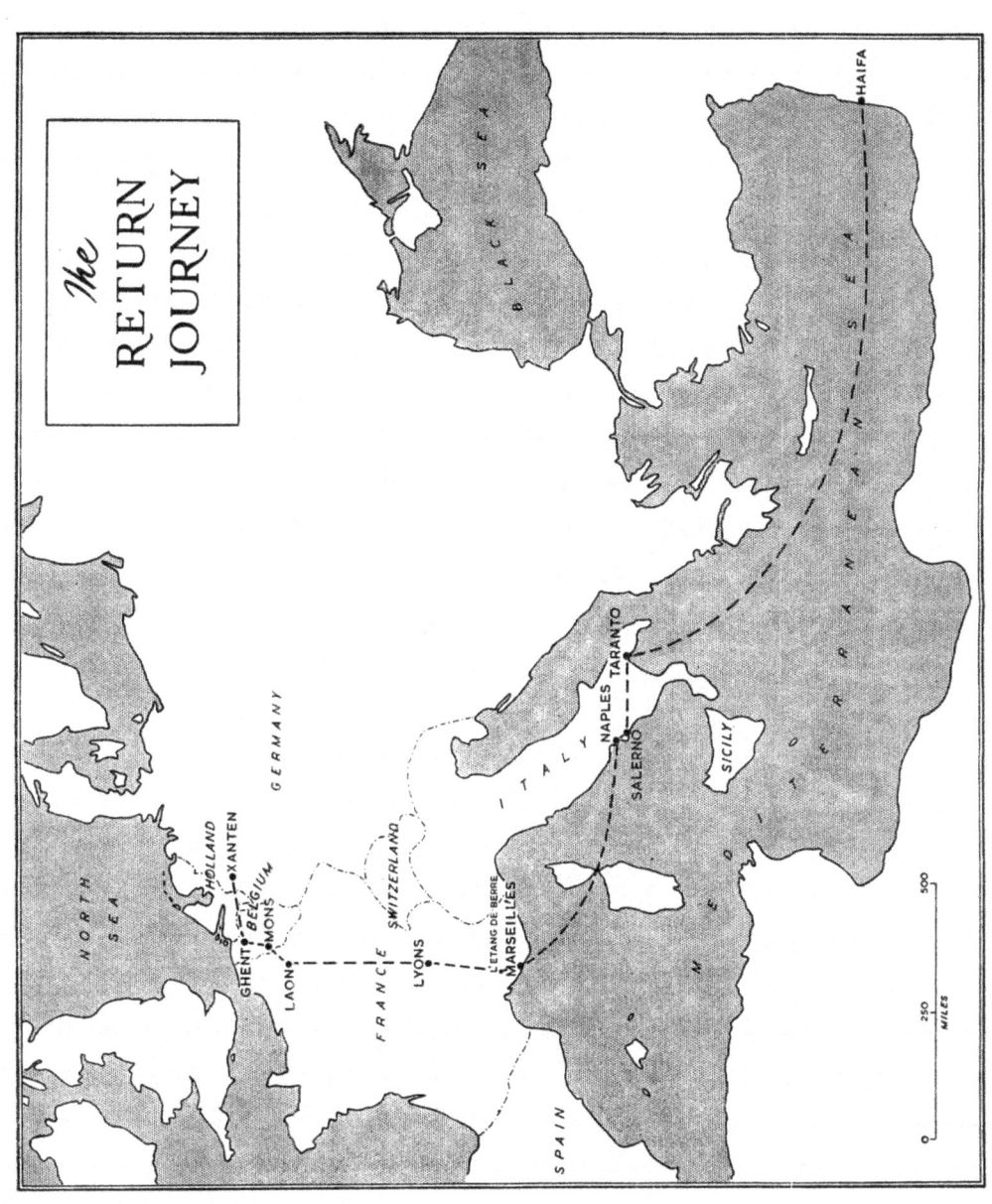

1959

Many years have passed since the Division fought its last battle just across the Elbe. Since then much has happened to disperse to all parts of the United Kingdom, some even farther afield, most of those who took part in the great journey. In all parts of Europe and the Middle East there are people who will never forget the quiet likeable men who wore the "Y" flash on their shoulder and who did their job well and without much fuss about it. Even the enemy has provided evidence, one instance alone is a simple entry in the Visitors Book at the Cemetery in Anzio.

Yet though memories come and go, the surrounding scenery has changed here and there to conform with the pattern of the new post war world. Nowhere is this more evident than in Anzio where now stand modern villas, hotels and bathing establishments in a continuous line almost from the Port to the Mouth of the Moletta. The glades around Divisional Headquarters are still preserved. All the woodland that once stood up to tremendous shell fire in "Gun Alley" has been cut back, the ground irrigated and fine new vineyards grace the landscape, with here and there a modern farm settlement. The house that was once occupied by the Military Police Post is now a large modern farm with a silo, the Lateral Road, still pot-holed as is the Coastal Road, shows little sign of the scars except for the farm of La Cogna and the Yellow Bungalow, neither of which has been rebuilt. To the north of the Lateral Road, there is a fine vineyard. The Fortress, the wadis around it and the Lobster's Claw have run wild and possibly still contain evidence of the grimly intimate life that was once lived there. The last body was removed for burial in 1950, six years after the battles in the beachhead. Those bodies now lie in what must be the loveliest of all war cemeteries, on the main road from Campoleone to Anzio, a patterned labyrinth of flowering pergolas backed by the dark pine and cypress trees of the Padiglione Woods. Elsewhere there is the odd reminder, the holes in the still battered fly-over bridge, the holes also in the Tower of San Lorenzo, but mostly, it is a new world almost too difficult to recognize in many respects. The fine new motor road that skirts the coast up near the Moletta sand dunes, the handsome villas lining the road around the old familiar "B" Echelon area and the town itself, a modern gay little seaside port with hardly a trace left of its terrible siege in 1944, have covered up most of the scars so well known to the Division.

Farther south the wounds have healed less quickly. Sicily remains timeless, as does Calabria and the hinterland to the south of Naples. New farms here and there, gained from absent landlords, but fundamentally, if he could remember it, the soldier of 5 Div would find little new. A mended crater, a fine new bridge here and there and particularly by Minturno over the Garigliano. If he were to stand on the mountain at Spigno, on the railway station at Campoleone, he would realize how much the Germans were able to see of his everyday life. If he were to stand upright on the Fortress, he would see how much that little hump of ground dominated, indeed comprised the last stand against a determined enemy drive against Anzio.

Nearer home, in Northern Europe, in the Gubrundsal of Norway the folk have almost forgotten the war but still remember the gallant stand of the men of 5 Div. The North Germans around Lauenberg, who owed so much to the help given to their sick and dying soldiers by the doctors of the Division on and after V.E. day in 1945, still remember, as do other Germans who, like the visitor to the cemetery at Anzio, found that he was fighting honourable enemies.

In Belgium there is many a farm around Ghent and Wytschaete that remembers the soldiers of the Division, and farther west in France, the people of Douai and Lille, of Tourcoing and Armentières have similar memories. Perhaps even farther afield, in South Africa, India, Persia, Syria, Palestine and Egypt there are simple folk who remember the part played by 5 Div in the great journey.

Scattered though they are, some of them still wandering or settled abroad, the men of 1939-1945 5 Div will always remember the little incidents of their journey, only a few of which have been described, inadequately alas, in these pages. May this account serve to keep alive the indomitable spirit of

"The Globetrotters", of "The Fighting Fifth", of the men of the "Fifth Division".

In 1959, twenty years after 5 Div started its long and adventurous journey, we are all glad to remember that the Fifth Division is active once more and that our "Y" is being worn so proudly by our successors.

APPENDIX "A"

Senior Commanders, 1939-45

General Officers Commanding
- 1939-40 Major-General H. E. Franklyn, C.B., D.S.O., M.C.
- 1940-43 Major-General H. P. M. Berney-Ficklin, C.B., M.C.
- 1943-44 Major-General G. C. Bucknall, C.B., M.C.
- 1944-44 Major-General P. G. S. Gregson-Ellis, C.B., O.B.E.
- 1944-45 Major-General R. A. Hull, C.B., D.S.O.

Commanders, Royal Artillery
- 1939-40 Brigadier J. H. Barry, C.B.E.
- 1940-43 Brigadier H. Greene, M.C.
- 1943-45 Brigadier W. Buffey, D.S.O., T.D.
- 1945-45 Brigadier H. C. Phillips, D.S.O.

Commanders, 13 Infantry Brigade
- 1939-40 Brigadier M. C. Dempsey, D.S.O., M.C.
- 1940-40 Brigadier D. N. Wimberley, M.C.
- 1940-43 Brigadier V. C. Russell, D.S.O., M.C.
- 1943-44 Brigadier L. M. Campbell, V.C., D.S.O., T.D.
- 1944-44 Brigadier F. R. C. Matthews, D.S.O.
- 1945-45 Brigadier W. H. Lambert, C.B.E.

Commanders, 15 Infantry Brigade
- 1939-40 Brigadier H. P. M. Berney-Ficklin, M.C.
- 1940-40 Brigadier J. A. H. Gammell, D.S.O., M.C.
- 1940-43 Brigadier H. R. H. Greenfield
- 1943-43 Brigadier G. W. Rawstorne, M.C.
- 1943-44 Brigadier M. H. Martin
- 1944-44 Brigadier J. Y. Whitfield, D.S.O., O.B.E.
- 1944-45 Brigadier C. T. Huxley, C.B.E.

Commanders, 17 Infantry Brigade
- 1939-40 Brigadier M. G. N. Stopford, D.S.O., M.C.
- 1940-43 Brigadier G. W. B. Tarleton, D.S.O., M.C.
- 1943-44 Brigadier A. Dudley Ward, D.S.O.
- 1944-44 Brigadier A. I. Finlayson, O.B.E.
- 1944-45 Brigadier C. B. Fairbanks, M.B.E.

(*Decorations shown are those held at the time of holding the particular appointment.*)

APPENDIX "B"

CORPS AND REGIMENTS WHICH SERVED WITH 5 DIV

1939–1945

In full	Abbreviation
The Royal Regiment of Artillery	RA
9th Field Regiment	9 Fd Regt RA
91st Field Regiment	91 Fd Regt RA
92nd Field Regiment	92 Fd Regt RA
156th Field Regiment	156 Fd Regt RA
18th Light Anti-Aircraft Regiment	18 LAA Regt RA
52nd Anti-Tank Regiment	52 A.Tk Regt RA
The Corps of Royal Engineers	RE
38 Field Company	38 Fd Coy RE
245 Field Company	245 Fd Coy RE
252 Field Company	252 Fd Coy RE
254 Field Park Company	254 Fd Pk Coy RE
The Royal Corps of Signals	R SIGS
1st Bn. The Green Howards (Alexandra, Princess of Wales's Own Yorkshire Regiment)	1 Green Howards
2nd Bn. The Royal Scots Fusiliers	2 RSF
7th Bn. The Cheshire Regiment	7 Cheshire
2nd Bn. The Cameronians (Scottish Rifles)	2 Cameronians
2nd Bn. The Royal Inniskilling Fusiliers	2 R INNISKS
6 Bn. The Essex Regiment	6 Essex
2nd Bn. The Northamptonshire Regiment	2 Northamptons
1st Bn. The King's Own Yorkshire Light Infantry	1 KOYLI

In full	Abbreviation
2nd Bn. The Wiltshire Regiment	2 WILTS
1st Bn. The York and Lancaster Regiment	1 Y and L
2nd Bn. The Seaforth Highlanders (Ross-shire Buffs, The Duke of Albany's)	2 Seaforth and 6 Seaforth
5th Bn. The Reconnaissance Corps	5 RECCE
Royal Army Chaplains' Department	RA Ch D
Royal Army Service Corps	RASC
Royal Army Medical Corps	RAMC
Royal Army Ordnance Corps	RAOC
Corps of Royal Electrical and Mechanical Engineers	REME
Corps of Royal Military Police	RMP
Royal Army Pay Corps	RAPC
Royal Army Educational Corps	RAEC
Royal Army Dental Corps	RADC
Royal Pioneer Corps	RPC
Intelligence Corps	INT Corps
Army Physical Training Corps	APTC
Army Catering Corps	ACC
Queen Alexandra's Royal Army Nursing Corps	QARANC

THE END OF THE JOURNEY.—Sergeant Coubey of 2 WILTS shares his tea with R.A.F. prisoners they had released on their way to Lübeck.

ANZIO AS IT IS TODAY.
The harbour where the Division landed from landing craft often under shell fire.

Part of the Coastal Road in the old "B" Echelon area clearly showing the filled-in shell holes.

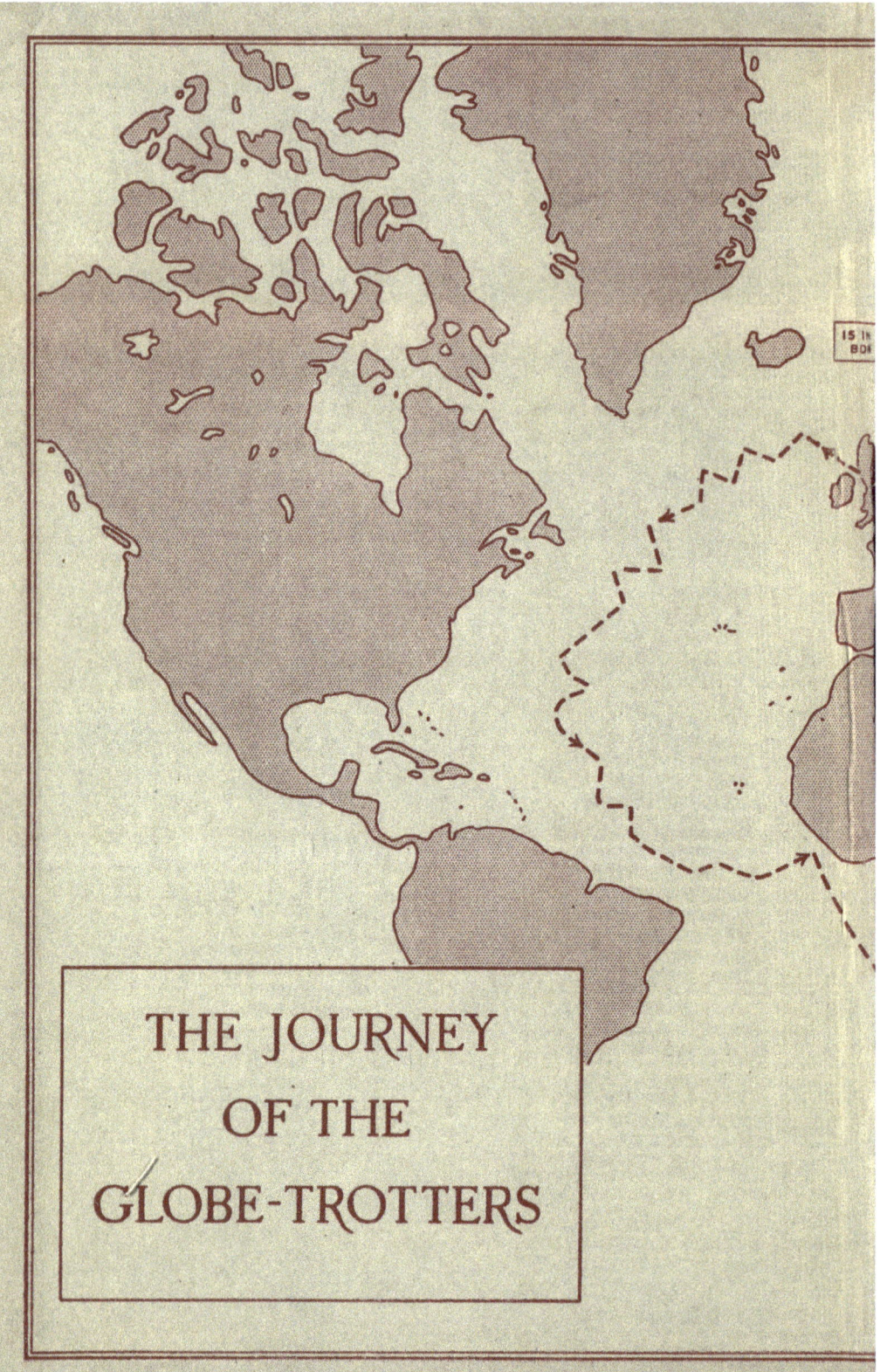

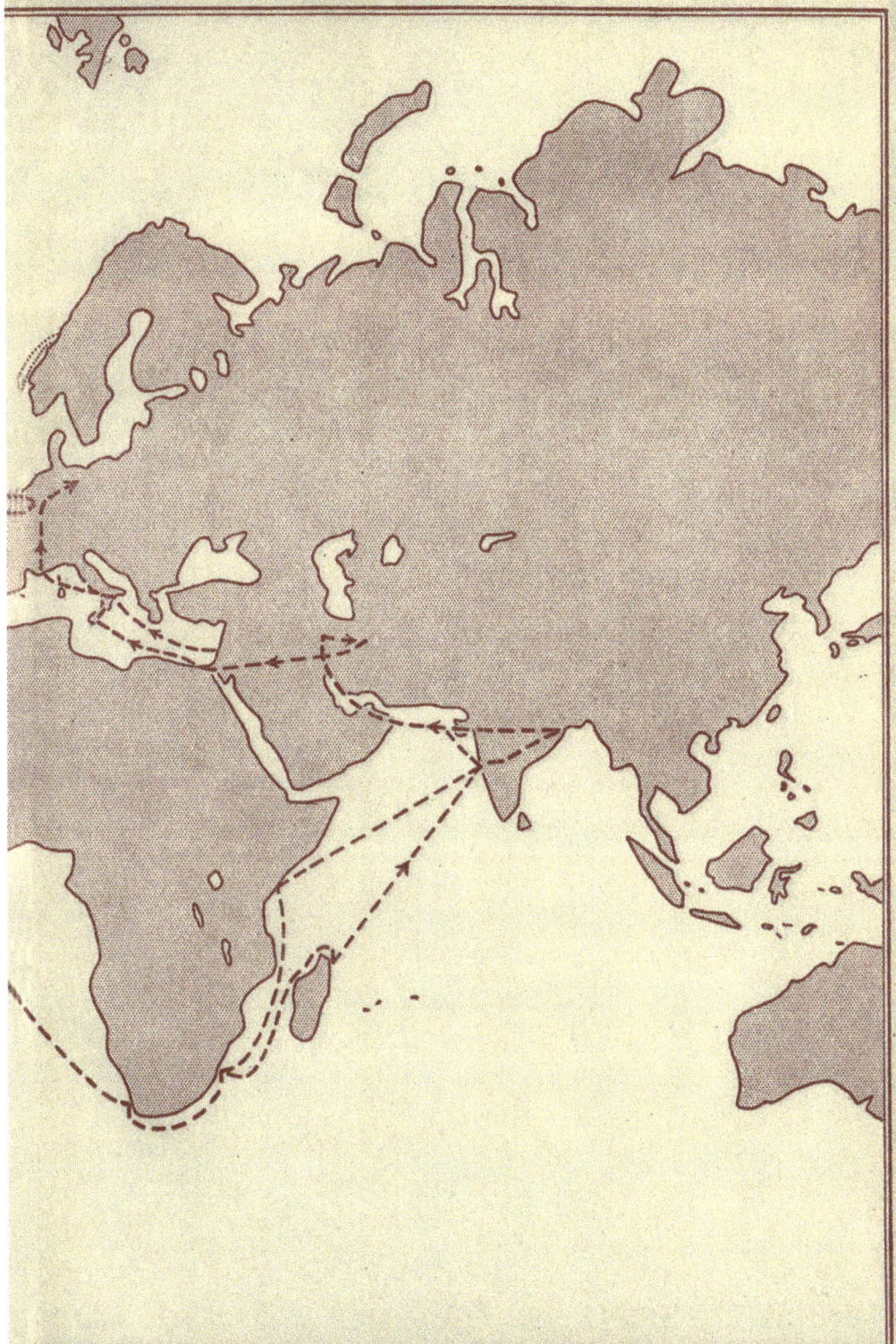

www.ingramcontent.com/pod-product-compliance
Lightning Source LLC
Chambersburg PA
CBHW061249230426
43663CB00022B/2949